Charles Joseph Bellamy

The Breton Mills

A Romance

Charles Joseph Bellamy

The Breton Mills
A Romance

ISBN/EAN: 9783337345402

Printed in Europe, USA, Canada, Australia, Japan

Cover: Foto ©Thomas Meinert / pixelio.de

More available books at **www.hansebooks.com**

BY

CHARLES J. BELLAMY

———

NEW YORK
G. P. PUTNAM'S SONS
182 FIFTH AVENUE
1879.

CONTENTS.

CONTENTS.

THE BRETON MILLS.

CHAPTER I.

A Picture and its Critics.

"LET'S take a squint in."

It is on the sidewalk in front of the fine residence of Ezekiel Breton. Surely everybody within the length and breadth of a hundred miles must have heard the name of the wealthy mill-owner, whose energy and shrewdness have passed into a by-word. The house is brilliantly lighted, and the windows wide open as if to invite the attention and admiration of the humble passers by.

Three men, laborers, if coarse, soiled clothes and dull, heavy tread mean anything, have come down the street and now stand leaning against the tall iron fence.

"Why shouldn't we see the show, boys?" continued the long-whiskered man, with an unpleasant laugh. "It's our work that's payin' for it, I guess. How long do you think it would take you, Jack, to scrimp enough to buy one of them candlesticks?

Hullo—there's the boss himself," and he thrust his hand inside the iron pickets to point out a portly gentleman whose bald head was fringed with silver-white hair. Mr. Breton paused a moment before the window.

"Come, let's go on," urged the man with a clay pipe, edging off a little into the shadow, "he'll see us, and be mad."

"What's the odds if he does?" and the speaker frowned at the rich man from between the pickets. "He can't get help no cheaper than us, can he? That's one good pint of bein' way down,—you can't tumble a mite. But just look at him, boys—big watch chain and gold bowed specs a danglin'. See the thumbs of his white hands stuck in his vest pocket, and him as smilin' as if he never did nobody a wrong in his whole blessed life—there now is somethin' purtier, though."

The old gentleman moved unsuspectingly aside, and revealed a young girl, large and fair, with great, calm blue eyes. She wore a pale blue silk, with delicate ruffles at her half bared elbow and at her neck, kissing the warm white skin.

"Well I suppose my girl Jane might look just as good in such clothes as them. But she wouldn't no more speak to Jane, than as if the girl wasn't human. And as for a poor man he might pour his life out for her purty face and she wouldn't give him a look. A few dollars and a suit of clothes makes the odds. Now look at that"—

"What's she laughin' at?" said the tall man taking his clay pipe from his mouth.

"Can't you see with your eyes? There's the boy standin' jist beyend her. Breton's young hopeful. Nothin' less than the biggest kind of game for her, I cal'late."

"I never seen him before," remarked the third man reverentially, "I 'spose he'll be our boss some day."

"He's been to college polishin' up his wits. 'Tain't goin' to be so easy as it was to grind the poor. The old man, now, didn't need no extra schoolin'."

"I aint so sure now," said the tall man, blowing out a wreath of smoke. "The boy looks more kind about his mouth and eyes. See him look at the girl. I cal'late she don't think he's very bad."

"Wait till he gets his heel on the necks of a thousand of us, as his father has. Wait till he finds we aint got a penny ahead, nor a spot of God's earth for our own, but lie at his mercy. See how kind he'll be then. 'Taint the nature of the beast, Bill Rogers."

Bill Rogers took a long look at the slight form of the mill-owner's son—at his fresh, young face and small, pleasant black eyes. "I wish the lad had a chance. I believe I'd trust him, Graves."

"You always was a fool," growled the man with the long whiskers called Graves. "I suppose you think he'll melt down those silver candlesticks, and the brass figgers that aint got no clothes on. Then you expect he'll auction off those oil pictures of cows and medders and the turkey carpet, and all them carved chairs, that look too good to set in, and divide the proceeds among us dirty devils."

"Hadn't we better be startin'? The meetin' will begin purty soon."

"What's the hurry? Curran is always late himself. Well, come along then."

Just now Mr. Breton is leaning lightly on the mantel near one of his pet heirlooms—the silver candelabra. Near him stands a tall, elegantly formed gentleman, only a trifle past middle age, whose clear chiseled mouth has the merest hint of a smile on it, as if he had just said something bright. It was a smile he always wore when he had spoken —a smile with an edge to it. But Mr. Ellingsworth had to make that smile do good service, for he never laughed. The funniest jokes had been told him—the most ridiculous situations described to him—but he only smiled. It has been supposed that he must laugh by himself, in the woods or behind double doors. Indeed he was once informed of the suspicion against him—and smiled, though several careful observers were sure, from certain premonitory symptoms, that a genuine laugh was at last coming.

"What am I going to do with the boy?" Mr. Breton's voice was always loud and sharp as if making itself heard above the roaring of his mills. "Why, marry him to your daughter the first thing. Eh! Philip?"

Would she be angry, proud and reserved as she was? Philip shot a furtive glance at Bertha as she sat at the piano idly turning over the music sheets. Poor fellow, all his cunning system of approaches come to naught; everything precipitated at perhaps the worst possible moment! But the girl might not have heard, not a shade of expression changed in her face. It might as well have been the sources of the Nile they were discussing so far as she was concerned, apparently, but as she pressed her white hand on the music sheet to keep it open, her lover's eyes softened at the flash of their betrothal diamond.

"I should think your hands must be pretty full already," suggested Mr. Ellingsworth in the low smooth tone, as much a part of his style as the cut of his black coat, "with a thousand unreasonable beings down in your factories. And by the way, I hear that Labor is claiming its rights, with a big L. As if anybody had any rights, only by accident."

"Sceptical as ever, Ellingsworth," said the mill-owner with all a practical man's distaste for a thing so destructive to industry. "But no, I get along easily enough with my help if quacks and tramps would only keep out of the way ; though there is some kind of an agitation meeting to-night ; somebody is raising the mischief among them. I wish I knew who it was," and Mr. Breton looked impatiently around the room as if he hoped to seize the incendiary in some corner of his own parlor.

He met Bertha's blue eyes wide open in a new interest. She had half turned from the piano, but her sleeve was caught back on the edge of the key-board, revealing the fair full contour of her arm which glistened whiter than the ivory beneath it.

"A mystery, how charming!" she smiled, "Let me picture him : tall, with clustering auburn hair on his god-like head—"

" Pish—excuse me, my dear—but more likely the fellow is some low, drunken jail-bird you would be afraid to pass on the street. Some day they will find out there is no good making working people uneasy. They want the work, and they ought to be glad the work wants them. Their interests are identical with ours."

" No doubt," assented Mr. Ellingsworth, in his suavest tones, that seemed too smooth for satire, " but perhaps they think you get too large a share of the dividends."

"You like to round your sentences pretty well," retorted Mr. Breton, flushing slightly, "but do you mean to say, you, of all men, sympathize with this labor-reform nonsense? Why, you will be marrying your servant girl next."

Ellingsworth smiled and shrugged his shapely shoulders just visibly.

"You ought to know me, Mr. Breton. I sympathize with—no body. It is too much trouble. And as for the sufferings of the lower classes—they may be very pitiable—but I don't see how the nether mill-stone can help itself, or for that matter be helped either." Then he smiled again and glanced curiously toward the piano.

"Why where are our young people?"

After considerable dumb show, Bertha had become aware that Philip had some intelligence of a startling nature to communicate. So it happened that, at the moment Mr. Ellingsworth inquired for them, the young people stood just inside the door of the cosy little room called "the study."

"I am going to have some high fun to-night, Bertha, I am going to that labor meeting. I want to see the business from the inside, when the public show isn't going on."

The girl looked at him in astonishment, "They won't let you in."

"That's just where the fun is coming. It is

going to be better than all the college deviltry, and —wait here two minutes and I'll show you."

Book shelves ran up to the ceiling on the side of the room, opposite the door. A long office table stretched across the centre almost to the high window looking toward the street. But all the business associations did not oppress this elegant young woman, who threw herself in luxurious abandon into the solitary easy chair. She apparently did not find love very disturbing. No doubt she only smiled at its poems fervid with a passion unknown to her calm, even life. Her young lover had often been frightened at the firm outline of the cold red lips, with never a thought of kisses on them, and at the sprite-like unconsciousness of her blue eyes that looked curiously at him when love softened his voice and glorified his face. She was not listening for his returning footsteps, not one line of eagerness or of suspense was on the dispassionate face, while she played with the flashing jewel her lover had placed long ago on her finger.

The door opens behind her but she does not turn her head—no doubt he will come in front of her if he wishes to be—there he is, a slight figure looking very odd and disagreeable in the soiled and ill-fitting clothes he has put on, with no collar or cuffs, but a blue flannel shirt open a button or two at his neck. His faded pantaloons were roughly thrust into the tops of an immense pair of cowhide boots which apparently had never been so much as shadowed by a box of blacking. His black eyes sparkle as he holds out to her a bandless felt hat which shows the marks of a long and varied history. Bertha looked at him in dull distaste. What a poor mouth he had, and how unpleasantly his face wrinkled when he smiled.

"I wouldn't ever do this again," she said coldly. A hurt look came into his eyes, he dropped his hat on the floor, and was turning dejectedly away. The fun was all gone, and her words and her look, he knew, would come back to him a thousand times when he should be alone.

But she put out her hand to him like the sceptre of a queen. "Never mind—you will generally wear better clothes than these, won't you?"

"But I wouldn't like to have that make any difference?" said Philip, looking wistfully at the cool white hand he held. "Supposing I was poor—"

She drew her hand away impatiently. If he had known how he looked then, he would have chosen another time for his lover's foolishness.

"Don't get poor. I like pretty things and graceful manners, and elegant surroundings; that is the way I am made. I should suffocate if I didn't have them."

"But?" urged Philip uneasily, "you couldn't love anybody but me, could you?"

She smiled charmingly. "You must not let me?" Then she rose as if to dismiss the subject.' "Are you all ready?"

In a minute more he was, after he had fastened on his yellow whiskers and bronzed over his face and neck, and white wrists. "Your own father wouldn't know you!" she laughed, as they opened the outer door. Philip went down two steps.

"You shake the foundation with those boots." He was quite recovering his spirits, now that she was so kind with him. "And you will tell me all about it, and whether the leader has auburn hair as I said? How long before you will come back—an hour? Well, I'll be here as long as that."

He pulled his great hat well down over his eyes and started,·but at the gate he turned to look back.

Bertha stood in the doorway, tall and queenly, the red gold of her hair glistening in the light like a halo about her head. He could not catch the look in her face, but as she stood, she raised her hand to her lips and threw him a kiss with a gesture of exquisite grace. And she was his; why did he like to persecute her for a confession she was ashamed yet to give, when soon perhaps she would warm his heart with a thousand times diviner words of love than any he could put into her mouth.

In a moment more he heard her at the piano, and he tried to keep clumsy step to the strain from "La Traviata" that came throbbing after him.

CHAPTER II

Masquerading.

PHILIP pushed open the door of "Market Hall" and looked in. About sixty men were scattered over the benches in all conceivable positions. A number held pipes between their teeth, filling the room with the rank smoke of the strongest and blackest tobacco. Here and there two men appropriated a whole bench, one at each end for a sofa. But more of them were settled down on the small of their backs with their knees braced against the bench in front. He saw in a moment, that though he was worse dressed than any of them yet there was a difference in kind also. There was more meaning in one wrinkle on their well worn coats, than in all his ingenious paraphernalia. He felt ashamed in the presence of these pathetic realities, and turned to go back, but his great boots creaked incautiously. Only two or three looked around; a poor man more or less does not count for much with the poor or with the rich. Two or three grave worn faces, two or three pairs of tired, hopeless eyes rebuked him for the idle freak that brought him there. What right had he there, who came out of curiosity to watch the unhealthy symptoms of the disease called poverty? What an insult to their bitter needs were his mock trimmings, in which he came like one masquerading among a graveyard full of ghosts!

" Hold on, friend, ye needn't go," and a long-whiskered man beckoned to him.

He found his way to a seat with a hang-dog air, the best piece of acting he had done yet. The same stolid look was on this man's face, bleached to a settled paleness from the confinement of years in the walls of the mills, and there was a bitterness about the mouth and nostrils as if he had not kissed the rod that smote him.

" No call to be shamed, young man. I suppose them's the best clothes you got. Your heart may be just as white as if you'd cheated out a better livin'."

The poor don't talk only when they have something to say. So Philip said nothing, to act in character.

" I suppose you think you're pretty hard up," resumed the big-whiskered man who was no other than Graves, the man who had peered into his companion's parlor window only an hour ago. And he glanced significantly at Philip's boots and soiled pantaloons.

" Jest look at that little chap over yonder all bowed up. He don't look very hearty, does he? Up to his house there's a wife all faded and broken and two little cripples for children, a whinin' and a screechin' from mornin' to night. He would chop his head off to help them, but he is slow and weak and don't git but ninety cents a day, and he can't save them babies a single ache, nor ease their poor misshapen little bones one twinge. It takes every penny to keep the wretched breath in 'em all, and him and his wife, once as purty a gal as ever you seen, has only to stand and see 'em cry. They used to cry themselves, too, but that was long ago. Why how surprised and sorry you look, young feller. Where was you raised that ye aint seen such things?"

Graves looked about him. "I could tell you something about well nigh every man here, that if some fool put it in potry the rich would cry beautiful over it. But their tears wouldn't loosen their grip on our throats, you be sure. Do you see that lean-faced man with the hurt arm at the end of the seat ye're on? Well, he's got the smartest little boy in town. All he wanted was schoolin' and his father and mother saved and scrimped so he could have it. You oughter seen how proud they was to see their lad struttin' off to school while they kept a thinkin' of him all day long in the mill. And they was never too tired to hear the boy tell them over the hard names he had learned. And then they would tell the neighbors who sometimes got jealous, how they was savin' every cent and how their boy was goin' to col-

lege like old Breton's son. But there was no call for
the neighbors to be jealous; the woman went to
work one day when she was sick and caught her
death o' cold and it took a mint of money to nuss and
then bury her. Then the man fell and got hurt and
the little boy cried enough to break your heart when
they took his books away." The face of the long-
whiskered man softened an instant. But he turned
his head away.

"He needn't a cried," he said gruffly, "I don't
know as he was any better than the rest of us."

Now there came a little commotion on the platform.

"Do you know what's up, young feller?" and
Graves looked at his neighbor curiously. "Why we
heard the other day we had some rights as well as
wrongs. We heard a crust of bread and a bare room
to sleep and die in—we heard that isn't pay enough
for all we do feedin' and clothin' the world. There's
Curran—shut up now."

A man who sat head and shoulders above the
group on the platform rose to his full height like a
young giant and came forward. He looked down
into the upturned faces for a moment in silence, and
Philip felt his steel-blue eyes piercing him like a
sword. Could he tell by some unknown sympathetic
sense, which was the man had no right there, which
one had come into the assembly of the poverty-

stricken only to mock them? He almost expected to be pointed out before them all, and to be made to writhe in every nerve and muscle at the depiction of his own careless life. Philip felt this young giant could do all this—there was such an idea of power breathing out of the man, with neck and shoulders like a Hercules and dome-like forehead above heavy overhanging brows.

"Men," he began. Then he stopped speaking a moment. "Yes, men you are, in spite of all the degradation the rich and the powerful can put upon you. The time is coming, when the principles of equality vaunted on the pages of so many lying con- stitutions, and breathed on the lips of so many false- tongued demagogues, shall be fully realized. The time is coming when the work shall not be on one side, and the reward on the other. We shall not always wear rags as the livery of our masters. Not always shall the poor rise early and toil late, wear their skin till it be shriveled like parchment, and their bodies till they be ready to drop into the grave for weariness, only to pluck the fruit of God's bountiful earth for the lips of the idle and the proud to taste. The gracious favors of ten thousand smiling hills and valleys are gathered only for the few, and those whose arrogance and hardness of heart have least de- served them. And they tell us it must be so; that the few who are more capable and prudent should thus be rewarded for their superiority. They point to six thousand years' oppression of the poor and say what has been must be. Yes, for six thousand years the groans of the poor have gone up, and as long the few, for whom alone all the beauty and bounty of the great earth seemed to blossom, have answered with curses and contempt." Now his magnificent chest seemed to expand; his voice lost its pathetic tone and rang out like a trumpet.

" But the knowledge they have given to make us better slaves, is bursting our fetters before their frightened eyes. The astonished people see at last the black and monstrous injustice of their subjection. They have numbered their hosts, as countless as the sands of the sea. It is the strength of their arms has girdled the earth with unceasing streams of wealth. It is the ingenuity of their brains has harnessed each of the untamed forces of nature to service. The infinite number of their cunning fingers has woven the fabrics to clothe Christendom, and their red blood poured out on a thousand battle-fields has bought vain triumphs for the pride of their masters."

His lips suddenly curled in majestic scorn. " And how long will your patient, calloused hands build palaces for the great, while you live in hovels? Ought not such strong arms as yours be able to win enough to make one modest home happy, if you

were not robbed? The world is full of cheap comforts; the harvests are boundless, the store-houses
bursting, but each worthless pauper has as good a
share as you, who make the wealth. You cause the
increase, your hands till the teeming lands and work
the tireless looms. Your shoulders bow beneath
the products of your toil—like muzzled oxen
beating out the grain for unpitying masters. Why
will you endure it? They tell you it is only right;
their books teach gentle submission; their oily-
tongued speakers soothe you with proverbs and con-
soling maxims, but all the wise men of centuries and
all the hundred thousand printing presses of to-day
heaping up books in every language like a new tower
of Babel, cannot turn a lie into the truth."

Philip sat leaning forward, his eyes fixed on the
speaker in a strange excitement. Curran's words
came into his soul like molten fire, consuming the
chaff of years and leaving a path of light behind.
He was full of wonder that he had been blind so
long, mixed with joy at his new piercing vision.
He had forgotten how he had come there, and felt a
sudden desire to take the hand of every poor man in
the room and pledge them his help. But no one
seemed touched as he was, the same hard look was
on each face, the mask the poor assume to cover
their distress, only the eyes of them all were centered
on their orator.

2

"But you are poor, and with your wives and children are hungry for even the crust of bread your masters cast you. Though you were a million to one, you are held to their service, no matter how unjust, by the daily recurring facts of hunger and cold. Look! the fields are white with their harvests, the shops filled with their cloths, but the lawmakers and their pitiless police are in their pay, and you must bow your meek necks and thank your masters humbly for the trifle their greed vouchsafes you."

Philip's heart thumped painfully behind his faded coat. Could the speaker give no hope to the wretched listeners hanging on his lips? Must they cringe forever at the foot of power? Their thin worn hands made the bread, but it was snatched from their mouths, and doled out in scanty allowance as the price of hopeless slavery. He had never seen it before.

"Who is he?" he whispered to his companion. The man did not even turn his face from the speaker.

"It is Curran. He belongs to the Labor League." This, then, was the agitator his father spoke of. And Bertha had pictured him rightly, with his clustering auburn hair. For a moment he stood silent, while under the divine light in his eyes, the souls of each one ripened for his next words.

"Alone, you can do nothing, alone ; whole fac-

tories of you cannot stand against the masters ; but
united, we can shake the world, and all over the
land the oppressed are banding together.   We are
weak now, but when the long-stifled voice of your
wrongs finds utterance, the answering moans of millions will rouse your souls to the resistless martyr
pitch.   Then it will seem sweet to die ; yes, to
starve, with your dear ones about you, inspired with
the same enthusiasm.   When the generation is
born, which dare starve, but has forgotten how to
yield, and even for the bread of life will not sell its
children into eternal slavery, then will the gold of
the rich rot worthless in their white hands till they
divide with us our common heritage."

He stopped and sat down, and as his enthusiasm
faded from his face, Philip saw he was not handsome.
The eyes that had seemed so wonderful, were too
deep seated beneath his heavy brows, and his
smooth shaved face was scarred from exposure to
sun and storm ; yet, while he had been speaking
pity and divine wrath in turn melting and burning
in his eyes and lighting up his rugged cheeks, he
seemed beautiful, like an archangel.

The audience sat in silence a moment, then one
man shuffled his feet uneasily, then another, and
then all rose listlessly to their feet.   Philip thought
their zest in life had gone so long ago that they did
not even miss it, then he remembered what his life

was, bright as a June morning. Did God love him so much better than these weary creatures, whose only refuge was in hopelessness? Then he thought of Bertha waiting for him, and he hurried out, glad that he seemed to be escaping notice. Where was the funny adventure he had to tell his sweetheart? A new world had been revealed to him; a world within the world he had played with, that knew no such thing as mirth, fed forever on bitter realities, and his little spark of happiness seemed smothered in its black night. Once outside the hall, Philip drew back into an obscure corner under the low hanging branches of an old elm, to watch the people scatter to their homes. Each one must have a family circle of his own. There were hungry eyes that looked to him for the cheer his poor heart was too dead to give. For each one there was a home without comfort, where nobody smiled, where children's voices were hushed, and even the sick had learned to stifle their moans. Philip thought he would like to see Curran once more; his heart was glowing so genially for him. As a devotee divides his love between his religion and the prophet who taught it to him, so Philip had a feeling in his heart for this man such as he never had known for any man before. His pulse came quick at the hope of speaking with him, of touching his hand; he longed to tell him how he honored him; he wanted to pledge him his friendship if he would stoop to take it. Suddenly a heavy hand was laid on his shoulder.

" Praps you aint got no place to go to, friend." It was his big-whiskered companion in the hall, Graves. Why couldn't he have kept away just now?

" I sort o' liked your looks in the meetin' to-night, and you're welcome to a bed at my house if you want it."

" Oh no," stumbled Philip, at his wit's end.

" Oh no? Why not then? Where be you goin' to stay?" and the man took his hand from the young man's shoulder and eyed him suspiciously. " Why, he wanted to go home and lay off his masquerade forever. Bertha, all radiant in all that wealth can add to beauty, was awaiting him. He had so much to tell her," but he had nothing to say aloud.

" I won't take no refusal," insisted the man, taking Philip by the arm. " No words, Jane will get along easy with an extra for once. I presume you've slept in wuss places."

CHAPTER III.

An Unwilling Guest.

PHILIP thought things were going a little too far, and as he walked along with his undesirable host, he began to plan escapes. He would select a certain alley-way or dark corner for an attempt at flight. But each time just as he was about to spring his tall companion happened to be just in his way. So finally he decided to see his adventure through.

The moonlight shimmered on the green leaves and silvered the commonest objects near their path. Up on the hill to his left he could see, now and then, between the houses, his own home and the lights in its window streaming welcome to him. The tense mood relaxed in him, old habits of thought and association made themselves felt again; the poor man walking heavily by his side seemed a thousand miles removed from him. No doubt the poor were unhappy, but as the vivid sense of kinship for them faded from his mind, Philip felt more able to comfort himself with good old proverbs and maxims. Probably his father and a thousand others as wise and kind as he, were as sorry for the unfortunate as himself. Unfortunate—yes, that was the word—and misfortunes of course are to be borne resignedly by everybody, including the lookers-on.

"Here we are," said Graves, as he led the mill-owner's son up a couple of rickety-looking steps to a doorway. A mat of what may have once been bristles lay there and the blank panels of the door stared the young aristocrat unpleasantly in the face. He was not pleased at all; he had seen enough poverty to-night, he did not care to particularize. What was the use of distressing himself over this man's private miseries and discomforts? Wasn't it written in all the books of political economy that—but Graves opened the door and waited for his unwilling guest to go in before him. The poor man's heart was warm with the unwonted exercise of hospitality. Far from him to suspect he was entertaining a man whose delicate taste would revolt against the best he could show him.

With an ungracious frown on his face Philip entered the dimly lighted room, his great boots sounding with startling effect on the bare floor. The top-heavy kerosene lamp was turned down, perhaps to hide the ugliness of the room, more likely to save oil, but with the heartiness of a true host, Graves turned up the lamp so that Philip could look about him. There was little enough to see—a round pine table with a little blue, cracked crockery on it, a rusty cooking-stove, two or three dingy, unpainted chairs. There was something more, a high-backed rocking chair with a faded shapeless chintz cushion, and what seemed to be a sofa in one corner. At first Philip thought the room had been unoccupied, but as Graves turned up the lamp a trifle more, he saw it was a woman lying upon the sofa, a woman with sunken black eyes, and wan colorless cheeks, whose loosely-bound hair, grey before its time, fell down over her shoulders.

"The woman is sick or she'd get up and speak to you?" said Graves with a new gentleness in his voice, as he looked at the wife of his youth. "They say she might get well if we could pay doctors' bills. All she says she hopes for now, is to die and rest. Eh, Jennie?"

Philip moved uneasily in his chair, the frown had left his face, the same expression had come into his eyes and upon his lips, that he had worn at the meeting, and even under his paint it made him handsome. The woman did not speak, but the questioning look in her beautiful eyes seemed to reproach her husband for bringing a stranger there. Was this the "Jane," Graves had spoken of, wondered Philip, when an inner door opened and a young girl entered.

"Ah, these poor people have one thing of beauty to solace their wretchedness." The courtly Philip fairly lost his self-possession for a moment at the unlooked-for picture. The girl who stood in the doorway was not tall, and the outlines of her figure were so perfect as to give perhaps a mistaken impression of slightness. She had her mother's eyes, not quite large enough, but with a rare sheen in them; it might be her mother's face, too, but with the bloom of perfect health lightening up its olive.

Involuntarily he rose to his feet and bowed, but as the girl only seemed to regard him as one might look at a circus tumbler, Philip relapsed into his seat, in the humiliation beauty can put upon the greatest of us.

" Nothin' but cold potatoes? Well I guess they'll do with a little salt and a piece of bread."

" But I am not hungry?" exclaimed Philip eagerly. " I had a hearty meal only two hours ago."

" More like you don't like what we can set before you? Perhaps you're one of them tramps that turns up their nose at anything but cake and pies."

And Graves looked at his guest in some distrust, and the daughter's red lips curled scornfully as she waited in the doorway.

Philip flushed hotly. "' Oh no, there is nothing I like better, I only thought I wouldn't trouble you." But the young man watched the girl uneasily as she prepared his strange meal for him. Would it be something he could not swallow? He had been a little hasty in insisting he liked nothing better. When a man is lying he does it too much at wholesale; if people would only lie in moderation, as they tell the truth, it would be so much safer.

" I guess he'll get along?" said the man, drawing up to the table, " bring a pitcher of water, Jane, aint you seen times friend, you would have smacked your lips for as much?"

Philip laughed in spite of himself, but nobody else smiled and the sick woman opened her eyes in astonishment, at the unusual sound of laughter. Then there came a period of silence. The startling echoes of his laugh were in Philip's ear, and he was thoroughly ashamed of himself. He tried to make amends for what surely was unnatural hilarity by showing his thorough appreciation of bread, water, and cold potatoes. He took up his knife and fork with nervous energy and cut off a quarter of a potato. Salt, at least, he was accustomed to, and he made the potato white with it, when he discovered Mr. Graves and his daughter were watching him very curiously. Why hadn't he known enough to have stayed at home? but here he was, and he must rise to the emergency. He put the uninviting morsel into his mouth. Good heavens! did the poor live on such food as this? He made frantic efforts to swallow, so that the tears came into his eyes.

" Be you sick, young man?"

" Did Curran speak?" interrupted the girl.

"Yes," answered Philip quickly, glad of a distraction. "And who is he—a common laborer?" Then he bit his lip.

But nobody took offence, no one suspected their guest of being anything above a common laborer.

The purity of his language or his accent would not betray him, there is no such plain badge of class in this country. The virtues and even the refinements are pretty evenly distributed. If the rich were poor, and the poor rich to-morrow, a month more might smooth over all incongruousness.

The girl was nervously picking at her dress, her head bowed away from him, showing a wavy mass of black hair. Why shouldn't so pretty a girl have a lover? But where were the lines of content and joy that love ought to give? Is even love turned into bitterness for the poor? Can their youths and maidens remember, even in the glow of love, that all paths for the poor lead to the same goal of hopeless wretchedness?

"Only a laborer," answered Graves, "a weaver, but he's got some book knowledge somehow. There aint many can beat him at talkin', is there?"

The girl's eyes were on Philip now, impatient, as he fancied, even for his poor tribute to her lover's praise.

"He is wonderful," he assented, "but what I

don't understand is, that he can be such a man and still a weaver.   Where did he learn it all?"

"Have you got enough to eat?   Well, knowledge has got pretty well through all classes now, for those as wants it.   It's there for all who have eyes or ears for it.   Why, friend, where have you been all your life? Brains and hearts don't go by station.   I've found smarter men in shops and mills than most we send to Congress.   There's thousands like Curran, if they only got the stirrin' he's had someway.   Now, Jane, it's about time you got this man's bed ready."

Philip's heart jumped.   Of course he couldn't stay, but what excuse could he give for coming at all, then?

"Be you lookin' for a job?" asked Graves, after his daughter had left them.

It occurred to Philip that he had one, if he wanted it—to put one spark of happiness into such lives as these, but he nodded.   The man looked him over rather disparagingly.

"Well, wash yourself up and black your boots a bit, and I guess I can do somethin' for you in the mill.   It's hard work and small pay, but we never had better, you and me.   We don't well know what we miss bein' poor, we miss it such a big ways."

"How long has Curran lived here?" asked Philip incoherently.   The man stared at him a moment.

"Oh! Curran, he aint been here more'n a six month. He's 'bout as queer a chap as you be, in his way ; he aint got no folks ; he lives down to one of them factory boardin' houses, but don't have no friends, or talk about anythin' but what you heard to-night. But it's all useless." Graves looked gloomily on the floor. "We aint got no show ; the rich are too many for us. I guess it's human nature for one man to boss the crowd, or it wouldn't a always been so. There's the girl, she'll show you where to sleep. Be up early in the mornin', now."

The only course for him seemed to be to follow the girl, and Philip rose to his feet.

"Good night," he said. The sick woman opened her eyes in surprise. Such people as they found no time for amenities in their dreary home. Graves looked around.

"What ? oh, yes, good-bye, but I'm goin' to see you in the mornin'."

His bed-room on which the roof encroached greedily, was newly whitewashed, or else was seldom used. His lamp sat on a wooden chair with no back to it, crowded by a tin wash-basin with his portion of water half filling it, and a round black ball of soap. Then Philip turned to look at the bed they had made for him on a slat bedstead with low head-board but not so low as the thin pillow. How many times must anybody double the pillow to

make it fit for his head? For a counterpane was the
girl's plaid shawl; he had seen it on a nail down
stairs. Poor little girl, she would want it very early in
the morning. Then he glanced in the eight-by-ten
looking-glass that hung on the white wall. Disguised! his own father would not have known him,
and he had a sensation of double consciousness as
he saw his own reflection. Perhaps Graves was
disguised too, and all the ill-dressed men he had seen
that evening, who suffered as much in their wretched
lives as he could, who could enjoy all that brightened his own life as much. And clothes made the
difference between him and them, apparently, perhaps really. The world managed according to the
clothes standard—for the man who could borrow a
broadcloth suit, comforts, consideration, happiness,
—for the man in overalls, weary days, cheerless
houses, hunger and—bah! Philip pulled off his
great boots and threw them angrily across the
room; he did not know what to make of it all.

He did not propose to spend the night here, of
course, and face the family and his job in the mill in
the morning, but he might as well lie down till the
house was asleep, and escape became possible. But he
could not lie down with all his paint on, and spoil the
poor little pillow. So he takes off his yellow whiskers
and makes such good use of the basin of water and the
ball of soap, that when he next looked in the little mir-

ror, he saw no longer the road-dusty tramp, but the fresh, kindly face of a young man who has never tasted of the bitter fountains of life. He started as if he had been shot ; the windows had no curtains, and any passer-by might have seen his transformation. Then came a heavy step on the stairs. He blew out the light and buried himself in the bed-clothes. In a moment more the door opened and Philip was breathing heavily.

" Asleep?" it was the voice of his host. " Well, I s'pose the morning will do. Pretty tired, I guess ; wonder how far he came to-day," and Graves closed the door after him and went down stairs again.

Of course Philip was not going to sleep, but there would be no harm in just closing his eyes, he could think so much better.

Here he was drinking in the very life of the poor, a strange, terrible life, he had never really imagined before. He had seen how worn and broken were their men, and read the pathetic lines of despair and sullen wretchedness written on their faces, as if in silent reproach to the providence that had inflicted the unsoftened curse of life on them. He had seen, too, their hapless girlhood, which beauty cannot cheer, which love only makes blacker, as the path of lightning on a starless night. And their sick, with no nursing, no gentle words, no comforts to assuage one hour of pain. Then he seemed to be in the hall once more, and thrilling under the eloquence of the man, Curran.   Suddenly he opened his eyes wide.   It could not be he was going to sleep, the bed was too hard—absurd—there could be no danger.   But in five minutes the heir of the Breton Mills was sound asleep in John Graves' garret room.

How long he had slept Philip had no more idea than Rip Van Winkle on a former occasion ; indeed it took him a ridiculously long time to separate dreams and facts enough to get his bearings.   Was that moonlight in the east, or dawn ?   Perhaps the family were all up and escape would be impossible. He bounded to his feet and clutched at his false whiskers, but, alas, his paint was all dissolved in the tin basin.   His only chance was in getting away unnoticed, and in two minutes more he was groping out of his little room and down the steep stairs, boots in hand.   He slowly opened the door into the sitting-room.   What if Graves stood within curiously watching.   An odd guest, this stealing out before day-break.   Again Philip wished he had stayed at home that night.

Thank God ! no one was in the room.   There was the cracked, rusty stove, and the sofa the sick woman had lain upon ; there was the dish of cold potatoes on the table, and the chair he had sat in while he tried to eat.   But somebody must be up in the inner room ; a stream of light made a white track through the half open-door. Would that bolt never slip—there. It slipped with a vengeance, and Philip drew back into the staircase in mortal terror. The light streak on the floor began to move and in a moment more a white figure stood on the threshold of the bed-room. It was Jane Graves with her long black hair about her neck and white night-dress, and her eyes glistening brightly. She held the lamp above her head, and let her drapery cling fondly as it chose about a form that would have charmed a sculptor. As she listened he could see her wavy hair rise and fall over her beating heart. Would she notice the open stair door, and come forward? What then? He must push her rudely to one side. He imagined her startled screams and the father's figure hurrying into the scene from another room to seize the interloper. No, she returns to her room. In another instant he has opened the door and is walking along the street. His escape was well-timed for the grey dawn of another day of toil and weariness is creeping over the factory village.

The houses were all alike, the front doors just as soiled, the steps equally worn, the paint the same cheerless yellow to a shade. Through the windows of one of them he caught a glimpse of a tall gaunt woman building the kitchen fire, her face and form lighted up by the flames she was nursing. His

3

ready imagination pictured the wan-featured man who must be her husband, out of whose eyes had faded so many years ago the last lingering gleam of tenderness. He imagined their old-faced, joyless children begrudged the scant play hours of childhood. Trooping behind them all, he pictured a long line of special wants and sorrows, the companions of their days, the spectres of their nights. Their houses looked all alike as he walked along, so their lives might seem just alike at first thought. Ten hours for each in the same mills—who got almost the same pittance for their hot work—and must spend their pennies for almost the same necessities. But infinite must be the diversities of their suffering.

CHAPTER IV.

Crying for the Moon.

THE strident voices of four hundred looms would seem to be too much for human nerves, but the walls of the weave-room number two of the Breton Mills are hung with soiled plaid shawls and chip hats, the livery of the factory girl. Their restless forms are busy among the rattling machinery, their swift cunning fingers moving harmlessly where mutilation would seem certain. It is a mere matter of habit, one look at most of the set pale faces, would show there was no brain force in exercise. Why, the overseer will tell you those girls are as much machines as the frames and belting; though they undoubtedly have one advantage for the employers, the girls are cheaper. The wonderful mechanism of those looms, the skillful system of belts and pulleys, and the enormous water-wheel cost a fortune; girls can be bought in the market any day for a crust of bread.

Is not that figure familiar—the one that stands this moment leaning against a dingy white pillar, while the rushing belts and sliding frames seem hurrying the faster all about her? Yes, on the piece of wall between the two jail-like windows nearest to her, hangs the plaid shawl Philip Breton had for a counterpane only last night. Her dress is soiled and ill made, and her hair tied up in the closest and ugliest coil to escape the greedy machinery, ever reaching out for new victims. But the warm soft tint of her cheeks, and the moist sheen in her black eyes, were always the same, and many a young man would rather look at her this minute than turn off an extra cut, they call it, of cloth at twenty cents. She is not gazing out of the window; Jane Graves is not the sort of girl that pines for the glories of the hills, or the speaking silence of the woods; she is only looking down at her own little hand and noting how stained and calloused it is.

Her days used to be more terrible to her even than now. She had wished every morning, that she might die before night, and at night that God would take her before morning; take her, she cared not where, no place could be worse, certain. Some women seemed made for sacrifice, better women than she, no doubt. She could only enjoy light and gayety, that was all her nature was pitched just aright for, and thoughtless pleasure. What a pretty hand it would be if it could only have a chance to get white and soft: it was cruel to make it work. But she was slowly growing, she thought, into the dead calm that all the rest had learned, and yet how she hated the great massive mills, irresistible giants that held her with deathless grasp, grimly contemptuous of her writhings, and foolish struggles. The overseers, too, how she hated them; their sharp words stung her like the lash of so many taskmasters, and the paymaster who doled out to her the few dollars, the wages of her blood and life, as if that could be paid for. She had longed so many times, to throw back his money in the smiling patronizing face, only the poor cannot afford the dearest of all luxuries, pride.

Suddenly the mill bell rung out above the roar of the wheels, and at its voice the looms stopped, the breath of their life taken away, and the belts ceased from their endless race.

Another day's work was closed, and the poor girls hurried on their shawls and hats as if at last something pleasant awaited them, and went out in chattering groups.

Jane Graves hated to follow the awkward throng, and preferred the longer way home, around by the hill. Besides, she could catch the breath of a different life, the life she knew she was meant for, the life of those who enjoy, rather than the life of those who earn. Wasn't she prettier than the other girls; and what good had her beauty done her yet, but won her a few more insults she was too poor to resent.

"What is it, Tommie?" A broad shouldered

young fellow had left the crowd, and followed her shyly up the hill.

"Nothin' much, only, may I walk home with you?"

"Will that do you any good? Hurry up then."

He was an honest-faced young fellow, and a little better dressed than most of the admiring group that waited about the mill-yard gate, to see Jane Graves go by.

"What you want to walk round here with me for, I can't see. They can't work you very hard, Tommie, if you want so much extra exercise."

It was rather a contemptuous laugh she had for him, but she showed a row of small white teeth, that poor Tommie thought were very beautiful.

"I wanted to say somethin' particular, Jennie?" And he reached down his big dingy hand for a stalk of grass, and began pulling it nervously to pieces, as he kept up with her quick feet. They were just passing Mr. Ellingsworth's house, and father and daughter stood in the doorway. No doubt Mr. Ellingsworth had just come home to tea. He held his tall felt hat in his hand, while he waited with his beautiful daughter, to enjoy the soft spring mildness. Jane Graves could see in behind them. How could they bear to stay outside. She saw a white spread tea table glistening with silver and rare china, soft-tinted carpets and pictures in rich gilded frames, far prettier, she was sure, than anything nature had to show. The girl's face, as she stood resting her white hand on her father's shoulder, was as calm as the twilight itself.

" How has she deserved it all more than I? She was never tired in her life, and I never lie down at night but my hands and feet ache. See what she gets for being idle; see what I get for my ten hours' work, every day since I was a child." The girl stopped a minute; the flash of resentment faded out of her face. " And I have got to keep it up till the end; there's no use fretting myself. If I only knew enough not to hope for anything else, I'd get along well as the rest."

The young man by her side was a good deal distressed; he looked at her flushed cheeks that were prettier than ever, and wondered vaguely what it was she wanted so much.

" Oh no, you aint like the rest," he insisted, and continued, " We've known each other pretty long, Jennie, and—and,"—he had pulled the grass all to pieces, " and I s'pose you know how I've—I mean what I've felt. I am doing a little better now." The young man's eyes brightened, " I've got a little money left me, and you know I'm just made second hand."

" What is that to me, Tommie?" she said impatiently. Her woman's soul was longing for the beautiful life of the rich, whose house she was pass

ing, and she felt too the admiring glance Mr. Ellingsworth had given to her graceful figure.   Why was
this awkward boy by her side to spoil the effect?

Tommie Bowler winced, but ducking his round
head to avoid the sharp look he feared was in the
beautiful eyes, he went on doggedly,

" I s'posed we'd been agoing together quite a
while Jennie, and I was goin' to ask you when you
was willin' to be married."

" Married—to you ? "

Ah, Tommie Bowler, what were you thinking of,
to want to marry a girl who had such a tone as that
for you?

Tears of shame started into his eyes.   " I aint
so low ; I never thought but what you would before."

She gave him a look half curious and half pitiful.
He might as well have cried for the moon, could it
be the lad thought that just because she was pretty,
she could make his home happy for him, his?

" I'm not going to have a hand at making another poor man's home.   People like us had better
be single, there's only half the trouble that way,
Tommie."

The broad shouldered young man, who did not
know what was good for him, fell back from the
woman his heart hungered for, as if he was shot.
And she walked on with hardly another thought for

the foolish lover who imagined they two could be happy together.

Why couldn't she be rich? They had always told her she was beautiful. If she only had a chance. There were plenty of women who could get along in the poorest homes, let them ; she could not. She hated every breath she drew in them. Sometimes she hated every creature she saw in them. They say men are fools over pretty women, and that is the only hope a woman has of winning her way. If she only had a chance.

A delicate grey mist floated over the river below the village, and the green forests and fresh meadows on the other side smiled through it like a fair woman through her tears. A tired soul might have drunk in its beauty, and been rested, and Jane Graves cast her eyes down on the dusty road before her, and walked along with a set bitter curl on her bright red lips, and did not once look at the gift of God's mercy to the poorest of his creatures. For her part she despised the poor ; she didn't pity them ; great, strong men who submitted to be trodden on and ground under the feet of the rich ; whose blood and muscles and quivering flesh were weighed in the balance against a few dollars of the speculators. It was good enough for them as long as they submitted to it. She didn't blame the rich ; they were the only wise people ; she only envied them. They did well to take all they could get and walk over as many thousands as would fall down before them. Oh ! if • she could only win her way to their ranks. But the rich men do not come into the weave-room for their enslavers.

Suddenly she heard a step behind her; a step she knew from all others in the world, and the whole air seemed to tremble with a new, strange heavenly impulse.

" Good evening, Jane."

She turned with a new sweet shyness. It was Curran the agitator who was beside her. A soft flush was on her cheeks, a warm light in her eyes that had grown larger for him, in delicious surprise.

" Who is that young fellow who just left you ? "

" Oh, one of my lovers," she answered coquettishly, dropping her eyes before his.

" He your lover ! " repeated Curran in his imperious fashion, " You're not for such as he, Jennie."

Her heart fluttered in sweet fear at the meaning she thought in his words. She was trying to walk very slowly, but how fast they seemed to pass the houses.

" So I told him," she said.

" You did well, then," and he looked down admiringly on the girl. You are a fine woman. I don't suppose you know it."

Jane Graves tried to look as if it was news to

her, and Curran went on. "Few women are prettier. There are fine prizes for such as you in this world if you will only wait." He continued thoughtfully, "Men have to work for distinction; a pretty face brings it to women."

"What sort of prizes?" And she trusted herself to look up at him. How grand he was, with his firm, strong face. If he only had a touch of weakness in him that might bend down to her.

"Position, money, power."

"No woman cares for those." And she believed it as she spoke, looking away over the river.

"What then?" he asked, smiling. "Those things are what all men are working for, I suppose."

"Women care for but one thing."

Sometimes the climax of a character is reached only in old age, when storms have wreaked their fury for a lifetime on a soul. Sometimes it comes in childhood, with threescore years of decline to come after it. It was at this moment, that this girl's life reached its moral height. If she could but have kept it.

"That is love," she added softly. "It is their lives; they hope only for that; they dream only of it."

Curran laughed, but gently, as he took her hands at parting; pressing them perhaps unconsciously,

but no man can be wholly careless to such beauty
as hers.

" It is only because women are more foolish than
men, not because they are more devoted, that they
are able to make such absurd mistakes."

She smiled on him as radiantly as a red-petaled
rose unfolding its glowing heart to the morning sun—
the sun that gives everything and wants nothing, and
stood half turned watching his retiring form. And
people called him poor, too, and friendless, him
whose eloquence made him each day new lovers.
And as for poverty, if a woman's love could smooth
its path, she would so joyfully shower on him all
the gifts of tendern essher heart was so rich in—for
him. She stood looking after him for a moment,
hoping he might turn for one parting glance, whose
sweet memory would thrill her foolish heart all
the night long. The road at this point passed near
a deserted ruin ; once a brick saw-mill, which had
shorn the hills and valleys around of their pride,
now a favorite trysting place for lovers of moon-
light-nights like this would be. Curran was just
entering under an arch, where once had swung a
heavy oaken door which long ago had served some
shivering family for a week's firewood.

He went in and did not once turn. How cruel
men are. Perhaps, she told herself, he is to meet
there some messenger of the Great League he had

told her about, and they will plan together some bold stroke. It was beautiful to have such power, even if it made him forget this one poor girl, whose heart longed so eagerly for another smile.

The whole world seemed glorified to the girl as she walked on. She had loitered so long that the sun was now almost setting, with his flowing robe of carmine about him, and the whole landscape seemed in a rapture of silent worship. Jane Graves was like one in a dream—her home, which she could tell from its cheap dreary counterparts, might have been a palace ; the path along in front of it, beaten by so many faltering footsteps, seemed only pleasantly familiar to her. She wondered vaguely why the mill-owner's mansion in the distance had seemed so grim and hateful to her. What had she seen to envy in anybody's life that had not her dear hope !

But down the hill comes a great white horse, tossing his mane and curvetting in the pride of his strength and beauty.

Its rider who held the rein so gracefully must be young Philip, the mill-owner's son ; he had just finished college, they said. So that was the young man Bertha Ellingsworth was engaged to ; not ill looking, and he rode well. The girl smiled to herself. " But Bertha Ellingsworth had not seen Curran."

" Did he lift his hat to me ?" She looked inquiringly about her. " There is no one else, and his

black eyes seemed to know me, too; how odd!"
thought the girl, as she walked on more hastily, and
the horse and its rider disappeared in a cloud of
dust.

.   "And it seems as if I had seen him somewhere,
too."

CHAPTER V.

A Ruin by Moonlight.

BERTHA lay back indolently in her favorite arm chair, watching the deepening twilight from her parlor window. Her eyes were almost closed, and Philip, affecting to be interested in Mr. Ellingsworth's conversation, thought he might look at her as fondly as he chose without discovery and rebuke. He was sure he was not noticed, but the girl was quite enjoying his silent offering—so long as he did not guess she perceived it. If a girl must have a lover, Philip did very well. At least he knew she was not one of the sentimental girls, with unlimited capacity for foolishness. Yes, Philip's manners were nearly as good as her father's, who had not kissed her for ten years. Not that she would have endured it for an instant if Philip had not wanted to make love to her—that would have been an insult. Her lover was no divinity to her; she saw all his faults as clearly as anybody; not with impatience, however, that was not her temperament. For example, he was too short, and his shoulders were too slight. She never forgot it for an instant. But then he al-

ways did what she said, and that was very convenient, and yet she was half provoked with him for it.
A man ought to command a woman's love, not try
to coax it from her. He thought quite too much
of her for what she returned him ; he ought to be
stern and cold to her sometimes, and give her a
chance to be something besides an ungrateful recip-
ient. But perhaps she would not like him at all in
that character. She suddenly opened her eyes wide
and looked curiously at her lover ; there is nothing
so chilling as such a look as that, and Philip winced
under it.

"Well, I suppose you two are bursting with
tender confidences," smiled Mr. Ellingsworth as he
rose to his feet, "I really won't stay a minute
longer." He moved towards the door, then he
smiled and looked around ; he had thought of something very funny. "Now Philip, my dear boy, you
mustn't be too sure of her just because she seems so
affectionate. That is where a young man makes
his worst mistake. As long as there is another man
in the world, he may have hope, that is, the other
man."

His daughter looked coolly after him, "Must
you go? why we shall die of ennui. We shall have
to take a walk ourselves. Excuse me, Philip, while
I get ready."

Left alone, the young man rose and went to the

window, and looked out at the evening sky. There
was a little frown on his face. "What an unpleasant way of talking Bertha's father had. One would
think he believed in nothing. There was no danger
of his feeling any too sure of her; how far away she
seemed to him. The idea of marriage seemed vague
and dreamlike, and yet he had her promise."

"You may adjust my shawl for me." His vexation fled, and he smiled with the sweet complacency
of possession as he laid the delicate bit of lace about
her warm shoulders. To-night would be a good
time to turn his idea into a reality, and ask her
when—

"But you must promise me one thing," she said,
standing close to him for one moment.

"What is that, Bertha, dear?" he asked with
guilty uneasiness.

She put her soft white hand in his so charmingly, that he was suddenly sure it could be nothing
hard she would require.

"I promise," he assented.

"No love-making in the ruin, if I let you take
me there."

"Why, Bertha!" he exclaimed, so sorrowfully,
that he showed his whole plan. The girl laughed.

"You are too cunning, by half, Mr. Philip, but
then you know love-making in the saw-mill is too
common. Why it is the rendezvous of all the fac-

tory hands.   No, I couldn't think of it for a moment."

"Then I won't insist on taking you to the old saw-mill."

"Oh, yes! it is charming by moonlight."

"One would think you hadn't any heart." Philip did not confess the peculiar charm this woman's very coldness had for him ; there was some quality in it that was irresistibly exciting to his nature.   Perhaps it was the presence of an unconscious reserve of passion, never yet revealed, that he felt in her, that kept his heart ever warm, and his eyes ever tender for its unveiling.

The round-faced servant girl had come up from tha kitchen, and stood awkwardly at the door.

"Yes, you may light the gas now, Annie, we are going out."   She laid her hand lightly on Philip's arm as they went down the walk.   "I must really have a maid.   That Annie is too clumsy for me to endure in the parlor or dining-room.   Oh, yes, I probably have got a heart, some time it will frighten you, perhaps."

They walked slowly along the street, passing the very spot where Tommie Bowler had offered his poor little all to Jane Graves only an hour or two ago. Their feet trod carelessly on the bits of grass the nervous lover had scattered along the path.

"But you haven't told me about the meeting.

Did the agitator have auburn curls as I said? That is the clearest idea I have got of a hero."

As he told her his adventure they reached the ruin and went in. The moonlight poured through the dismantled roof, and made a white track for itself over the uneven floor, leaving the rest of the interior in the shadow. Such as remained of the fallen rafters, made convenient benches for visitors, who might easily enough imagine themselves in some old-world ruin. And the young mill-owner's son and Bertha, the hem of whose garment had never touched poverty, seated themselves where many a penniless young fellow had wooed some pretty weaver maid to share his destitution, all for love,—soon starved out of both their lives.

Philip felt all his last night's enthusiasm coming over him again, as he described the meeting of the hopeless poor and the life of the family that had taken him in. And he seemed to be again thrilled with Curran's eloquence as he pictured his noble presence, and tried to repeat his vivid sentences. Was Bertha listening so patiently to him or only idly watching the shadows as they shifted with the moon? He hoped she was touched. She could help him so much to do something for the thousand souls in the mills if there was anything could be done. And then it seemed so sweet to have an earnest thought and hope in common—one more bond to unite them.

"But what can I do, Bertha, it is all so mixed up? Do you suppose my father would listen to me—but if he would, what can I propose? If I tell him the people are poor and unhappy, he knows all that. I can't ask him to divide all his wealth with them, that wouldn't last so many very long, and then he couldn't employ them any more; they would be spoiled for work, and we would all starve together."

"I wish I could see him," said the girl slowly.

He looked at her blankly.   "Why?"

Hadn't she heard what he had just said so eagerly? He felt like one who had plunged into what he thought a rippling river and found it ice.

"Curran, you called him."

Suddenly a double tread of feet without and the forms of two men, one much taller than the other, blocked the doorway.

"Hush, then," whispered Philip, excitedly. "There he stands."

The men came forward till they stood directly in the path of the moonlight, which seemed to clothe them with its silver sheen.   No need to tell her which was he; the girl bent eagerly forward and fixed her eyes on the majestic figure that stood with folded arms.

"I am very late," began the shorter man, apologetically.

Curran did not reply and the man went on in a

minute more. "What is the news? I want to report your village, you know."

"There is no news. It is the same old story. What is the good of reporting and reporting, and then doing nothing?" The words escaped between his teeth like the staccato tones of a cornet. "I am sick of the word 'wait,' it is the resource of the weak."

"But we are weak. Give us time."

Curran unfolded his arms with a gesture of impatience.

"The injustice has got its growth; it has fattened on our flesh and blood, and sucked out the life of untold generations before us." His eyes shone fiercely on the man of caution. "I believe the time has come to destroy it, and the crime of murder lies at our consciences for every crushed soul sacrificed for our delay."

Philip fancied Bertha trembled.

"But," began the stranger in the metallic voice of the objector, "the officers of the League think the laborers are not ready."

"No, nor will they ever be; they have submitted too long. But they are always good for action if somebody will lead them. They hang on our lips, but we do not speak."

"Yes, we are spreading intelligence, sending out orators like you; we are arranging political campaigns. By and by capital will be more reasonable."

"Do you fancy then," retorted Curran bitterly, "that the rich will willingly open their coffers to the logical workmen, out of whose earnings they have filled them? Isn't it too delightful to be able to build a palace for a home, and create another paradise for a garden; to marry off their sons and daughters when the first coo of love trembles on their young lips? Then will they divide," and he raised his voice with terrible emphasis, " when there is no escape from it. As long as the people submit, if it be till the trump of doom, so long the lords and masters will defraud them of the price of their labor; so long their wives and daughters will look down complacently on the sufferings of the million, one of whom starves for every piece of finery they smile to wear."

Philip felt Bertha tremble again, but her eyes never once wavered.

"What do you propose?"

"I don't know," muttered Curran, turning his head half away, "but when I see the silent raging in the hearts of the poor, when I see the riches squeezed out of their scant, ill-fed blood, I am mad with impatience. But I suppose all great changes come most beneficently if they are slow. Then there are no heart sickening reactions. Come out into the open air. It seems close here."

The two men went out and the indistinct murmur of their voices was all could be heard.

"How do you like my hero?" said Philip, pleased that Bertha should have a chance to learn from the same source he had been so stirred. Now she could sympathize perfectly with him, in the new idea that he felt must have such a great influence over his life.

"He is coming back," she whispered breathlessly, "alone."

Curran looked in astonishment at two figures starting toward him, out of the shadows. He recognized them at once.

"Well, I hope you may have learned some useful truths," he said scornfully, looking the young man full in the face.

Bertha's lip quivered, and she came close to him in the moonlight and laid her white hand on his arm. "We did not mean to overhear your secrets," she said earnestly, "but surely it could do no harm to listen to such beautiful words. They seemed to be wasted on the one you meant them for."

Philip looked at Bertha in startled surprise; he hardly knew her: then he glanced at Curran whose curled lip softened its stern lines. The girl's bonnet had fallen back on her neck, and her face was turned up toward his in the perfection of graceful entreaty, her big blue eyes showing dark in the evening. The agitator glanced at her sparkling diamonds, and the rich lace shawl that lay over her shoulders, then back into the beautiful upturned face, and at last his eyes fell before hers. His boldness was gone; his scorn and contempt for the women of the rich changed to timidity before her.

" Don't distress yourself, my dear lady," he said at last, " there is no harm done, I am sure."

As his tense mood relaxed, the charm that had so transformed the girl seemed broken, and she drew back as if in surprise at finding herself so near him.

"But I want you to tell me what I can do," said Philip, rather vaguely, hesitating a moment in the doorway.

Curran looked keenly into the young man's kind face.

"And you want to do what you can?" he repeated thoughtfully, " I hardly know where to begin, there is so much."

The walk home was a silent one, till almost the end.

" Do you know what I am going to do to-morrow, Bertha? I am going to put on the old clothes again."

" Don't you think it rather boyish?"

"I'm in earnest this time. I am going to learn how to make cloth, and find out just how hard the work is, and just how—why Bertha, are you yawning?"

They had reached her doorway. She looked very

sweet, even when smothering a yawn with her two fingers, as she stood on the step above him, and gazed off on the river. His foolish heart began to beat.

"Bertha, we are not at the saw-mill now, and—"

She smiled. "But you were not to say anything if I let you take me there, and I have let you, haven't I?"

"But aren't you ever going to consent to—"

"There," she stamped her foot playfully. "You are almost breaking your promise," then she looked at his reproachful face and let him take her hand and kiss it all he chose. "You know there is a sort of solemnity in the kind of business-like talk you want so much. But I'll promise this, if you will be patient for just one month, you can say what you please to me."

Philip went off in great glee, and his horse Joe could not leap too high to suit him, for what Bertha had said was almost what he asked. One month from to-day, that would be a Friday early in the morning.

CHAPTER VI.

A Day Off.

JANE GRAVES was putting on her hat and faded plaid shawl for another dreary day's work. It was a cloudy morning, and even for a girl in love it is hard work to be sentimental such mornings. She wondered what she ever could see poetic in life. If she only did her work well, so as to escape reprimand, she might come to take a kind of pride and pleasure in it as the rest did, till their strength and spirit was broken. But as it was she hated it with all the passion of her nature. She saw nothing in it but slavery and degradation, and in her impatience, thought she would rather die than drag out her life thus. Somebody must do the work, but not such as she, surely.

"Come here, my dear."

She had been lingering aimlessly, only that she dreaded to turn her feet toward the factory, whose tolling bell rung sternly in her ears. Now she approached her mother's bed with a gentler expression on her face.

The thin hands were laid on her arm, and the

sick woman drew the girl's head down on the pillow beside her own.

"Was I ever so pretty as you, I wonder," she said wistfully. "They used to say I was the prettiest in the village." And the sunken eyes brightened at sweet memories, the sweetest in the world to a woman.

"It did you little good, mother," said the girl in a muffled voice.

In a moment more she started up—

"There, mother, I am late again ; a quarter days pay lost, and a scolding gained."

The sick woman's eyes opened wide, and the girl waited one sad minute more, to see how terribly white the poor face looked even against her pillow.

"I had something to say, I thought," said the woman eagerly, "but I can't remember, I am so sick. But perhaps it wasn't anything. You may go now, dear, I am sorry I kept you."

The girl pinned her shawl about her. What good of looking in the glass. It could only tell her she was pretty, as her mother used to be, and remind her what a fool she was to expect a different fate. Fifteen years, and she might be sick and broken on this very bed, perhaps telling her own unhappy child, how pretty she used to be. The girl shuddered at the picture, as she went .out of her mother's room.

"Oh! I remember now," called the sick woman.

"Did you want the tea put near you?" asked the girl, coming back wearily.

"It is not that—but—but you are not to go to work to-day. Somebody is coming to see you. He wants you to live with him."

"What, to marry me?" exclaimed the girl in astonishment.

"He didn't speak of that," smiled her mother languidly, but I can't talk any more, I am so tired."

Jane Graves had learned one lesson of poverty, not to hope. So after this strange announcement of her mother's she only laid off her hat and shawl, and waited. After looking idly out of the window for a while, and seeing nothing that had not worn itself into her very soul years ago, the vague woman instinct stirred in her, and she moved about the house arranging things. She found a little map that hung in the sitting-room, a little awry, and straightened it. It was a dingy map of China that had come once with a pound of tea, and she wanted to throw it away, but the wall looked too bare without anything. She took down a couple of ugly little gift chromos her father had placed on the mantelpiece, and tore them up in disgust. There seemed nothing else to do, there was so little to arrange. She wasn't so sure but it was better in the mill, —perhaps it was a blessing the poor were kept so

many hours in its grim walls, where at least there
was but little chance to think. What was there to
long for in such homes and such leisure as this?

She stepped to the closet and took out a well
thumbed book, and sat down. She turned two or
three pages, and then counted how many times she
had read them before, and she felt sick with the
foolish hopes and dreams the oft read book had
used to wake in her.

She laid it away with a sigh and picked up an
old newspaper. How slow the forenoon went.

She read down the advertising columns; how
many beautiful things in the world, and all for sale!
Somebody must have the money to buy them
or the stores wouldn't be running. Where was it
all? did anybody work any harder for it than her
father and herself? Jane Graves opened her little
pocket-book and shook it over the table; but it was
as empty as the day she bought it.

Then there came a light tap on the street door.
This must be the " gentleman," this tall, elegant
figure in a checked summer suit; and he actually
lifted his hat to her.

" My name is Ellingsworth." He needn't have
told her; he had figured in the girl's fancy for years
as the very impersonation of rank and wealth.

" I called about a maid. Mr. Graves gave me
leave to speak with his daughter. Is she in?"

"I suppose I am the one.   Will you come in?"

She watched him as he crossed the room to the nearest chair. How much lighter he walked than she could ; and one might have thought from his unconsciousness that he had been used to just such a miserable room as this all his life. He showed no surprise at her being the prospective maid servant ; no doubt he knew it all the time and the way he spoke was only a part of his good manners. But then she could not imagine his showing surprise at anything.

"There will be but little to do," Mr. Ellingsworth continued, looking at her face and not seeming to see how ill she was dressed. "There is only my daughter ; you may have seen her, yes ; and myself. The wages will be small," and he named them and smiled apologetically, as if he expected her to decline. "Your father spoke to me as if you did not like the factories."

Out at service ; well, why not ? Could it be any more degrading than the life she had lived ? and such wages, too. Why, she could dress quite prettily then ; and her girlish heart fluttered. And she could leave ugly things and rude people ; and breathe perfumes and have only graceful surroundings ; what matter if they were not hers.

She would be lifted right up into the very atmosphere she longed for ; yesterday she had envied the

Ellingsworths, to-morrow, perhaps, she would share their beautiful life with them. Why not?

She lifted her bright eyes to his face. It was in half profile at this moment, and she could see his hair was just touched with grey; how could men in his world ever grow old! He was smooth shaved, showing in full effect the delicate cynical curve of his thin lip and the clearly defined outlines of his chin which struck the girl as having a touch of weakness in it. He must have been very oddly affected by the poverty pictured so unmistakably about him; but there was not the smallest sign of it on his well bred face.

"I will go," she said abruptly, "when do you want me?"

"I shall be away for a fortnight," he said rising, with his own admirable smile. "You can come when I return."

She rose too; but could think of nothing proper to say, but how poverty-stricken she would look in her factory clothes. Her spirits had fallen already.

"By the way," Mr. Ellingsworth turned, as if a sudden business item had struck him. It was a peculiar expressionless monotone he used sometimes when on delicate subjects that seemed to have as little personal quality as a printed page. "I always pay in advance; be kind enough to accept your first month's wages and our bargain will be closed."

The girl found herself alone, looking at the crisp, fresh-looking bank bills he had placed in her hands. " How thoughtful these rich people are. They have time for it, I suppose."

The tea hour passed long before dark that day, the mills letting out earlier on Saturdays ; and Mr. Graves had pulled his old hat down over his eyes as he always wore it, and gone over to the grocery store to talk politics with his friends. They all had long accounts there ; accounts the boldest of them never expected to catch up with ; nor was at all afraid of the keen-eyed storekeeper losing anything on them either.

Jane Graves was in her mother's room, but dressed in the best she had ; a faded plum-colored silk, a remnant of her mother's youth. Did it make her sad to see it? The girl stood a moment before the mirror and fastened a cardinal ribbon in her hair, for wouldn't Curran be sure to come to inquire after her? It had been a great while since she had missed a whole day's work. How he would admire her dress ; he would say he never knew how pretty she was. But this was nothing to what she would have soon. Then she began to look over her scant wardrobe ; her mother's feverish eyes watching her from her pillow. On one chair lay the cheap calico dress she had just laid off ; every spot and wrinkle reminded her of some dreary, hopeless hour. But now all would be changed. She would see only beautiful things, and graceful, smooth-voiced people. Poor mother, it was too bad she had to stay here. Never again would the daughter be a part of the jostling, chattering swarm that poured out of the factory gates. Oh, she never half knew how she hated it; she hadn't dared confess it to herself. She was sorry for the worn girl faces, old some of them at twelve years; and wrinkled and wan at sweet sixteen. But probably there were not many, she complacently concluded, that suffered as she did. Custom must dull their feelings and habit for most of them overcome their longings for free breath and brightness.

Her wardrobe was very simple. There hung over the back of a chair the dull check of a merino, chosen long ago to endure the most service with the least show of it. On the bureau before the mirror was a paper box holding a discarded ribbon or two, pink or cardinal, and two or three pieces of cheap jewelry the girl was too proud to wear. There was in the box besides a grey veil that she had never worn.

" It won't take me long to pack," she said aloud.

She suddenly took a pretty attitude of listening. She had closed the door into the sick chamber in a moment more, and stood in the middle of the sitting room when Curran came in.

" Why, you don't look very sick, Jennie. I have to walk to Lockout by eight o'clock; but thought I would look in just a minute."

" I am going to leave the mill." How preoccupied he seemed to-night. " I am going to leave the mill, Mr. Curran," the girl repeated with beating heart. He might not like her new plan, and at the very thought of his disapproval, she felt all her bright hopes taking to themselves wings; and the old dreary picture of factory gates and soiled calico dresses came back.

" Going away, little girl? " He seemed to speak with a slight effort, as if his mind was not on what he said. " Well, I suppose you can't be any worse off, but we shall miss you."

And was that all he had to say when he thought she was going forever out of his life—had he no reproaches for her?

" I am not going far," she began, hurriedly.

" There would be no use going far." He had seated himself on the other side of the table from her, and rested his face on his hand. " It is just the same everywhere, wherever there are a thousand souls, ten will grind the rest. I don't suppose the rich mean to be so unjust, not all of them, they don't stop to notice that they are getting all the good things in the world. It never occurs to them to wonder why the great earth seems to produce only for them."

Jane Graves sat back in her chair, her hands crossed in her lap. Why didn't he talk about her just a little? She looked up at his absorbed face wistfully. She wished he was not quite such a great man, or perhaps if she was a greater woman she would not mind it.

"Why, Jennie, sometimes I get so tired trying to stand up against it all, so sick of my own heart-ache that I can make nobody share with me." He had risen to his feet, and was walking moodily across the room. That very night he must pour out all the precious energy of his soul into dull, stolid ears, that seemed so slow to understand—a hall full of strange faces would look up coldly at him, and his hot words would be quenched, as they fell from his lips, in the unmoved depths of their hearts. It seemed so vain, all he could do or say, and he felt so tired to-night, longing, instead, to rest his head on some gentle breast, and be soothed with some foolish words of comfort and tenderness.

The girl had risen, too, and stood resting the back of her hand on the table. But her eyes dared not lift to his. She tried to speak, and her lips trembled so that her voice came strange and unfamiliar.

"I am sorry for you. Is there no one, no woman?" she half whispered.

"Women do not care for such as I," he said,

smiling a little bitterly. " They love light and pleasant things. I am too serious. I should only
frighten them ; they could not understand. And
then a woman would ask more of me than she
would give. And I am not my own."

Then he came toward her with a softer light in
his eyes.

"You are a good little girl, Jennie." He had
taken her trembling hands, which only trembled the
more. " I shall miss you very much. What is the
trouble with your eyes, Jennie, can't you look at
me? I am going now."

Then she raised her eyes, like lightning, to his
face.

"Oh, let me comfort you," she cried, " I would
die for you. I will ask nothing back, but a smile
now and then. Nobody can ever love you like
me."

His face was troubled, but cold and impassive as
rock. He still held her hands, as she sank in a
heart-breaking flood of tears at his feet.

After a moment he bent down in pity, and gathered her trembling form in his arms. How the sobs
seemed to shake her. He smoothed back her wavy
hair from the low forehead, and even kissed her wet
cheeks. But all he said was,

" Poor little girl, poor little Jennie."

For an instant she lay still as a nestling child.

Then she sprang back from him, and fled into her mother's room, and wept and moaned for shame and heartache, until the calm of weariness came over her, as nature's blessed gift to her hopeless children.

CHAPTER VII.

A Test.

"ISN'T your father going?" It was the same evening, and Philip Breton was assisting Bertha into his beach wagon for a twilight drive.

" Father has left town for a few days. Didn't you know? Suppose you let me have the back seat. The world is large enough to afford us a seat apiece to-night."

Bertha adjusted her wraps and the horses stepped off down the street as gayly as if their driver had not been disappointed. It almost seemed as if Bertha took pleasure in giving him the heartache; no doubt it was only her innocence of what the feeling was, and her aversion to being disturbed.

There was not very much conversation to-day, indeed there never was unless Philip afforded it. Bertha considered she did her part in looking well, smiling prettily at his witticisms, with now and then a remark, if she felt inclined. But to-day Philip was moody and silent, pretending he could not make himself understood, sitting with his back to her, implying, of course, it was all her fault. So Bertha gave herself up to the sensuous delight of riding, and only spoke in mild exclamations of admiration of the scenery as they left the village behind, and followed up the winding river.

Philip was beginning to feel the oppression of silence, and to be conscience stricken at anything so near rudeness to Bertha. He knew, in advance, just the look of surprise she would have for any confession of fault on his part. He must only act as if there had been no break in their talk; and it became easy for him, for the mere consciousness of her presence warmed his heart, so that no coldness or fancied grievance could live there. But before he found the word he wanted, they had passed through a wood and were coming into an open stretch of country, and suddenly Philip saw a man's form swaying easily, while he took great strides along the footpath.

"Curran," he exclaimed, and stopped his horses close beside him. The man turned, and one might have thought he did not recognize the occupants of the carriage, only there was the least bit of a flush on his face, which bore the lines of interrupted meditation. Then he bowed slightly to Philip.

"And you don't recollect me I suppose," smiled Bertha.

"I am not so stupid," he said, letting his steel-blue eyes rest admiringly upon her.

"We are going to Lockout too. Aren't we, Bertha? You must get in with us."

"No, I won't crowd you, don't move." And he turned a little away from them as if to continue his walk.

"Certainly you must!" said Bertha, "see I have a whole seat to myself and it is so stupid—Please."

And Curran took the seat she offered him, holding back her wraps till he was seated, and then releasing them.

"Do you think I shall ever learn to weave cotton cloth?" asked Philip, to call his attention to their day's work together.

"I presume so, if you really mean to. But it is lucky you haven't got your board to pay meanwhile."

But Curran did not smile, and was very ill at ease. He seemed to be lifted, body and soul, into the very life he was accustomed to rebuke. The beautiful horses of the rich were harnessed to-day to his pleasure with their gold plate trimmings. What right had he here? He said nothing of it, but felt intensely the falseness of his position; the delicate springs hurt him, and every sign of lavish wealth in the dress of his companions. He had tried that very day to give this young heir to the Breton Mills the impression that there could be no intimacy between such as they. He wanted no interests with the rich, his life work must be against them, he desired no association with a luxurious manner of life he ought to upbraid, there must not be one chain of gold to unite him with the wealthy class in whom he saw the enemies of the people.

And yet he was taking delight in this woman's presence, a new delight, such as the women of the poor had never given him. And was not she the very essence of luxury and refinement. He hated himself for it, but for all he tried to look elsewhere he kept seeing the sparkle of the diamonds on the whitest hand he had ever seen. He enjoyed the lilies of the valley set in mosaic at her throat, which showed its creamy white against the delicate ruffles, and the comb with its band of Roman gold almost the shade of the rippling hair it restrained. But were not these the very extravagances the poor had to struggle to earn for her? He ought to be fulminating withering sentences for such as she.

" I will get out at the rocks and walk the rest of the way," said Curran at last, as they could catch a glimpse of Lockout in the distance. " The workmen I want to talk to would hardly understand my coming with a carriage and pair."

The " rocks " came but a mile from Lockout and the horses had trotted so well that the spot was reached in a few moments more. The road at this point had been cut through a side-hill of sandstone, by dint of great blasting, and the jagged edges jutted out angrily at the passers by.

"There must be a wonderful landscape on the other side of the rocks," said Bertha, as Philip stopped his horses for Curran to alight.

"Have you plenty of time?" said Bertha before the workman could express his thanks.

"An hour to spare."

She looked wistfully at the envious rocks that shut them in, and then at Curran's grave face.

"I would so like to see that view from the top of the rocks if I had some one to help me."

Curran's face suddenly flushed with pleasure, "I should like to help you."

In a minute more Bertha was climbing the rocks with her strange escort, and Philip sat holding his horses quite a little distance back.

"You didn't talk very much during our drive," said Bertha as she stood with her companion looking off down the valley. "Is it so wicked of us to be rich?"

He shot a sudden deprecating look at her. "Don't force me so far. I can not say it now."

Bertha smiled. "Then leave me out of it, say Philip instead."

"He is enjoying the fruits of terrible injustice."

"But would his father have been rich unless he had deserved it?" asked Bertha.

"Is it a just reward of merit, then, that a thousand human creatures should well nigh starve, and he be rich? If he has deserved to be rich, you must say they have merited starvation."

The girl liked to hear his earnest, thrilling tones, and watch his eyes flash and his nostrils dilate with such rare passion.

"Is it just," he went on, "that no matter how unweariedly a laborer works, his idle neighbor, as surely as the sun sets, should lay intolerable tribute on his profits; so that he must stay forever poor? Is a day's work worth nothing, then why does it bring in some capitalist thousands of dollars for a stroke of his pen?"

Bertha understood but little of what he was saying, but she could look intently at him with wide open blue eyes which had a pretty trick of changing expression as if in closest sympathy with a speaker. Curran felt no one had half listened to him before, that at last every word told, and he was strangely excited by the sweet mystery of their common inspiration.

"Great wealth is made up of ten thousand trickling streams, drained from the paltry earnings of as many defrauded workmen. Mere cunning scheming ought not enable a man to turn aside the great river of plenty which flows for all men. Why these shrewd business men, whom so many praise, have so ingeniously placed their chains on the laborer, that the harder he struggles to escape from poverty, he only

turns the faster the wheel that grinds out fortunes
for his masters, and draws him in at last to be
crushed."

He hesitated for her to ask him some questions,
but perhaps it was already as plain to her as to him.
At any rate, she only looked off to the west where
the glow of sunset was fast fading, and then back
into his face regretfully.

" I suppose we ought to go down," she said.

" Why, yes, I had forgotten whether it was night
or day."

He took her hand gently as if he touched a holy
thing, and his face softened like a child's. He would
not have let her fall for the world. She had taught
him, how he did not stop to think, that there was
a rare and exquisite strain of joy in life. She had
spiritualized womanhood to him ; he suddenly saw
in it an essence so pure and fine it might redeem the
world. An hour ago, he had been so wretched, and
now a vague, sweet hope he cared not to define was
born in him. As he stood upon the road-bed, and
reached up his hands to help Bertha down, their eyes
met for a moment, and then she trusted herself to
him in such gentle surrender that a mist floated
before his sight. She almost fell, and he must needs
gather her perfect form in his arms to save her.

Philip had been idly snapping his whip, and
looking up the road. He thought he saw in the dis-

tance a number of men with guns hurrying in his direction, and before them—yes, it must be a dog, an odd hour of the day for hunting. He might as well have his horses turned about; he could see Curran and Bertha clambering down from the rocks. So it happened that at the moment Bertha came so near falling, in fact did fall, into Curran's arms, Philip was sitting with his back toward them, faced towards home.

But by this time the hunters with guns were nearer, the blacksmith had rushed out of his shop to look at the dog who bounded along with his mouth to the ground dropping foam as he ran.

The dog was mad. Bertha saw the great white creature, and grew pale as death, and pressed back against the rocky wall in despair. Curran saw him too, and had not even to make up his mind to die to save this woman. It was a matter of course. He stepped out directly in front of her without one word, and bending forward waited. The mad dog might pass them by. But no, in an instant more the beast was upon him, and like lightning Curran had reached out his hands of iron, and caught his shaggy throat as in a vise.

The creature rose upon its hind legs, and snapped ravenously at his captor, great drops of foam specked with blood, dropping from his jaws. With one rapid glance Curran saw the men with guns,

running at full speed, and almost at hand.   If he
could hold him but one moment more, he might yet
be saved, if those glistening teeth, distilling poison
and madness, would spare his flesh one moment
more.   His arms and wrists were corded like a
giant's ; his head thrown back to escape the venom-
ous fangs, while he listened with fast sickening
heart, to the sound of approaching feet. He heard,
too, the quick breathing of the woman behind him ;
thank God, he could save her from such a fate, and
she might think kindly of him sometimes, even if he
must die like a dog, since it was for her.

But now his arms trembled with the terrible strain
upon them, and the dog struggled more fiercely, so
that the man felt his hot, fetid breath on his cheek,
and in an instant more the deadly jaws seemed
closing over his arm.   Suddenly there came a loud
report and a cloud of smoke, and the mangled creature fell upon the ground in his death agony.   The
madness had gone out of his big brown eyes, which
looked up pitifully at the man he would have slain.

"They were just in time with their guns," exclaimed Philip, rushing up, and wringing his hand.

But the man made no response, nor even looked
around for one sign of gratitude from the woman he
had risked his life for.   He had no answers or smiles
for the admiring crowd that had seemed to gather so
quickly when the danger was over, but his face grew

quite pale as he walked up the road. At the black-smith's shop a thought seemed to strike him ; he hesitated a moment and then went in.

When the crowd came up and followed him in, they found him before the glowing forge. His sleeve was rolled up, revealing an arm almost like the smith's, but how closely he was studying it. Just below the elbow were the marks of a dog's fangs, out of which slowly oozed two great drops of blood. No one dared to speak, all looked on him as a man devoted, and half expected to see already the signs of madness in his calm, pale face. The men with the guns had come in with the rest, and stood under the rows of horse-shoes that lined the blackened walls, with horrified eyes riveted on the print of the poi-soned fangs. The blacksmith stood by his anvil, ham-mer in hand, as if frozen, and even Philip Breton was stunned and baffled at the sudden revelation of the fate stamped on this man who had given his life for Bertha's. Philip had been devising how rare a gift of undying friendship he could give him in token of his gratitude, and now a terrible death must be his only reward.

But the face of the victim was as composed as if death had already claimed him. He did not seem to see one of the silent forms that thronged the little shop. Then he looked carefully at the wound in his arm, and pressed out the drops of poisoned blood.

In another instant he had reached out his right
hand toward the forge, and grasped the end of a bar
of iron that shone at white heat where it touched
the coals. He drew it out before one could catch
his breath, and held it close against the death mark
in his quivering flesh.   A sickening hiss brought a
cry of sympathy from the astonished crowd, but his
lips never moved till the cure was completed.   He
threw back the iron, and grinding his teeth in his
agony, turned on his heel and went out.

At the door was a face paler than his.   Bertha
Ellingsworth had seen it all.   As he looked at her
white face and golden brows and lashes, Curran
thought of wreaths of strands of gold on the driven
snow.   But her eyes had a new fathomless expression in them, and her lips were parted as if to speak,
if there were only words sweet and gentle enough.
His face flushed with a delicious gladness deeper
than his pain, as she made him hold out his arm for
her, and touched it with mysterious tenderness, and
bound her handkerchief about his charred and aching wound.

" And you can't disappoint your audience ? How
brave you are.   But you will come to me to-
morrow ?"

"If you wish it." The crowd had gathered outside the door, and stood a little way off, curiously
watching them.

" I wish I could repay you," she said, looking wistfully up at him.

But Curran's face flushed crimson, and he drew back from her as if he had been stung.

As she looked at him, a flush slowly came into her face, too. " Would you like to kiss me, just once ?"

The man turned and drew her to his heart before them all, and her eyes fell till their long golden lashes touched her cheek, as he stooped and kissed her pouted red lips.

CHAPTER VIII.

His Mistake.

IT was quite dark when the carriage turned the last bend in the winding road homeward and the lights of Bretonville came into view. The lights in the windows of the poor danced out to meet the tired horses as gayly as any. There might have been a sobbing woman behind the cheeriest of them all; nature shows no sympathy for human suffering. If her poor children have no rest and joys their hearts must break; that is one of nature's laws. Neither can light lose its gladness and cheer because gladness and cheer are so absurdly out of place in poverty-stricken homes. As if the circles that were gathered within most of those windows deserved the name of home, with never a smile of contentment to light up a face, or a word of hope to make music for a dulled ear. Ah, that human nature is so terribly logical and cannot let a creature be happy unless there is something light or pleasant in its life! Home to such as they is the place where the cravings of hunger are quieted and the tired cords and muscles are relaxed for a new strain; where they can complain, and

where they can sleep and die. But save the word
to them at least, for a time when it shall be a reality.

Suddenly the sound of fire bells fell upon Philip's
ear and startled him out of his melancholy revery.
The same instant he saw a little cloud of smoke
above the brick mills, and then a bright tongue
of flame leap up toward it. The bells pealed out in
short nervous strokes as if in tremulous fear, and
at their impulse the young man's blood coursed
through his veins in uncontrollable excitement. It
was but two minutes more when Philip drew up
short at the mill-yard gates, to escape the engine
which swept by with a rush, dragged by a crowd
of shouting men. The people hatless, coatless, and
some even bare-footed in their haste, poured out
of every street and alley-way, and into the wide open
gates, everybody talking and nobody listening.

But Bertha had hardly spoken during the drive
home, and now seemed very little interested in the
disturbance.

"The mills are on fire," cried Philip, dropping
his reins and turning his excited face toward her.

"So I see," she said coolly, "and hadn't you better drive on?"

"Why, I ought to be here." He looked nervously at the hurrying crowd and back into Bertha's
cold beautiful face. "Couldn't you wait in one
of these tenements? these are all nice people?"

But she made no motion and only looked at his flushed face in annoyed surprise. " What are you thinking of? I stop with these people?"

" Or drive on home without me. The horses are gentle and you are such a good driver, you know."

Philip was growing terribly restless; the people came faster and faster ; and his eager eyes followed each man and woman into the gates with increasing anxiety. Even Bertha noticed the curious looks the passers-by gave to the carriage that blocked the way.

" I couldn't think of it," she said in measured tones that reminded Philip, even at such a moment as that, of her father's. " You had better drive along; there, not so fast. Why will you run the horses ? You almost frighten me."

It took but a few moments to reach Bertha's home, but it seemed a long time to Philip, who kept looking back over his shoulder at the flames which to his excited fancy seemed rising higher at every glance. He stopped the horses at Bertha's door at last, and leaping to the ground, assisted her to alight. The horses were panting, but there was no time even to give them breath, and in an instant more Philip was back in his seat. But Bertha stood as if she had something to say, and he waited before he drew up the reins.

" You will make a mistake in leaving me to myself to-night."

He thought there was a mysterious touch of self-distrust in her voice that was soft and almost tender as she looked fixedly at him. Ah! he had never seen her so lovely; as if the warm passionate woman soul had been born in her; and he longed in his rapture to fall at her feet and kiss them. He was forgetting the mill in flames as he drank in the new sweet hope she seemed to give him. He could not leave her thus with that wonderful light in her eyes. No doubt the fire was subdued, and how little he could do at best ; there were so many stronger than he.

But suddenly a tongue of flame leaped up into the black sky like lightning.

"I would so love to stay, darling, but the mills are on fire—my father's mills. I might save them. Don't you understand—it would be infamous in me to—"

"I only said you make a mistake."

Till he dies Philip Breton never will forget that scene; the darting flames beckoning him away, and this beautiful woman, for whose first fond caress he would have given everything but his manhood and honor, inviting him to stay. And in her changed face he thought he saw such sweet promise of love if he stayed and such sure presage of evil if he went.

"Good night," he said with faltering voice as he drew up the reins.

"Good night," she answered slowly as she turned

to go in, and he thought he heard her other sentence over again, "You make a mistake."

It was number 2 mill on fire, but all that ingenuity and strength could do seemed doing as well without Philip. The men were as busy as bees. Fifty manned the brakes of the hand engine and pumped as vigorously as if there were no such thing as lame backs and aching muscles, while on top of the engine beside the bell, which rang with every stroke of the brakes, stood their foreman keeping time with his arms and whole body and encouraging them with his hoarse, excited voice. Then there were three hydrants in full operation and a crowd of men to keep the hose in condition, and four more in rubber suits to hold the nozzles and direct the streams of fast flowing water where it would quickest subdue the fierce flames. There seemed nothing for Philip to do. He was worth no more than the crowd of chattering women, who stood as near the fire as their rough-voiced men would let them. How odd their thin white faces looked half hid by the shawls tied about their heads. It was a great event in their dull, monotonous lives; the very foundations of their world seemed shaken, and they could not talk fast enough to express their crude thoughts at the breaking up of old associations.

"Carry the hose up to the next story," shouted the foreman.

"The ladder is not long enough," answered one of the men in rubber suits.

"Can't you climb? Who can then?"

This was Philip's opportunity, and he hurried up the ladder two rounds at a time. Then he swung himself off on the lightning rod. Its sharp edges cut his tender hands, but in his eagerness he did not notice it. In a moment more he had pulled himself up on the window-sill and burst in the sash. Then he reached down for the hose and a cheer went up for the rich man's son who was not afraid of work.

He heard his father's voice below thanking the men for their devotion, as the sullen flames seemed to give way before their tireless efforts. But it was no time now for idle felicitations, the fire seemed under control, but if the mastery were relaxed, it would leap high again in its fury, and the other mills must go too, for all they stood so cold and proud. The smoke grew thinner in the window where Philip stood, so he could look down on the sweaty faces and bending forms of the men at the brakes. Every thing depended on them, and how strong they sent the water through the hose he held, and forced back the fire inch by inch from its prey. If they could only keep it up a few moments more, the other mills would be out of danger. Each stroke of the brakes made the hose throb against his side almost like a

giant's pulse.   God grant them strength a few moments more.

Suddenly he heard a loud voice raised above the
murmur of the crowd.

" Wise boys ye be, to clench the nails in yer own
coffins.   Aint this mill yer jail and its bosses your
jailers?   Is there a fool of ye all, but knows old Breton who grins so nice to-night on ye, but knows him
for a tyrant, who grinds us to powder ? "

Philip saw a short, burly man whose hair was
cropped close to his round head, shouting and gesticulating wildly, as he made his way up to the
engine and then leaped upon it.   The brakes stop
moving and the fire sends up new tongues and leaps
along the smoking beams and rafters in fresh fury,
while the men listen breathlessly to this stranger.
The women too gather nearer, and look in curiosity
at their husbands and brothers who drink in so
eagerly his poisoned words.

" I s'pose ye thought ye didn't work long enough
for yer ninety cents a day.   But ye hev.   Aye boys,
that big heap o' brick stands for that old man's mean-
ness ; it's the machine to crush ye.   It s the way he
bleeds ye.   But how sweet he is to-night.   Ye never
noticed it before, did ye?   He's seed you a starvin' on
the wages he paid, and yer purty darters gone to
the bad for the want of a few things all gals kinder
like.   Some on ye, too, has got old and cripples in

his service. He aint ever guv in a mite, has he?
Now it's your turn."

And the man shouted loud above the hissing,
crackling flames that leaped out of a dozen windows
in wild glee. "Let his mills burn fur a warnin' to
such as he who make so much sorror and misery in
this ere purty world, that if Satan tortured their cruel
souls forevermore, it wouldn't be a feather in the
balance. Let him know the despair of a poor man
for once."

It was almost madness that glittered in the fellow's darting eyes, and his voice grew hoarse and
terrible as he pointed his thick fingers at the mill
half hid in smoke, lit up in spots with forks of flame.

" Let every plank of it go. It's only served to
make him richer each month, and ye poorer. Such a
machine as that don't desarve to stand. Let his
riches he's used so poor turn to ashes this night.
Tears and prayin' couldn't git equal rights for us; the
fire will do it, though."

Ezekiel Breton elbowed his way into their midst.

He had lost his hat, and stood pale in his agony
in the presence of the men who thought he had
wronged them. He was conscious of no guilt; he
had only made his money as others made theirs;
fairer indeed than mere money-lenders, who added
nothing to the world's productions. He knew, of
course, the poor suffered, but a man can't be too

squeamish, and the same road was open to them that he had taken. And as for wages, who could blame a man for getting help as cheaply as he can? That is business.

Mr. Breton knew but one argument for them.

" If you want pay," he shouted, " here is money, a dollar an hour to each man."

But not a face relaxed, he looked fearfully from one to another, and then up at the grinning face of the stranger, " only save my mill." The old man put up his hand to his white hair in a piteous gesture as he glanced at the sheets of flame and lurid smoke that shut off the sky above his devoted mill.

" See the fire grows every second, we are lost unless you go to work; I will pay ten dollars an hour."

The brakes began to move slowly up and down. Philip felt the water throb through the hose as it touched his side, but it was only one fitful spurt, for the stranger, who seemed to hold the mills at his mercy, had found his voice again.

" Keep yer money, old man, you will need every penny of it, for you've cheated yer last out of yer help in them mills. Yer mill hez got to go."

Philip saw his father turn toward his mills, the pride of his life, and look as fondly at their grim walls as a man on the woman he loves, and the tears of futile agony wet his cheeks. That moment the young man aged ten years.

The crowd fell back again, and another speaker mounted the strange rostrum. He looked young for such a crisis, but there was a new suggestion of power in his lips and the sullen crowd wondered what he thought he could say to persuade them.

" I suppose," began Philip slowly, as if every minute might not be worth a fortune, " I presume," and his voice sounded dry and hard, " you will want your wages as usual, next pay-day. Is there any one of you foolish enough to imagine you will get them if the mills go ?"

Then the young man glanced at the burly stranger, who, clearly enough, was taken aback by this new style of appeal to a crowd.

" Possibly this broad-shouldered friend of yours is going to find a living for you. You have got to find it somewhere, and you won't have particularly good characters to recommend you to new tyrants.

" Mind, men, I don't say it is quite fair, but mill-owners manage their business about the same way. It is all very well to complain, but the first necessity is a place to work ; if there isn't that, you surely can't have any rights. I may as well tell you, the mills are heavily insured, and you can't quite have the rare satisfaction of seeing that old man ruined. But I doubt if he will care to put any more mills under such extra risks. Some of your women and ignorant people, who don't see the fun of starving, may think you had done a poor night's work."

The stranger have disappeared, and the faces of the men, clustered about their engine, had lost their sullen cast. The young man's black eyes glistened in the new ecstasy of an orator's triumph.

"One thing I will promise. I will do what I can in your behalf. I know the lines of most of you have fallen into hard places, and I promise if I can see any way to lighten the burden of life on your shoulders, I will help you."

The men returned to their work with a murmur of approval. Was it too late?

The brakes started up again. The men ran up the ladders again, with the hose in their hands, in the renewed battle with the fire. Philip had moved the crowd. He had chosen instinctively, the only method for the crisis, while the flames crackled and flashed in high carnival. But was it not too late? The men were working with new energy; new hopes were in their hearts. The mill-owner's son had promised to help them; he sympathized with their cheerless poverty, and who could do more than he?

If the whole line of mills went, it would be upon their consciences, and the thought put fresh strength into their weary arms, and more fearless courage into their hearts. But precious time had been lost, and the wind had changed, so that now the red, greedy tongues of flame lapped the frowning brick walls of the next mill, and lavished their hot, wanton kisses as if it were love and not hate whose fury would consume them.

When the moon was setting in the west, that night, Mr. Breton found his son all grimy with smoke, with clothes torn, and drenched in water, out of all semblance to the gentleman of elegant leisure. He stood by the smouldering ruins of number 2. mill.

"Aren't you coming home to-night, Philip, my dear boy? How proud Bertha would have been if she could have seen her hero to-night."

Bertha! What a strange influence her words and manner at parting had left upon him; as if, someway, in leaving her just when he did, he had lost her for-ever. God forbid! He could not shake it off; it was with him yet as he waited almost alone in the great mill-yard; all the excitement and responsibilities of the night had not dispelled it. He looked down moodily into the smoking mass of crumbled walls and roof and blackened timbers, and watched for the little forks of flame that started up boldly, now and then, as if it were not yet too late for a new battle, and then seemed abashed at finding themselves alone in the dark, and sank back.

"You have saved the mills," said his father, wringing his bruised hand till he hurt him. "God bless you, my son.   I didn't guess how much there was in you."

Philip looked up at the scorched walls off on the right, and the long pile of massive structures away to the left, unshaken by the whirlwind of fire. In a few hours more they would be alive with rushing belts and wheels; and with the feet of the men and women, telling how strange there was a place left for work to-day.   Yes, he had saved them " But at what price? "   He spoke half to himself.   If he only knew what Bertha had meant.

"What price?   Oh, your promise to do what you could for the men and all that.   It was guardedly put, my boy."   And his father laughed appreciatively.   " Inexorable parent must be considered, though, ha, ha.   You will catch your death of cold. Well, if you will stay, good-night."

CHAPTER IX.

Weak Man.

IT was at dusk a few days after Jane Graves had come to the Ellingsworths, that she stood at the dining-room window.

It was almost in sight of her old dreary home, and yet another world; how strange that the two should be so near and not change or shadow each other. But Jane Graves was not the girl to trouble herself over hard questions. She breathed her new atmosphere in unmixed delight, while latent senses awoke each day only to be gratified. What difference if she did not own the pier glass mirror that reflected back her neatly clad young figure; it could not tell her she was ill looking. The exquisitely carved chairs, upholstered in the rarest designs, into which she could sink in delicious abandon, were not any softer for her master than for her.

At this moment she stood in a very charming attitude leaning lightly against the window casing, her prettily rounded arm raised to play with the ·curtain tassel. Her master rather liked to linger in the dining-room and read his evening paper. Occa-

sionally he would glance at the girl who had such
pretty poses ; he had quite a taste for pictures, and
then she afforded him an excuse for not a little
cynical philosophy, and then—well that was all
he confessed to.   Mr. Ellingsworth had one pecu-
liarity that would certainly seem very commenda-
ble.   He never spoke rudely to any one; it would
have been impossible for his finely grained nature.
Not that he had a particularly kind heart, indeed
the world quite generally agreed he was a very
unlikely man to ask a favor of; and there were some
whispers afloat of cruel and unrighteous things he
had done before he retired from business.   Not a
few could have told an unpleasant story of how
coldly he treated the wife of his youth when sick-
ness faded her fair cheeks and spoiled her Madonna-
like beauty.   No husband could be more polished
or correct in words, but her heart was broken, they
said, by the cold steel ill-sheathed in his smooth
voice and elegant courtesy.   None of his servants
ever heard a surly word or sharp rebuke from him,
but somehow they all seemed afraid of him ; all
but this new acquisition who presumed on his
good nature in the most audacious fashion.   The
new maid did not seem to understand it was her
duty to withdraw timidly from a room when her
master entered or lingered in it, or to modestly
drop her shining black eyes when he glanced at her.

She thought him polite and kind, and in her innocence imagined his was the usual manner of the
well-bred with their hirelings. The other servants
knew that humiliation was a part of their required
week's work, which their wages were considered to
pay for; and expected to see the thunderbolt fall on
this foolish girl who did not know how precious was
the purchased privilege of being cringed to. But
strange enough the thunderbolt did not hasten.

No, there were no lightning flashes in the eyes
that looked at her over the newspaper to-night. He
was speculating curiously on the change that had
come over the girl with changed surroundings, and
congratulating himself on his shrewdness in foresee-
ing it. He hadn't studied life for,—well never mind
how many years, for nothing. Given a healthy
physical organization, and not too much of the
morbid high moral quality, and the woman will
display an absolute delight in all the conveni-
ences and embellishments wealth can lend, that
seems almost uncanny. Such a woman appreciates
love, but it is only as a device to make the world
turn its softest side to her. Love without the ac-
cessories of comfort and elegance is very pretty for
poems and songs, but for practice she would cool
her divine frenzy, and marry a man who fired her
heart less, but pleased it more. Ah, it is the man
who has the means and inclination to satisfy her ex-

pensive tastes, who is alone rewarded by the passion of her heart. And she is right, too, soliloquized Mr. Ellingsworth, love to such a woman is only one of the elegant tastes, and is in keeping only with poetry and refinement, velvet divans and solid silver service. If coarse, disgusting realities worked themselves into the delicate web of its day-dreams, it couldn't exist.

It would be rather pleasant to see the effect of silk and jewelry on her rich type of brunette; dress wouldn't be thrown away on her. The girl looked pretty in ginghams and calicoes, a few hundred dollars now, would make a perfect little queen of her. Her bright olive cheeks and neck would be positively dazzling in a cardinal silk with Roman gold in her delicate ears. The great majority of women might as well wear their morning wrappers all day; full dress only makes them more conspicuous. Even lovely blondes, like Bertha, gain but little by rich dresses. Bertha looked almost her best when she seemed to take the least pains to do so. But how dress would tell on this little maid!

Jane Graves had no idea her master was looking at her. She was thinking of the last time she had seen Curran. Why she never expected that night, ever to be happy again, and now she wasn't sure but she should be happy in such a beautiful place as this even if he died, or loved another woman instead of her. But no, she could never endure the last. Perhaps he would find her out some day, and come to her, and he would tell her it was all a mistake, that he really loved her all the time ; only that he was ashamed to ask her to share his poverty. It is hard for a woman to believe a man cares nothing for her, that melting dark eyes and tender tones, breathing the wildest of worship, can be nothing to her hero.

Suddenly the girl started, and a deep flush lit up her dark face. Up the walk, to the front doorway, came the man of whom she thought with his own lordly stride as if he were a prince, indeed, as he deserved to be. Her heart was in a sweet glow ; he had found her out, and had come for her. She would leave all these beautiful things with rapture for him.

Mr. Ellingsworth saw the man's figure at the front gate, and the girl's start, and smiled rather disagreeably to himself. He had wondered before why her lover didn't come, and here he was at the front door, no doubt expecting to be entertained in the parlor. Certainly Jane Graves must know too much to marry a poverty-stricken man, just because she liked having a lover. She wasn't the sort of woman to be happy in that kind of madness. Somebody ought to tell her, it would be a boon to the young man, too, who no doubt was fancying he was going to marry right into heaven, because the girl could talk foolishly to him now.

Jane Graves glided into the hall. Suddenly

grown shy at the maiden passion of her own heart, she slowly opened the front door. What would he say first? Would he take her hand which had grown so white and soft lately? Would he ask to kiss her, and with beating heart she stood in the open doorway.

It had now grown almost dark, perhaps he did not see her plainly.

"Did you ring?" she asked foolishly, while her heart sank down, down, would it never stop?

"Is your mistress in?"

What was this—some strange mistake? Could he not see who it was held the door open for him?

"My mistress, Miss Ellingsworth? why yes, she is in the parlor." It must be a joke, but now he had frightened her enough, and how they would laugh together over it. She was attempting to smile, when she heard the parlor door open behind her.

"Yes, I am here." It was Bertha Ellingsworth's voice, and if her face was in keeping with it, it must have been soft and beautiful as an angel's. The visitor passed in, and Jane Graves shut the outer door heavily and sank upon the floor, pressing with both her hands against her bursting heart. Then she leaped upon her feet in sudden madness, and hurried along the hall to the parlor door. What right had this rich woman to steal away her lover? She would care only to amuse herself with him for a few days,

and then her servants would be told to shut the door
in his face. Such cold creatures as she never love;
passion they know nothing of, only the passion to
break honest men's hearts. Why not warn him?
Oh, but what was Jane Graves to him? he might remind her how he had spurned her from him once.

The girl turned and came back. It wouldn't
hurt him any to know how a broken heart feels; he
might, by-and-by be sorry for the poor little factory girl he had put away from him. She opened
the dining-room door. But the woman who would
break his heart, who would entangle him in the
perfumed meshes of her golden hair, who would
tempt him to look deep into the eternal calm of her
great blue eyes, and dream it was love he saw, and
then laugh him to scorn—was there no punishment
for her? Jane Graves went back into the dining-
room, now grown dark, and threw herself into a chair.
The poor cannot fight against the rich. Ah! but
she could hate her mistress' white face. She could
curse her in her thoughts with all the evils in the
universe. The girl burst into a passion of tears.

"What is the trouble, little girl?" It was her
master's voice. She had forgotten him.

The girl heard him draw a chair near hers, but she
did not uncover her face.

"Was your beau unkind to you? Well, don't
have anything more to say to him, then, Jennie."

Why! the elegant Mr. Ellingsworth was actually kissing his maid! What difference did it make? the one she loved had thrown her away, and trampled her devotion under his feet. She even let him draw her shapely little head to his shoulder, and take her hands away from her face. They hid her lips, he said,—when the door-bell rang.

Mr. Ellingsworth answered the bell himself—a breach of etiquette not frequent with him, even under the liberalizing influence of village manners.

"Mr. Breton, charmed to see you," and there was not the faintest trace of ill-humor in his perfectly trained voice. The old gentleman might have been the most opportune of guests.

But his daughter had not been schooled enough, by a great many years, for such self-control, and she started to her feet as her parlor door opened, almost in consternation   There was quite a study for character in the room at that moment. Curran had not arisen, his lips might have been closed a little tighter than usual, but his face did not even reveal surprise. Mr. Breton had reached the centre of the room before he saw whom Bertha had been entertaining, but now he stood in astonishment—he had no concern to hide—snapping his black eyes from the young lady who was soon to be his son's wife, to this weaver in the mill, who did not seem so much out of place in this fashionable parlor, either. The crisis had come, and Bertha was entirely unprepared for it. Her heart was fluttering wildly, and for the moment she wished she had never seen the man whose presence embarrassed her. A moment before, she had forgotten there was such a thing as wealth or rank, devoutly confident such a man as her guest could stand before kings ; but the door had opened, and let in the breath of pride and caste, scattering the halo about the poor man's head. Suddenly she looked with new repugnance at him she had just thought so sublime. Why did he not go ? She was flushed with vexation at his stubbornness in delaying. Had he no sense of propriety, to court a social meeting with her aristocratic father, who would ridicule him without his guessing it, and the blunt mill-owner, who would be sure to insult and browbeat him plainly. She expected to see him rise awkwardly, and shuffle out of the room, perhaps pulling his forelock respectfully to the company that was not for such as he.

If he had.

CHAPTER X.

Weak Woman.

CURRAN glanced keenly at the face of his beautiful hostess, whose wonted serenity had all gone, then he rose to his feet, and stood, while she spoke his name in the briefest form of introduction. He did not seem offended by the stare of surprise Mr. Breton had for him. It was a new experience to the mill-owner, meeting his workmen in fashionable parlors.

"Curran, is it? I was sure I had seen you in the mill, but you had on a white apron then." Mr. Breton laughed familiarly, but he did not hold out his hand.

Couldn't Curran see how rudely he was treated? Mr. Breton's laugh and tone rasped Bertha's finer sensibilities, so that she was at once indignant with him, and disgusted with Curran, who seemed to bear it so unconsciously. Curran's brow was unruffled; he had only folded his arms across his breast, sometimes a sign of excitement with him, she had noticed. He must be made of stone or stubble not to writhe under such treatment, before her. But was the man foolish enough to think he was obliged to stay here and endure it ? The girl's full under lip began to curl in contempt. No doubt he was flattered at being in such company, and would endure any insult of manner in unconscious vanity, or perhaps he thought he might curry favor with his employer. Apparently, he had forgotten all about her ; he had looked at her once, that was all, since her father and Mr. Breton had come into the parlor.

But her father had looked at her more than once, and there was considerable material for study in the changes that passed over her face. There was a half puzzled and half amused expression in his eyes, as if he had just fallen upon a phenomenon, which seemed to prove almost too completely, some pet theory.

" Mr. Curran had the good fortune, I believe, to do my daughter a great service." Mr. Ellingsworth's manner was the perfection of that peculiar tone so thoroughly well bred in its variety of rudeness. It expressed the infinite elevation and polish of the person who assumed it, far above the very natural feeling of disgust at the presence of so vulgar a person as this workman. It suggested irresistibly, the great contempt such a person ought to call forth, but at the same time that Ellingsworth was unapproachable by even as vulgar a thing as contempt.

" Indeed !" exclaimed Mr. Breton, as he seated

himself, " I will thank you, too, it was a good job for
you, and I will see it don't hurt your interests any,
either."

What further was he waiting for? His calculations
had turned out to be judicious. Mr. Breton had
promised to look out for him. If Curran knew how
every new insult or familiarity made her despise
him, he would not linger. Bertha stood waiting for
him to go, but instead, he stepped back to his chair
and sat down. He had not spoken yet, but his arms
were folded tighter than before over his chest.

"How do you like your work?" went on Mr.
Breton in his harsh mill voice. " I hope you aint one
of those who don't know when they are well off."

" I can keep from starving ; that is well off, I
suppose."

Mr. Breton was at loss but for a moment.

" But you poor people don't save what you get.
You ought to economize."

Curran's eyes flashed dangerously, but he bit his
lip and kept silence.

Mr. Ellingsworth saw a scene was imminent.
How little tact Mr. Breton had, patronizing the
young man so provokingly, before the golden-haired
goddess, he had no doubt fallen in love with. Something must be done.

" Excuse me. Have you had any serious trouble
with your wound, Mr. Curran? "

"I have only lost a few days, that is nothing," he answered quickly.

"But it must be considerable for a poor man!" broke in Mr. Breton with his grand air, " I will direct my paymaster to make it up to you."

Curran glanced across the room at Miss Ellingsworth. He expected to see her face flushed with anger. She would leap to her feet in indignant remonstrance to shield him from such impertinence, all the generosity of her nature in revolt against such return for his devotion to her.

She was looking at him, but much as a girl looks at a strange animal she has been petting, when suddenly they tell her he bites. Curran turned away from her and ground his teeth. Then he looked at Mr. Breton.

"Can't your paymaster make up for the pain, too, as well as the lost time?"

Mr. Ellingsworth was at his wit's end. He saw the cloud gathering in the workman's eyes, and that his lip trembled with suppressed feeling when he spoke.

"How long have you been in town, Mr. Curran?" he said to change the conversation if possible into safer channels.

"Only six months."

"Why," volunteered Mr. Breton after an awkward silence, "that is about as long as the mill hands

have been fault-finding so loudly." The old gentle
man looked sharply at him. " I don't suppose you
would tell who has been making the trouble."

Mr. Ellingsworth was almost out of humor. His
friend actually seemed only fit for his own factory.
What is the good of riches to a man who has no
conception of the amenities it cultivates, and is
capable of treating a person he meets in a parlor as
if he were playing overseer. Not that he need have
any consideration for the man, but certainly he
ought to have some respect for a parlor. Once out,
of course such a person as Curran should never outrage the elegant precincts again, what could Bertha
have been thinking of? But so long as he was here—

"Yes sir." Curran had risen to his feet, the flush
of offended self-respect in his cheeks, " when I came
here I found the mills paying you twelve per cent
dividends, while the help who ground them out for
you, were crushed almost to the earth. I felt bound
to tell them as I now tell you, that the owner has
no more God-given right to all the profit of their
work, any more than they to all the profit of his
investment."

" And you are the man who has been stirring up
this mischief here!" cried Mr. Breton, almost starting from his chair. He had caught him at last then.
" And do you say that a man isn't entitled to the interest on his money? My money represents a thou-

sand such lives as yours, it ought to have a thousand times the pay." He had more terrible guns than of the batteries of logic for the rebel, but he could not resist the temptation to explode the fallacies of his class before he let him go.

The young man's eyes flashed beautifully. As for this girl who had suddenly grown ashamed of him before her own class, she might learn he could bow and scrape and cringe to no one. If she had no care to shield her own guest in her own parlor from insult, thank God, he was bold enough to vindicate his own manhood, no matter what it cost him. And what gentleness had any of them deserved of him? One had cut him with his keen sarcasm and his two-edged politeness, and another heaped impertinence on rudeness till now he fairly challenged him to a battle of words. Why should he not with rough hand lay bare the cruel falsehood on which this great man's wealth was built?

"Your money represents a thousand lives, then, out of which you have sucked the life blood? And at how much do you value a human life? As much as a thousand dollars for a soul? A thousand dollars for all the joys and hopes and possibilities of a human life? Your valuation is too miserably small. I tell you," and Curran threw out his right hand in a magnificent gesture, "I tell you, a human creature ought to have for its service a good portion of the comforts and delights the world is so bounteous with. Anything less is slavery, a slavery worse than negro bondage. Do you call it pay, that you give the hopeless men and women that weave gold for you on your looms? Rather say the daily recurring fact of hunger chains them to your mill."

Mr. Ellingsworth had sunk back in his seat in despair; he might as well resign himself to the situation since it seemed beyond his power to change it. Mr. Breton was likely to hear some startling truths before he succeeded in refuting this dangerous young man. Perhaps it was just as well, too, there is no sense in a man's making his money as the rich do, by one kind or another of imposition or injustice and then affect such ridiculous unconsciousness. There is no sense in being blind and stupid about how one comes to be rich, the comfortable fact remaining. What was the use of Breton wrestling with such a young giant as this?

"I pay my help market prices of labor. I don't propose to make them gifts." The old gentleman handled his cane nervously, but he could punish the man enough later. He felt Ellingsworth's sharp eyes, he must think of something to absolutely overwhelm the arguments of his workman. He ran over in his mind the smooth axioms of his class, and tried hard to recollect some of the perfect syllogisms of the political economists.

Curran stood, his elbow resting on the back of the chair he had been sitting in, in an attitude so dignified and graceful that Mr. Ellingsworth glanced across at his daughter to see if she had observed it. It was not quite so inconceivable, after all, that Bertha might have taken a fancy to him. But then his whole associations had been with the poor, and what possible harmony, even for a moment—then Mr. Ellings worth remembered the maid servant crying at this moment in the dining-room.

" Naturally you prefer to let your half-clothed ill-fed hands make you the presents ; they earn you big dividends ; you throw them a crust of bread, the market price of labor you call it, and put the dividends in your own pocket."

" But it's my money made the mill, and my management runs it."

" As for the money," retorted Curran, " perhaps you inherited a part of it, saved by the tax laid on the poor of the last generation, or you borrowed it, perhaps, on interest, and made the help in your mill pay the interest every penny of it, how else could it be paid ? Then from that start which the stolen profits of the poor gave you, you managed, as you say, to squeeze a big enough fortune out of the rightful earnings of your laborers to pay back your borrowed money, and leave the mills free to grind their grist for you only. You did not make your money ; no

man can till two million of dollars out of his farm, or
dig it out of a coal mine. You simply took it. Your
new mills are paid for out of wages you ought to
have given your help ; you call them yours ; the new
machinery comes out of them. They are the real
stockholders in it all. If it were possible for one
man's brain or muscle fairly to win a fortune, it could
be done on a farm. It cannot be done till a man
manages to make hundreds of unwilling suffering
creatures contribute of their wretched subsistence."

Mr. Breton had sprung from his seat, but Curran
went on unflinchingly. "It isn't earned, it is simply defrauded. The management is doubtless good,
but no management could, in the righteous course of
justice, bring such vast fortunes into the hands of a
few men ; while the thousands who work for them
live and die with the consuming thirst for happiness
never for one hour assuaged in their souls."

The old gentleman had come up close to him as
he spoke, and as he finished, Curran looked down
calmly into a face almost purple with passion. It
occurred to him that Mr. Breton was about to have
an attack of apoplexy. The hand that held his
gold-headed cane fairly trembled. Could a man never
be so rich that unpleasant facts must not touch him ?

"You have earned your last penny in my mills ?"
the old gentleman shouted at him. "We ought to
have laws to shut up such men as you."

But Curran looked away as if he had not heard him. Of course, what Mr. Breton had threatened him with was a foregone conclusion.

" Mr. Ellingsworth," he said, as that gentleman rose to his feet, " I am very sorry to have brought such a scene into your parlor, it seemed unavoidable after what was said to me, and it seems likely to prove more unfortunate for me than for anybody else." He moved two or three steps toward the door. " The most I can do is to promise never to come again."

No one thought of anything to say. Mr. Ellingsworth vaguely wondered where the man picked up his neat way of talking, but then the wealthy, after all, have no monopoly of talent ; it isn't like the old world.

Curran cast a withering look of contempt on the mill-owner, who had nothing more to say. " I am sorry too, to be deprived of the chance to win my daily bread, but I may serve as an illustration of the workings of the slavery I spoke of. And by the way, Mr. Breton, you will have to modify those directions to your paymaster you were good enough to offer me earlier in the evening. Miss Ellingsworth, good-bye."

He did not notice that the expression of the girl's face had changed, or that she had started to come to him, and there was a grandeur of wrath in his face and bearing that awed her. She stood in the centre of the room, with heaving bosom, and frightened, troubled eyes, watching him out of the door. Then her father came back through the hall with his sarcastic smile finely curving his thin lips.

Why should he spare his ridicule? Had she not deserted her guest in shame, suffered insult and impertinence to be heaped upon him, and sat by in contemptible silence? But how beautifully he had known how to preserve his own honor. It would have been base and ignoble in him to have crawled out of her parlor at the entrance of her father and Mr. Breton, self-confessed unworthy to sit in their presence. And for all their wealth and power and vantage ground, careless of what it must cost, he had thrown their insults in their teeth and shown himself a grander man, a thousand times, than either of them.

The warm flood of returning feeling swept over her soul. She could not bear one more cruel word against him now. Before her father could speak she had hurried into the hall and shut fast the door so that she should not hear the bitter sentence that was just parting his lips.

What strange impulse moved her that she should go to the outer door and look eagerly down the street. But her insulted guest had not lingered. In a moment more she was at the gate, and saw his tall form only at a little distance. No doubt he was thinking sadly or perhaps angrily of her, as he walked, and he could not guess that she had repented, and was eager this moment to beg his forgiveness, with all the sweet words she knew. Bertha glanced back at the house in hesitation. She could see the slim outlines of her father's figure shadowed on the curtains. She could not hear what he was saying. It was this :

" It is one of Bertha's freaks. All women are subject to them."

" But I don't understand," insisted Mr. Breton, wiping the perspiration from his heated face. " I don't understand how she can bring herself, a girl of her notions, to entertain a fellow like this. How long do you suppose this has been going on? Ever since the dog adventure, very likely. If I were Philip —."

" But you recollect I am only three days returned from my trip, and am entirely unable to tell you how many times she has met this very striking individual. Don't hurry yourself into mental decline by trying to explain on logical principles a woman's performances," smiled Mr. Ellingsworth. " And I wouldn't take the trouble to suggest misgivings to Phil. I would rather trust the girl's nature, and I think I know it, than depend on a jealous lover's reproaches. Why, my dear friend, I would stake my life on the girl's attachment to the traditions of her position. Our wives and daughters are thrice more intolerable, unreasonable aristocrats than we. If she has been guilty of a touch of foolish sentiment, reaction is certain, and she will only despise the man the more because of her season of blindness."

"But supposing the reaction come too late," suggested Mr. Breton anxiously. "Then it better not come at all," he continued. "The very character you give her would make three people perfectly miserable—the man she refuses, the man she marries, and herself."

"Excuse me," answered Mr. Ellingsworth, with his most unpleasant smile, "I doubt if a daughter of mine would be unhappy so long as her physical comfort was unabated. That would suppose a certain over-sensitive moral quality that doesn't go with our blood," and the proud father slightly shrugged his shoulders. "But be satisfied, I think I saw unmistakable symptoms this evening that the reaction of custom against nature has already set in."

But the girl who had stood at the gate, in her slippers, and with no covering for her head only her golden hair fastened low on her neck, had hesitated but a moment. She could not let Curran leave her thus ; perhaps she should never see him again, if he went away without one word from her to soften the blows she had let them give him. And then he seemed to be walking slowly; she could overtake him in a moment. The uneven walk hurt her feet, her slippers were so thin, and as she lifted her skirt to walk faster, a rude briar tore her soft flesh, and then hung greedily to her, to impede her steps. She stopped, and called his name. She had hardly murmured it, but it seemed so loud spoken, and so tender toned, she blushed at herself, and dared not speak it again. She might run a few steps, and then he would hear her voice more plainly. But her dress clung so closely, and then her excited breath came so fast, that she gained on him very slowly. There was no use, she must lose him forever out of her life ; he must always think her cruel and ungenerous. She leaned against the fence and sent one more hopeless cry after him. It was more a sob than a cry, a piteous sob, trembling with gentle heart-broken reproach. Why, she was sure he must have heard that ; she had never meant to speak so loud. What could she say to him when he came back to her? She must try to be very cold and dignified. But wasn't he going to turn? why, her cry was piercing enough to go a mile on the still evening air. No, he was farther away, he had not heard her.

Then she looked back, and was frightened to see what a distance she was away from her home. And as she stood looking, now at his tall form drawing unconsciously away from her, and then at the distant lights of her home, the first hint of the desolation that broods over millions of hopeless hearts, came upon her soul. Her slippers were torn, and wet with dew, and each step she took bruised the tender feet that had never known hurt or weariness, only of pleasure. Her heavy masses of hair had been shaken from their fastenings, and hung at full length to her waist. She fancied herself some lost, friendless Magdalen, for whom the world, that fawns on the fortunate and proud, had only taunts and cruel blows. And were there women who had to face the world alone? fight their own battles with timid hearts? earn their own right to breathe, with shrinking hearts?

"What was that, a step, a man's step coming toward her?" To her excited imagination, at that moment, her beautiful home and the elegant life she loved so well, seemed things of the past. Why had she never been more pitiful to the poor and the hopeless, whose name was legion? Now she knew what they might suffer. There were but a few, after all, who were favored of fortune, the rest were weary, and faint and broken, as she was to-night.

She gathered her hair into a loose coil, and let her dress trail on the walk to cover her feet. The man wore workman's clothes. She had hoped he might be a gentleman. She tried to keep on the

outer edge of the side-walk; she would have taken
the road, if she had dared. She looked away from
the man, but she could see with beating heart he was
coming directly toward her. But perhaps he did not
see her, and he might turn aside yet. God grant he
be an honest man, whose wife's loving face was in
his thoughts at this moment! There were such men.
But instead of moving aside, the man stopped short
just before her, and she raised her big, scared eyes
to his face.

"Why, Bertha, I thought it was you."

Sure enough, it was Philip Breton. He had
come from the mill, where there had been some
extra work.

"Let me walk home with you," he said very
gently, as if he had no right to assert any privilege with her.

"I came too far, and got frightened," she said
dreamily, as she rested her hand on his arm.

Her hand was cold, but its touch sent his young
blood tingling through his veins.

"I am so sorry." How he longed to catch her
white hand to his lips, and warm it with kisses. But
lately she had treated him with a new coldness, and
her coldness he dare not meet. He dreaded to face
it, it pained him so past endurance, and he had
called on her but seldom since the night of the fire.
But now his heart was full of eloquent love; so full,

he could not conceive of her not sharing in it. It
was she called it forth, she must have something for
him.

They had reached her gate. She would surely
invite him to go in with her. Then she could tell
him if he had done anything to displease her. He
could remember nothing, but women are so gentle,
there might have been some unconscious cold word
or tone, as if, poor fellow, he had not been only too
tender with her.

"Good-night," she said. She had lost the tremor in her voice fright had given her, and all the
softness of heart of her loneliness.

"I thank you," she added coldly, as he did not
go, but stood looking at her as if he did not quite
understand.

"Good-night," he answered, with a great throb
in his throat. He stumbled awkwardly, as he went
down the steps ; he could not see very well for the
mist in his eyes.

CHAPTER XI.

Ungrateful Populace.

PHILIP BRETON sat late over the tea table, one evening some days after. His father had been detained down in the village, and had come home with a good deal on his mind apparently. Indeed, the old gentleman, who generally laid aside his hardness outside his own doors, had sat in silence wrinkling his forehead very inartistically almost through the meal.

"Poor folks are always ungrateful," he exclaimed harshly at last as he shook his head severely at the maid servant who offered him the cake basket. The little maid started violently; what had he given her that she was ungrateful about? But the young master Philip gave her an amused smile that calmed her fears; somebody else, then, had committed the unpardonable sin, according to the code of the rich. And she tried in vain to think of some poor people who had any blessings.

"Here I have whitewashed every house for them and they needed it enough, too, and it was only to-night I heard some grumbling old woman tell her

husband, she wondered how old Breton would like
to live in one of his own tenements."

He pushed back his chair in a movement of perfect disgust. "What has that got to do with it? I
don't undertake, and only a fool would expect it, to
provide an elegant house, with all the modern im-
provements, and an acre of land for a front yard, to
every laborer in my mills that earns ninety cents a
day."

Philip said nothing, it had been his habit lately
when his father got on this theme, to keep silence.
He was puzzled to know what to say. His father's
logic seemed correct, but then there was all that
debasing poverty to stare it out of countenance.
Was there not an occasion for another line of logic,
or if not, for something besides logic, if logic shut
out a thousand strong, big-hearted men, and gentle
souled women, and joy loving children, all to make
one family rich beyond all conceivable wants. But
his father took his silence for the expected assent
and went on.

"Why, look at it, Phil. The insurance on the
burned mill won't make up for the lost time in re-
building, and this is the time they select to ask for
fire escapes. Yield them an inch and they want an
ell. You are in the mill a good deal, you must see
it for yourself. I suppose they think I ought to run
the factory for a big benevolent institution. Every

man that is poor curses me for it, and not one shift-
less family in town, I'll warrant, but would lay the
fault on my shoulders. By the way, Phil, you have
been to college, you ought to know if there isn't any
way I can stop the tongue of that tall brown-haired
fellow. Can't the law touch him? I have discharged
him, but he does more mischief than ever."

"Discharged Curran!" exclaimed Philip. "You
don't mean it! why he is the man that saved Bertha's
life," and he continued hurriedly, "You must take
him back at once, it would be the most outrageous
return, you must take him back at once, no matter
what he has said."

"No matter what he has done either, I suppose,"
said Mr. Breton with some heat. "Perhaps I know
more of the interesting young man than you do," he
went on indiscreetly. "It may be as well for you if
I open your eyes a little—What is it, Mary?"

"Three men at the door, sir. They want to see
you, sir."

"Say gentlemen, not men," corrected Mr. Breton sharply as he rose from the table.

"I think they are workmen." To be sure. The
mill-owner found three of his workmen in his study;
all standing when he entered because they felt less
awkward on their feet.

"Send my son in," he called to Mary. "He might
as well learn how to meet this sort of occasion."

The delegation of workmen did not look very fierce; one of them kept gazing longingly out of the window, and smoothing his napless felt hat; another, out of whose soiled coat pocket stuck the stem of a clay pipe, was studying the ceiling of the room with an intensity only explainable by his fear of his master's eye. They were two of the men who had peered into the parlor windows of this very house on the evening our story commences. The third was John Graves, whose eyes were fixed unflinchingly on the mill-owner for whom he had a message. When Philip came in he was a little startled to see his quondam host, but the man had other things to think of than the possible identity of this elegantly dressed young gentleman with the ungrateful tramp he had kept once over night.

"There's a meetin' of the mill han's down in the hall, sir, and they sent us up to ask a favor."

Mr. Breton had seated himself before his long office table and pulled up a file of business letters.

"You have too many meetings," he said loudly. "You talk so much you aren't fit to work. Some of the noisiest of you will find themselves out of a job, some fine morning, one man did the other day."

Philip drew away a little from his father's chair where he had been standing. That didn't seem quite the way to treat intelligent human beings. That was hardly permitting free speech and why had one man any reason to conclude his talk was correct and a thousand others, false. And then Curran's discharge; he must certainly restore him instead of boasting of something so like the black ingratitude he inveighed so much against.

The two other men looked anxiously at their spokesman. If they had dared they would have begun to make excuses for coming; for their wives and babies must be fed; and talking about their rights wouldn't ever feed them; and the master looked so stern. Let others who could afford to offend him go to the meetings. But the poor fellows were afraid to raise their voices, even in apology.

" But the willingest of us all don't want to be roasted to death; and it aint a bit pleasanter to us men folks to think of seein' our wives and children burnt up before our eyes. Our women aint quite so purty as those of the rich: but a few on us prize 'em as much. We come to ask for firescapes on the mills. So if there should happen to come a fire in daytime when the mills were full, the poor critters could git out." It was quite a long speech for John Graves in such august presence; and he delivered it in the monotonous Yankee drawl which carries high tragedy or low comedy without a distinction of accent.

Mr. Breton was well accustomed to the blunt form of speech of the common people who have

never had time to study fine shades of expression.

"There is no danger," he answered with a gruff
laugh, "and in business we can't spend much money
providing against very unlikely events. Fire escapes
would be a piece of useless extravagance." Mr. Breton looked sharply at his visitors over the file of letters. "It would make necessary another cut in your
pay."

Bill Rogers fingered his pipe uneasily in the significant silence that followed and finally drew it half
out of his pocket through force of habit in distress.
Then he found his voice.

"Yer jokin', squire, yer wouldn't cut us poor
devils down again. The last cut seemed as if it
would kill us, till we found out how little it takes to
keep soul and body together if a critter don't expect
nothin' else. Why, squire, a dog has the best of
some on us now; for folks let him steal." The tall
man thrust back his pipe into the depths of his
pocket, and his face hardened into a sullen expression as he added solemnly, "I cal'late another cut
would fill all the jails in the county. Yer might as
well give us the least we can live on here, as support
us in prison."

The mill-owner rose to his feet with a bustling
movement of impatience. When would he learn
that men like these were incapable of appreciating

sound argument. It was much more judicious to say no, in a tone they could not question. The unreasonable beings had no conception of the principles of political economy, but always had some particular hardship of their own to urge against its beautiful theories, as if what made the rich more rich must not in some way help the beggars even that cringed at their feet.

" Well, well, I don't mean to cut you again if you don't bother me too much. I have lost so much that I really can't afford another dollar of expense." He rang the bell for the servant.

There was a gleam of sarcastic humor in John Graves' black eyes.

" But wouldn't it now be quite a loss to burn up a thousand such good cheap factory han's ? I wouldn't thought you could afford that. These fire 'scapes now—"

" Show them out, Mary," interrupted Mr. Breton angrily. " You might as well know, I could find a thousand as good and as cheap, in a week," and he shut the office door after them with a slam.

" But you have let those men go away thinking you had just as lief they would be burned to death," expostulated Philip, flushing with excitement.

" Nothing of the kind sir, only that—but do you take sides with them, that is the last thing I expected, that my own son would take part against me."

Possibly the old gentleman was a little ashamed of having spoken quite as harshly to the workmen as he had. It would be repeated all about town. And it was certainly incautious, but his very uneasiness made him the more provoked at Philip's suggestion. " I presume you picked up a few socialistic ideas at school. No doubt you would like to put on the fire escapes out of the money your mother left you." He rang the bell violently.

"Yes I would," exclaimed Philip, his eyes lighting up. " I will be very glad to pay for it all. It seems unjust somehow to crowd the men and girls into the mills as thick as they can work, and not provide so but that they all may be burned to—"

" Mary, bring those three men back," interrupted Mr. Breton.

" But they are on the street by this."

" It makes no difference," and the choleric old gentleman brought his fist down with a crash on the table. " Go after them, if you have to chase them a mile. Bring them back, I say."

The little office clock ticked its loudest to break the silence, till the door opened to let in the returning committee. What could it mean? Mr. Breton stood with his back turned to them, drumming on the window pane, while Philip, pale and uncomfortable, looked nervously at his father, and then at the three awkward figures in the doorway, with the breathless servant girl behind the mwaiting for startling developments.

"You can report to your meeting," said Mr. Breton in a constrained voice, without facing the workmen, " My son will put on the fire-escapes at his own expense. That is all."

The men were astonished. So the young mill-owner's son had begun to redeem his promise of the night of the fire. There were rough words of gratitude on their lips, their hearts were in a glow, after the first chill of disappointment, but there was an influence in the little office that hushed their eager speech, and they only ducked their heads in awkward acknowledgment, and followed the maid out.

" Did you suppose," said Mr. Breton in a calmer tone as he left the window, and took his chair by the long table, " that I was going to let you pay for those fire-escapes ? Not a penny, my dear boy, but you can have the credit of it, discredit I should call it." He opened the drawer and drew out a sheet of business paper.

" The Breton Mills," was printed at the top. He dipped his pen in the ink, and wrote in the date.

Then he wrote the address, as follows: " John T. Giddings, esq. Attorney at Law, 42 Loring Street, Lockout."

" Please sit down, Phil. I am not much in the habit of talking of my business, to anybody, but I

9

presume it is your right to know this." Mr. Breton
laid down his pen, and clasped his hands behind his
head. "I want to make this mill four times its present size ; I haven't the money, but other men have.
I am going to take those other men in with me, and
then turn the whole thing into a corporation. Giddings is managing it for me."

Philip's face fell. A corporation! Then all his
thoughts of some day letting a little light into the
lives of the villagers, so far always in the shadow, his
dreams which had lent a new dignity to his life, and
his promise to them, were all for nothing. A soulless corporation, with nobody to blame for an act of
injustice ! How it would rivet the shackles of the
poor past any power of his hands to loose them.

"What is the trouble, my boy?" smiled his
father, in his superior wisdom. "One would think
you wanted the tough job I have had, over again.
It is too much, too much for a man ; why, I thought
I was doing you a kindness. A man thinks, at first,
he is strong, that he won't care for the murmurs
and the threatenings of his help, but he gets tired.
The amount of power, almost like God's, Philip,"
said Mr. Breton excitedly, " almost like God's ; a big
fortune gives a man, is too much, too much." He
came around the table, and put his hand on his
son's shoulder.

"The people are so poor and unhappy, we can't

shut our eyes to it. Don't we all wonder," he went on
in this new, strange mood Philip was fairly startled
at, "don't we all wonder what life is worth to them,
that they are so hungry for the bread that keeps the
breath in them? And they all blame the men who
own the mills; they think it is our hardness and injustice. A man may know he is all right, that rich
men have always done as he is doing, that the few always have the best of everything, and seem to deprive
the masses of their rights; but it wears on a man;
he wants to get behind somebody."

The little office clock ticked on restlessly, for another week, and Philip had come to feel that to be
in love may be the most terrible misfortune of a
man's life. His pride had not let him call again on
Bertha for days of distress, days of hot, dry wretchedness, whose dawn was a new, pitiless reminder of
his quenchless passion that met only insult. It was
insult, as he felt it, for a lover has sensibilities painfully acute, and can detect the slightest change in a
woman's relations with him, by signs too subtle for
unstimulated observation. A hair's breadth varia-
tion in tone makes mysterious revelations, sweet or
bitter to him; a shade of expression in the beautiful
blue eyes, has a meaning clearer than words, to
thrill him with hope, or plunge him into despair.
And in those days, too, he found time to remember
how unlover-like Bertha had always been to him, and

every time she had met his ardor with coldness,
with all the instances of hardness and neglect she
had meted out to his devotion, rose up in his mind
like hideous sins that will not be forgot. How he
had fooled himself, and he had been so happy in his
delusion.

The beginning of love is an arch of flowers, whose
rare perfume seems fresh wafted from heaven—what
danger can lurk in such tempting portals? The
eager traveler steps lightly in ; he pushes aside, with
fingers trembling in new delight, the low hanging
boughs of unfaded green. He tastes the honey on the
roses that half open their petals in ravishing tenderness for his clinging kisses. But when, all of a sudden, the roses close their sweet mouths to him, and
the boughs swing up in some strange chill breeze,
beyond his reach, and he turns to go, now each green
leaf reveals a thorn to torture him, and beneath the
graceful garlands many a poisoned spear-head is
pointed at his heart. Philip's face had lost its merry
humor, for now he was continually either determin-
ing dark and cheerless purposes never to see Bertha
again, since he knew at last she had never loved him,
or else starting at some voice that sounded like hers,
or a sudden association of memory that made her
seem near him. Sometimes, in despair of subduing
a passion that only grew the stronger for his struggle against it, he would resolve to go to her and fall at

her feet, with all the suicidal humility of a mad lover, and beg her to marry him—to marry him for the love of God, for he could not live another day without her. Again, as to-night when he sat in the little study, he would try to laugh at the folly that set a pretty face above all the glorious aims in life, and a face, too, that had never once lit up with love for him. Was a man such a weakling that he could not get along without a woman's soft perfumed breast to lean his head upon? Suddenly a thought struck him. Wasn't that pretty picture of Bertha as a young girl in one of these drawers? Very likely she had loved him no more then than now; he was sure he could tell from the eyes in the photograph. He threw himself into the chair before the table, and pulled out one drawer after another, in morbid eagerness to drive another knife into his heart.

There came a light tap at the door. He closed the drawers and turned about in his chair, in time to see Mary, the maid, enter with a letter for him. He glanced at the writing, and then was so angry at the sweet glow about his heart, that he tossed the letter carelessly on the table.

The maid had lingered with a woman's unwearying taste for sentiment; but now she slammed the door on him and went bridling down the hall in high dudgeon.

" He's a pretty beau, he is," she muttered, " if I

was that girl of his, I'd teach him to treat my love-. letters that way."

But the maid did not see, for the door was shut, what might have better suited her ideas of propriety. Her young master had torn open the envelope, and read the three lines of the letter, before Mary had finished her disgusted soliloquy. Then he re-read it a dozen times, and behaved generally in as foolish a fashion as the most exacting sweetheart could have desired. But there were only three lines.

" I have not deserved it, I do not deserve it ; but will you call before seven to-night ?—BERTHA."

But where was his sullen determination never to see her again ? Had he forgotten so soon that she had never loved him ? But he remembered that moment, that to-morrow was the day she had promised to let him talk of marriage to her, the month would be up. She had meant it in joke, no doubt, but might it not be she remembered it now, and perhaps was blushing as she wrote this note of reconciliation, for fear he should put her in mind of it ? Ah, to be sure he would, he had been too timid a lover, altogether, she should see after this. There was a new flush on his face, which any woman might have thought handsome this moment, and a new bright light in his eyes. Why, it was near seven o'clock, now. And he rose to go out.

" Bah !" It was his father who opened the door

and came in, tearing a scrap of paper between his fat fingers.

But Philip thrust his letter into his inside pocket, and then made sure it was safe, as if it were a precious ticket of admission.

"My dear Phil, if there ever was a man fool enough to try and give the poor what they want, they would lead him the wildest kind of a wild goose chase, I can tell you. You'll see yet I was right about those fire escapes. Since they have got those, the help are clamoring for something new every day. They devote all their spare time trying to think of some Right they are kept out of. I suppose the ninnies imagine the mills ought to be run in their interest," and Mr. Breton smiled at the absurdity of the idea conjured up. Then he tossed the torn bits of paper into the waste basket. "There goes one of their warnings ; I have burnt a dozen within a week. ' If I don't do this or that, my mills will stop, they read. I wouldn't wonder if a strike was brewing. I only wish they would give me one more day, they might scare some of the capitalists if they should make a disturbance to-morrow, but after to-morrow it will be too late. They can do their worst, we will always have the whip hand of them."

" Is your corporation actually going to be started to-morrow," exclaimed Philip, breathlessly, " I didn't know but it was given up."

"I never give anything up, my son. But you can help me a good deal, if you will. The hands trust you, they would do as you urged them. You understand how to talk to them. Yes you do, don't stop me, didn't your ready tongue save the mill once, the night of the fire? Now just you run down town, go into their meeting, if there is any, calm them down some way, I don't care how, Philip, all I want is one day more. If they should happen to strike to-morrow, good gracious, Phil, it might knock my corporation scheme all to smithereens. Little mercy they'd ever get after that, from me, though. You see they won't gain anything either way, strike or no strike, but you see I might lose."

Philip moved toward the door in silence. To-morrow good-bye to hope from any help of his, and his father expected him to—

"That's right, my boy, don't delay, I am expecting a man here every minute, and I—"

"But, father, I can't—"

"Yes you can. Ah! good evening, Mr. Giddings. My son, Mr. Giddings, my lawyer."

"But I must say one word to you."

"No, positively not one moment, Phil, later on. Good-night."

CHAPTER XII.

A New Galatea.

BERTHA rose from her chair slowly like one in a dream, and looked long and earnestly at Philip as he came toward her. There was a red spot on either cheek, and her eyes seemed preternaturally large and bright. At first he fancied it was out of joy at seeing him. Then she smiled as if she had not thought of it before, but with a strange gentleness that was intensely pathetic.

"You don't come as often as you used, but you have always been very good and kind to me, Philip," she said vaguely as if rehearsing the virtues of the departed.

His heart came into his throat, and he could not speak. Was this her coming back to him? It was more like a funeral. She motioned him to sit near her, and then she started and seemed to listen.

"Have I been very cold and hard with you, Philip, when you wanted me to love you?" She laid her hot fingers on his hand, but her eyes wandered lingeringly around the parlor walls.

" It is nothing, my own sweetheart," he answered
her anxiously, " only say you love me now."

She did not seem to hear him. "I must have
made you suffer. I did not understand, you know,
what it all meant."

She had taken his hand, and bent over toward
him with a troubled look on her face. She rested
one hand on his shoulder, and her lips almost touched
his forehead.

" Do you forgive me ? " she said softly, and yet
her voice was as dispassionate as an angel's whisper.

" Why, there is nothing to forgive," Philip answered, his words of love frozen on his lips, there
was something so terrible in the mysterious mood
that was upon her. " But do you remember," he
added with a forced smile, " what you promised for
to-morrow."

" To-morrow ? " she drew back from him fearfully,
" to-morrow," she repeated as if the word had some
strange mystery in it. " Have I promised you anything for to-morrow."

It was not Bertha Ellingsworth at all, as he had
known her, it was rather as he had dreamed she
might be. In the commonest of women are elements of character, germs of emotions, that in their
height and fused together can glorify her to a creature of resistless power and dignity, with holy fire
shining in her face. It is the sleeping goddess, men

worship in women, for worship is the truest form of
love, and when that worship is lost, the part of love
for which a man would make a hero of himself, and
rise above every grovelling taint in his nature, is lost
too. A woman may sin and not repent; she may
seem as shallow as the surf on the shining sand just
before its ebb, but so long as a man believes in the
goddess in her, he waits on her folly, he strives to
gild over her sin, in ennobling reverence for her possibilities.

" Why, to-morrow was the day you promised to
let me talk of —"

" I remember." She drew back from him, and
clasped her white hands for a moment over her forehead, " and have you been thinking a great deal
of it ? "

" Why not to-night, Bertha," he begged in sudden
fervor.

But she started to her feet like one in mortal
terror. " Oh no, not to-night ! "

Then she came near him again, and looked down
with a new sad smile as he held her hand to his lips.
" You don't mind very much, do you ? I am not very
much of a woman really," she said wistfully, " if it
wasn't for the habit you have fallen into."

Then she glanced at the clock on the mantel,
that had presided at so many sweet interviews between these two.

"Aren't you going to the labor meeting, it must be begun before this?"

Her voice had changed, there was a sharp and uneasy tone in it that brought Philip to his feet.

"I didn't know there was any," he repeated stolidly.

"I must have been mistaken then," she looked troubled.

How fortunate that she should know. Well he might as well go and attend to his father's business. Bertha had nothing for him that did not break his heart.

She followed him to the door.

"How sad the moonlight is. I am afraid of it," she said as she held out her hand to him.

He did not see it, but stood looking out into the still night, the moonlight making his face show wan and set as if that moment he was crushing forever the dearest hope of his life.

Then he heard a broken voice coming, it seemed a long way to his ears.

"Oh, Philip, aren't you going to kiss me good—good-night?"

His passion he had thought crushed came over him in a storm. He gathered her yielding form in his arms as if he never would loose her again, and kissed her trembling answering lips a dozen times, and her wet anxious eyes.

"Bertha, I will not go," he whispered hurriedly. "I can not leave you thus."

But she had gently released herself from his embrace. She tried to smile at him through her tears. "No, no, you must go." Still he hesitated till a strange eagerness came into the blue eyes. "No, no, you must go. Good-bye, Philip."

As he went down the steps and out of the gate, the chill of the last expression in her eyes hung about his heart. Then he stopped and looked about. She had closed the door, but something white fluttered on the step. It was her handkerchief, with the perfume she always used in its delicate folds. He carried it to his face—it was almost as if he touched her. He stood hesitating a moment—a moment big with issues to them both. He remembered her tender words and the rare caresses she had had for him ; he forgot the undertone that had so painfully interpreted them. It was as if he had tasted of some priceless vintage of wine. He would return in an hour and taste again. Ah, he had waited patiently for the moment when this woman of stainless marble would turn to flesh! And now his foolish heart counted all its hard lessons for nothing, but beat high with triumph. "To-morrow." She understood him, then, but how modest and timid she was ; to-morrow would be for them both the brightest day of their lives. But she was startled at herself now, no wonder, at the revelation of the depths of such a heart. She wanted a little time to calm herself; to get wonted to the new woman that looked out of her eyes.

He had made up his mind, and the moon went under a black cloud for anger. But it was only for an hour: then he would come back.

Market-hall was crowded, and Curran was speaking at a pitch of impassioned eloquence beyond anything Philip had ever heard.

"What overwhelms you is your own energies fused into weapons of deadly warfare; it is their cunning which turns your myriad hands against yourselves. Where else can they find the force to vanquish you? The rich are but few. Whose hands but yours are strong and numerous enough to carry out their plans? The longer you submit, the stronger they entrench themselves with your flesh and blood. Every week some new trade or profession is invented to make respectable and steady some new discovered method of living out of the poor; every month some new law is passed in the interests of the money power."

He paused for a moment and then went on with more bitterness. "Every month the upper classes grow more indifferent to the foundation on which they rest—of throbbing, agonizing human flesh. Not satisfied with the terrible natural distinction between

wealth and poverty, they invent codes of manners
and devise elaborate systems of what they mincingly
call etiquette. Marriage with the poor is inexcusable. Even familiarity with inferiors—a great breach
of " propriety " they call it. They ask not, is a man
honest and true hearted, is he kind, but is he
wealthy, or did he ever soil his hands with work?
Not is a woman beautiful, is she modest? these are
of little account; but is she well, that is richly, con-
nected? If her father cheats others she may be
admitted to their circles, if he is unfortunate enough
to be cheated, never. Ah, the shame of it, that makes
no account of hundreds of million of human creatures
of untainted blood, of unclouded intellects, only as
mere beasts of burden; to deny them social privi-
leges, and whip the boldest of them back into the
darkness of ignorance and contempt. All the lights
of knowledge must burn for the few alone, all the
soft influences of culture, and the elevating pleasures
from art and genius are for the few alone." He
folded his arms over his broad chest and threw back
his head in one of his grandest gestures.

"And how have they earned the right to call
themselves mankind, to drink alone at the fountains
of knowledge and inspiring beauty, with never a share
for the millions sweating under the burdens their
white hands have put upon them? No carpets of
priceless web are too fine for their lovely women's

feet, rubies not rare enough for their jewels.   Music
beats out its heavenly harmonies for them alone,
with its treasured meaning of uncounted centuries.
Painting ravishes their eyes alone with the pictured
realms of inspired fancy.   Literature scrapes and
cringes before them, with its stores of wisdom.   Deserved!   God himself, in the full glory of his om-
nipotence, would not outrage his creatures thus, and
yet they are our creatures and we suffer it."

Then he threw out his arms and came forward to
the edge of the platform, for one last personal appeal.
A hundred that could not understand all he said,
thrilled in vague revolt under his irresistible magnetic force.

"Your bodies, whose only pleasure is sleep,
whose only gratification is to still the daily recurring
necessary hunger, your bodies could enjoy every
luxury and beauty, ah, and the common Christian
comforts would be sweetest luxuries to you, which
have palled on the sated senses of the rich.   Your
minds and souls could grow fine and broad and
calm, in the education their pampered children scoff
at ; and the world progress more in a year, than in
centuries before.   And you are a thousand to one ;
the joys and comforts, the blessed possibilities of a
thousand lives, against the insensate greed of one
man for more, and more he cannot eat, or drink, or
enjoy.   It is his madness, but they do not confine

such as he, who sets the world back ten years for one he lives. But when he opens his great vault to-morrow and sits down to count his ill gotten gains of the yesterday, let his heart sink within him ; he has refused his workmen the common rights of humanity, and they will leave his mills to rot in idleness."

He took his hat from the table and strode down the aisle amid the excited applause of his audience, and went out, not even once looking back. An awkward silence followed, but it was several moments more before Philip braced himself to do what perhaps was his duty. His father depended on him, and besides it was a terrible conflict, when labor and capital came to open battle ; it ought to be averted. Every eye was fixed on him as he made his way forward ; not one there but believed he was their friend. Had he not put on the fire escapes out of his own money in spite of his father? Many a whisper of commendation brought an answer of hearty good feeling. One or two of the women in the galleries actually said he was handsome.

" My friends," he began, but somehow he did not care to lift his eyes to meet the kind look in the trustful eyes, " I don't think there is any occasion, I mean, friends —"

What did he mean, he knew better than they what occasion there was. How dare he ask them

10

to wait and hope, for when had a corporation a heart for mercy? He knew better than they, that to-morrow would be the last day when a strike would be likely of any effect. They might defeat his father's scheme if nothing else, a scheme that would make them servants no longer of a man, but of a pitiless business principle.

He looked about the room at last; he read aright the confidence in the eyes of the company. He believed he might make them wait, but had he a right to ask it? Here were a thousand souls in the mills, impatient at injustice, as they thought it; he could offer them no hope, not one straw; his hands would be forever tied after to-morrow. Had he a right to restrain them?

"Friends, I know not what to advise you, since I am so weak to help you." He sat down and a cheer rang loud and hearty to the roof, but he felt himself in an agonizing position. On the great questions at issue between the employers and the workmen, the rich and the poor, his mind was slow in coming to a conclusion. He admitted most that even Curran said, while he listened, but what then, how to help it, was the question he ever asked himself. Surely nobody was profited by flying in the face of great economical laws. But then what were laws, and what were fallacies. Well, if he did not know what was right, could he not follow his father's

urgent wishes? Was he making a generous return
for the love his father had lavished on him, if he
should disobey him now? Well then if he told them
all he knew, it might be fair for him to ask them
to submit one more day, but what arguments had
he in that case for them? As he sat there his
vivid imagination pictured the corporation in operation. Some little injustice was being done, and he
mentions it to the overseer. "Them's orders, you
must see the superintendent." He could see it all so
plainly. He knocks at the superintendent's door and
is received with the attention due the chief stockholder's son; he sees his bland smiling face, strange
but familiar, his sleek well paid smile. He speaks
of the rule which perhaps works to rob some particular set of hands, wholly without their fault. "But
I have no authority to change it, though it does
seem hard, better see the agent." Philip imagines his
discouraged step, as he makes his way to the agent
to be referred to a set of indifferent directors, who
"really know nothing about the matter, but I do not
feel like running against the interests of the stockholders." There would be no responsible human
being to listen to the cries of the poor, who contrib-
uted their meagre portion of the air and sunlight,
and all their hopes of joy or rest, to be woven, no
doubt, into the matchless fabric of the Breton Mills.

While Philip sat trying to grasp his duty of that

moment, he became conscious that it was very still, and no one seemed disposed to follow him. Not a few impatient faces were turned askance toward him. Well, they were afraid of him ; no wonder, if they knew what was passing in his thoughts. He rose and crossed the room to go out, but almost at the door he hesitated. He must say something.

"Perhaps it is not all quite as plain as you think. If by higher wages or shorter hours you made the profit on the mills smaller, are you not afraid other mills would leave us behind, being able to sell cheaper, or else the capital invested go elsewhere, where it can make more profit ? Now you get small wages for long hours, but in the other cases you might lose work altogether." Then he looked anxiously around and added hurriedly, "Mind, I don't say do this or that ; I will not ask anything of you. But if there is a loss it will be on you."

When he left the hall he felt like walking about a little while, to calm his mind. He chose the route that would lead past the little tenement house where they had fed him with cold potatoes. It was only a month ago. He looked in through the windows. The sick woman yet lay on the sofa, the same soiled plaid shawl for her coverlet ; there was the same bare deal table, and a pair of dingy chairs before it. The desolation made his heart sick. Then he looked up at the windows of the attic chamber where he had

slept that other night. It was all dark, but he imagined the glaring white walls, with the queer little
block of a looking-glass hanging there, and the back-
less wooden chair that had to serve for a wash-stand,
then there was his low bed, and the girl's shawl for
his counterpane. What great things he had dreamed,
that night, he should do for the new cause that had
fired his heart, new to him, but old as civilization.
He turned away with a pain in his heart, a pain for
the wrongs of the millions of the sons of toil, who
have never come into their inheritance. He turned
up the road that led to his own home on the hill; he
could see the gleam of bright light from his father's
study, where with his smooth-faced lawyer, he was
perfecting his plans for the morrow. And then he
seemed to hear his own words, and his own tone as he
had spoken in the meeting, echoing oddly in his ear.
Had he undutifully sacrificed his father to his help,
and would it be from his fault, the strike he feared
would come to-morrow? Could his father point his
trembling fingers at him, when the mills should stop,
and the prospective stockholders decline the investment to-morrow, and say, " My own son is to blame.
With one word he could have prevented it."

Then Philip turned his back to the lights that
seemed to reproach him intolerably, and walked
slowly down the hill again. Ah! what fear for capital, it always shifts its burden upon labor.

A woman's form came quickly out of a shadow, and laid a hand on his arm. It was Jane Graves, with a shawl over her head, servant-girl fashion, but was it the ghastly effect of moonlight on her face that made it so pale?

"Wasn't you at Miss Ellingsworth's this evening?"

"Why, yes," he looked at her in astonishment, "and I was just going there again."

"I didn't know but she might be with you. I was at my father's, and when I came back, I couldn't find her, and her hat and shawl were gone."

"She has gone out with her father, perhaps," suggested Philip, startled more by her manner than her words.

"But he has been up at Mr. Breton's all the evening. And you know she never goes out alone."

"Sometimes she does," he said, as he went with the girl. "I met her quite away from home one night, but she seemed a good deal frightened."

"When was it?" Jane Graves stopped short, and when he had told her, a quick, involuntary cry escaped her lips, and after that he had almost to run to keep up with her.

Now and then he tried to laugh at the terrors this foolish servant girl had put into his mind. But could it be Bertha had taken another evening walk? She was too beautiful for the exposures of common life ; mankind was much too weak to be tempted by such delicious loveliness as hers. Was heaven envious of such happiness as he had expected in their reconciliation ? Why not strike him, then, and not her ? Why, it might have been she had tried to overtake him, to call him back. " Hurry faster," he muttered, catching the girl's arm roughly.

CHAPTER XIII.

Class Prejudice.

BUT the house looked so sedate, and altogether respectable, that it seemed impossible but that everything was as usual inside. The door stood invitingly open, as it should on such a balmy summer evening, the light streaming bountifully out on the walk. A catastrophe surely would have left some sign, some fatal mark somewhere to curdle one's blood from afar. How foolish of this black-eyed maid and him, to rush at the top of their speed, in an agony of suspense, only to find Bertha sitting at the parlor table, mild eyed and serene as he had used to know her. She had only stepped across the street, perhaps.

How she would wonder to see him hurrying in his unreasonable fear, into her presence, but he would pour into her ears such a torrent of words of love, that she would bless him a thousand times that he had come back, and their happiness would date from to-night. Perhaps she had tender confidences for him, too, of how wonderfully she had grown into the love he had longed for, and she would whisper to him that the few weeks of estrangement had been a blessing of God for her, and he need never again complain of the coldness of her love. Life is not so serious and tragical an affair as one sometimes thinks; things don't always plunge into the ruin they are pointed toward.

By the time Philip stepped into the door, he had fully discounted his expected relief; indeed, had almost persuaded himself that he had had no misgivings, there seemed so little sense in misgivings.

But he did not find the blue-eyed woman he loved at her parlor table. He looked for a crochet needle or a square of canvas, which might show the marks of recent work; but the round table was in perfect order. The little book-shaped card basket stood near the bronze base of the drop lamp. A large red morocco bound volume, called "The Dresden Gallery," was tilted up a little by a blue and gold book of Swinburne's poems, on which it had been laid. The gracefully carved book-rack was full, all but one space the volume of poems might have fitted into.

"Just as I arranged it after tea," said Jane Graves, moving uneasily about.

"For heaven's sake be still," he exclaimed. He stepped out into the hall.

"Why, here is her shawl," he said, with a lightened heart.

"It is her heavy shawl that is gone," the girl

looked peculiarly at him when she added almost under her breath, "the one she takes on evening drives."

Philip shot a glance of sudden intelligence at her, and terrible suggestions and recollections came crowding their hateful meanings upon him. The mad blood seemed congesting about his heart, and yet his face blazed like fire. "Good God!" he shouted hoarsely, "if you dare to breathe it, I will choke the envious life out of you." Then he caught the bell knob at the door and rang it fiercely, and then again, before its echoes had ceased, and again and again.

"And is there another fire, your honor?"

The broad-faced chambermaid had come up from the kitchen, and stood with arms a-kimbo, trying to make her rich Irish voice heard above the sounding gong.

"Do you know where your mistress is?"

"No-a; if she be not inside, indade."

"Didn't she go over to a neighbor's somewhere?" questioned Philip, eagerly.

"Not that I knows on, sir."

"Has anybody been here? Didn't you tend door, you ninny!"

"The bell didn't ring till now, sir; but lave me think a bit," and the woman rubbed her head meditatively.

"Quick," cried Philip, between hope and fear.

" Don't scare me, sir, or I can't do nothink."

He moved his feet restlessly on the inlaid hall floor ; and he had bowed his head as if studying the artist's design ; but it was for fear he should catch some terrible significance in Jane Graves' black eyes. He could hear her dress rustle ; he knew she was looking at him, waiting for him to lift his face ; but he would not have met her eyes at that moment for all the world.

" Yis, there was a rumblin' team come up, and I thought I hearn a man come to the dure and thin go back ; but the bell didn't ring, sir, and I didn't make no count on it. No sir, I hevn't hearn missus movin' roun' sence, and I knows she be all over the house before."

The creature's tongue was unloosed and she kept on talking, but Philip had bounded up the broad stairs and thrown open the door of the room he thought was Bertha's.

In another moment the gas blazed up to the ceiling and he stood, wild-eyed, looking from side to side as if he thought to find a heart-breaking story written all over the gold papered walls. Then his eyes became fixed on the black walnut bureau with its long mirror coming down through the centre. On the marble slab at the foot of the mirror he saw a satin covered handkerchief case ; and pinned into it —

In three steps he had clutched a little perfumed note, with a ribbon fastened on it as if for a signal, a delicate bow of white ribbon. Mr. Ellingsworth's name was written on it. It was all here, and yet he hesitated a moment as a man would hesitate to cut off a maimed and poisoned limb. And it was almost unconsciously at last that his nervous fingers tore the note open and let the bit of white ribbon flutter to the floor. He seemed to read very slowly and the flush faded from his face and left it very calm. There could be nothing very thrilling written there surely. But every line and curve was branded forever on his heart.

"I have gone with Curran. I knew I could not stand your reproaches, but I can only be happy with the man I love. Society will disown me. He is more to me than them all. BERTHA."

He crushed the bit of paper in his hand, and looked up to see Jane Graves standing in the doorway, pale as death. Beside her stood the red-cheeked chambermaid, speechless again, this time with astonishment to see the young man make so free in her mistress' chamber.

"Gone with Curran, oh yes, it is all written out. Well, that is a joke; a man who don't wear cuffs, and Bertha loves him! Why, I never could dress to suit her." And he threw himself into a chair, and burst into convulsions of laughter till the tears came.

"Well, there may be something else," and he stepped jauntily up to the bureau again.

"Certainly, a jewel box with my name on it; oh! to be sure, our engagement ring." He held it up to catch the sparkle of the solitaire diamond. "Yes, yes, a very proper and delicate spirit. I wasn't mistaken in Bertha, she always had a nice sense of propriety."

He came a little unsteadily toward the two women. Jane Graves was pale and still as death, with her two little hands pressed tightly upon her bosom. Philip wondered impatiently what was the matter with the girl. If he could treat the whole wretched business like a huge joke, what the deuce was the use of her playing tragedy queen over it? What child's play life's solemnest woes and failures are, after all a man's dread of them! It is mixing up flesh and blood with them, spoils their grand effects; men and women are only fit for the cheapest kind of low comedy. How it must amuse the immortal gallery gods, when a man attempts to sustain the tragedy pitch in his experiences. If one can only get the true point of view, there is no such thing as a noble situation, a glorious victory or a desperate dilemma. The dignity of sorrow is a ridiculous misnomer. Everything is only more or less funny according to its pretentiousness—for example the astonishing denouement of his love episode.

Now Norah the chambermaid, with a face like a pumpkin, and eyes that stuck out like saucers, say of the cheap blue kind, was a suitable lay figure for such an occasion.

"Why here, Norah, this is really a very good diamond. I bought it for the best, permit me to present it to you. Bertha, your late mistress I mean —was a large woman, no doubt you can wear it over your little finger. Consider it as a reminder of this charming evening. Ah, let me put it on, you are not used to jewels—thus. Now, my love, you may run down stairs and show your pretty present."

He turned his strangely bright eyes to the wall at the foot of Bertha's bed.

"My picture, too. How the girl's heart must have glowed night and morning over it." He took it down and held it before him a moment.

"A foolish face," he muttered between his teeth, the wild merriment fading out of his features. He bent and laid the picture glass upwards on the floor, then he ground it viciously beneath the heel of his boot, and walked away without deigning to cast another look at it.

Bertha's pure bed, which her graceful form had pressed so many years—an inscrutable awe crept over him; it seemed impious to look, he fell on his knees and buried his hot face in the pillow where he fancied her head had rested.

"Oh, my lost darling, my lost Bertha, you have taken all the joy and hope of my life with you," and his slight frame shook with tearless sobs, like the death throes of a breaking heart.

Then he rose in bitterness of soul to his feet. Was there no way to drown the deep settled pain about his breast? Were there no other women in the world? He had heard times enough, there was no salve for a broken heart so quick and sure as another woman's kisses.

He almost stumbled over Jane Graves, who lay across the threshold in a dead faint. It was but the work of a moment to bend over her, and lift her in his arms. But he would not let her lie on Bertha's bed, no, not to save her life, and he bore her through the hall to another chamber. It was a slight girlish form he held and need not have been so unpleasant a burden. But he laid her down on the first resting place he could find, and lifted her feet with delicate gentleness on the bed. He removed the high pillows from under her head, so that she could breathe more easily, and, true gentleman that he was, covered her pretty feet and ankles with some light wrap.

A green tinted cologne bottle stood near by and he bethought himself to dash the cool contents into her face, and felt quite a doctor's surprise to see any good result follow his ministrations. The banished

blood stole slowly back into her olive cheeks. He
bent over her and lifted her shapely little hands, as
dainty as a princess', and tried to arrange them in
some graceful position. She would know how to do
it the instant she opened her eyes; he could think
of nothing only as she had stood at the door of
Bertha's room; so he crossed her hands lightly
over her bosom that was beginning to pant in returning consciousness. How pretty she was; if
her lips were a little full that was a very pardonable
fault.

It was very odd her fainting out of sympathy
with his sufferings. Not impossibly the little maid
might have a soft spot in her heart for him. A sudden
mad thought warmed his blood; why not wait till .
she opened her eyes, this charming little girl, and
then, swear to her that he loved her. What was love
then that such a pretty face and form as this should
not have it? She was no cold woman: her kisses and
endearments—but his eyes had grown cold and hard
while he looked at her. If she were a Cleopatra she
could be nothing to him, her kisses would only stifle
him with their passion; her clinging soft arms about
his neck would only strangle him. He knew to his
sorrow what it was to love, and no pretty sham, no
matter how its voluptuous artifices made his hot
blood surge through his veins, could still for one
moment the immortal longing it only mocked. She

moved a little as she lay; and he started and went out.

The girl's eyes opened slowly on the rich blue lambrequins, and the rare frescoing of the room. She vaguely wondered for one delicious moment if she awoke some rich gentleman's wife, and her old life of poverty was past forever. Why, she was in Mr. Ellingsworth's bed chamber; how came she here? And her hair was wet; and the ruffles on her neck were damp—it was cologne. Then she remembered everything, and rose from the august couch she had unworthily pressed. She laid back the great pillows and tried to smooth out the outlines of her form on the spotless counterpane, and then made her way down stairs. The house was so still it frightened her; it was as if everybody in the world had died while she lay in her faint. The hall below was empty too, and the outer door shut. As she passed she brushed against Bertha's light shawl, the one that had relieved Philip Breton's fears when he saw it. She opened the parlor door; she felt as if she must find somebody to ease the tension of her nerves.

Mr. Ellingsworth sat with his head bowed on his hands; he knew it all; his home was desolated, his pride outraged. At the noise he uncovered his face for a moment and looked up; and the cruel light falling on his distressed face revealed the marks

11

of age his tranquil course of life and selfish and complacent philosophy had so long softened and covered. He saw the graceful figure of his maid in a pretty attitude of hesitation on his pleasure. He was alone in the world but for her, deserted in his own home only for her.

"Come here, Jennie," he said in a broken voice.

She came into the room, and a few steps toward him. Then she stopped. Her face was almost as pale as when she fainted, but her black eyes shone with unusual feverish brilliancy.

"Give me your hand, dear."

The girl started, and half turned as if to escape. Then strange thoughts darted through her brain. A warm, red flush mounted from her neck, and spread itself in tingling waves of shame to the very roots of her black hair. She came up to him, and reached out her little hand. He pressed it gently, then he laid it against his cheek. Her heart bounded in sudden revolt, but she controlled herself with an effort of sheer will, and did not move, but her startled eyes sought the floor. And so this was her proud master. But what harm if he wanted to be foolish and sentimental? it was no matter to anybody now, no one cared for her unkissed lips.

"Jennie," he said at last, "come nearer to me."

And she kneeled by his chair, in a sudden impulse she dared not define, not yet. She put her other hand in his, and lifted her dark, wet eyes to his face. But the cold man of philosophy and subtle analysis was transfigured, and she was suddenly afraid of the spirit she had evoked. The next moment he looked in sudden terror at her face, in which reckless daring and maidenly timidity were blended into the most bewitching and tantalizing of effects. Then he bent down to the upturned face, that never flinched, and in another instant he held in his arms her form that seemed to shrink only that he must clasp her the closer.

"Will you be my wife, Jennie? I never loved a woman as I do you. Will you be my wife, Jennie?"

"Yes," whispered the red lips that never once turned away from his thick raining kisses.

In Bertha Ellingsworth's own parlor, it was, with her mother's face looking down from the painted canvas, in the room where the daughter of the house had so coldly entertained the heir of the Breton Mills. Ah! yes, and where she had taught Curran, the prophet of the poor, to love her, and she the very essence of the spirit he taught them to hate. But how her proud face would wince now! If she were only here! Her father, the haughtiest of men, to everybody in the great world beneath him cold as an iceberg, they said, arrogant as any duke of courtly circle, could it be he praying, with hot breath, the love and the hand of his servant maid! Could it be he holding her so fondly in his arms, where he might have gathered coy dames of the stateliest rank, lavishing honeyed words and mad endearments on his poor servant girl, whose only nice dress it was he was crushing so recklessly! Ah! it was worth the cost, if she had to tear her heart out, for all that wealth can buy will be hers.

She nestles her burning face on his shoulder, and tempts him to new caresses and new words of folly, that he may not remember yet what a strange thing it is he is doing; that he may not think of repenting until his enthralled senses shall let him forget everything else, rather than this sweet hour. She will now be able to comfort and restore her dying mother, give her tired father rest, and show them both that there is such a thing as happiness in life, even for them. Her wildest dreams are realized. She will be one of the rich and the great, whom the rest of the world bow down to. She will make her husband's—yes, this man is to be her husband, why should she be ashamed with him—she will make his friends all envy him his beautiful wife, and as for their faded, fashionable women, with limp backs, and bloodless veins, how it will please her to study the signs of jealousy on their listless faces. And Bertha Ellingsworth's proud, false heart will ache with shame over the low-born woman whom her father has made his wife. Curran had scorned her, now she could scorn the woman he had preferred to her, and with wealth, how countless the means of revenge! The poor can only kill, if they hate, the rich can torture and crucify alive.

" Has the train gone for the west?" asked a breathless voice at the Lockout station.

" It's thirty minutes behind its time," growled the ticket agent. It was Philip Breton, who went back to the post to tie his horse more securely. "Poor Joe, poor old boy," the big white horse seemed more like to fall dead in his tracks than to try to break away. " A pretty hard gallop, wasn't it, Joe, your breath will come easier in a minute, old horse."

His time was precious, but he lingered in an uncontrollable terror of what he had come so far to see. He had thought he wanted to make sure. There might be some mistake in the note, or even now, if she had changed her mind—but it was all folly, he saw it now. He had forgotten all reason in one wild longing to see Bertha again. But what was the use of harrowing up his soul with new pictures he would pray God in vain to wipe out of his memory? But he had come so far, perhaps it would do no harm to look at her once more, and who knows? strange things have happened in this world. He had turned and was walking along the platform, toward the ladies' waiting-room. He glanced up the long stretch of straight track and saw in the distance the headlight of the engine, which seemed to him a pitiless monster, hastening on to seize his darling and bear her to some hopeless region of eternal night. He must hurry. Who knows? it might be fate had kept her rescue till this moment, and meant him to save her. He pushed the waiting-room door open. The seats appeared all vacant and expectant; a big russet apple had been dropped on one of them by some interrupted traveler, and in another place the carpet upholstery was specked with the white litter of a cracker and cheese luncheon. The whole atmosphere was too commonplace for a pair of runaway lovers. Philip took two or three steps into the room, but it was only as he turned to go back, that he saw the settees were not quite deserted.

It was a group for a painter's loftiest genius, but the artist must have a faith in love, such as the world have learned to scoff. The figure of the man may embody strength and dignity, in unconscious perfection, it is bent now in a beautiful protective attitude toward the woman whose head rests on his shoulder. Her lips are parted to reveal the pearly gleam of her white teeth, but she does not smile. She has golden hair like a crown sitting well down on the broad forehead, and there is the tint of red gold in her cheeks like a perpetual glow of sunset. But what painter can catch the holy tenderness in the eyes that drink in her unsullied beauty, the breathless wonder, the rapt mystery in his softened face? What inspired brush can picture the quiver of the long golden lashes against her cheek, and then the dreamy stirring of the eyelids that now open wide, so his impassioned gaze may thrill the liquid depths of blue. Let the artist fix then forever if he can—the smile that ripples at last over her fascinated face, a smile of trust too perfect for shame.

What was that sound so like a human sob, that startled the lovers from each other's arms? Why, it almost made them sob for sympathy, as if it came from a broken heart. Who ever heard the wind moan like that, so short and sharp it was? But it must have been the wind, for they were quite alone.

CHAPTER XIV.

The Mill-Owner's Triumph.

THE grey mists broke and the eastern clouds blushed red at the coming of the most ardent lover in the universe. His fruitful bride, earth, smiled her glad welcome up to him, but gave place to settled peace and love as the early hours went by. But it was the saddest day of Philip Breton's life, so terrible a thunderbolt had fallen upon him out of the clear sky.

A woman's hand had struck him; and he had looked to her for all the most precious experiences of life. Humiliation might have stirred in some hearts a blessed reaction to relieve their aching consciousness of loss; but the blow to his love and his hopes was so much heavier than the hurt of his pride that he did not think to be insulted, he was only overwhelmed. Other men and perhaps sometimes a woman must have met with such misfortunes; Philip wondered curiously how they managed to endure them; but they could not have lost one like Bertha; she could have no exact counterpart to ruin other men's lives. There

could be no escape for him ; he had been so simple
to give his whole heart to a woman before he had
married her; to teach every taste to incline toward
her; to suffer every little rill of tenderness and worship in his being to pour into his ideal of her. And
all his plans touched her somewhere ; and all his
thoughts, even such as she never could understand,
wound about her personality as he conceived of it at
some point in their processes. And now every hour
of his life must be embittered by some reminder of
what he had hoped for and lost. The balmy south
wind that morning was like her breath; the soft
murmur of the water in the raceway below the mill
was like her voice ; a blonde face looked down from
one of the windows of the weave room, there was a
flitting expression on it like Bertha. And so it must
be forever.

At the head of his counting-room table sat Mr.
Breton, smiling and bland. Before him were piled
the heavy tomes containing the records of his great
manufactory; by his side stood two clerks to assist
in handling and explaining them. Around the table,
attentive and eager, were gathered as many as could
get there, of shrewd, hard business men. A dozen
more, of the same unmistakable species, stood about
the room and leaned against the windows, quiet and
observant, listening to all that could throw any light
on the matter under discussion. It was the moment-

ous meeting of the prospective stockholders in the corporation looming up in magnificent proportions before their fancies.

The paymaster and the attorney stood at hand apt with suggestions ; one of them had the smile born of fond hopes of unlimited fees ; but the other an awkward fretted air at the sudden change from one to so many superiors. The mill-owner was detailing to this most interested audience the history of the flourishing industry he desired to enlist them in, and their eyes shone eagerly at the prospect of buying such stock at par. They imagined their thousands doubling on their hands in such an investment, doubling without an effort of theirs, doubling in spite of their idleness, which added never one stroke of theirs to the sum of the muscular force that furnished the wealth of the world. Their dollars would double in five or six years, whether they were sick or well, virtuous or vicious, even if they violated the most sacred laws of society. They rubbed their bald, shining heads in dignified delight. Ah, but isn't it fine to be rich, with no care but to invest one's money and count the income the inert gold can breed? Isn't it beautiful to have laws that look out so well for those who pay most of the taxes ? To be sure the laws seem to bear hard on the poor ; they find it pretty slow getting a start, but of course if everybody was rich, why, nobody would be. And the same set of laws and the same principles of government could not possibly help the poor get large profits from their labor, and also enrich the capitalists so rapidly out of the labor of the poor. And then what a comfort it is to feel no fear that the laws may change, no matter how loud the lower classes complain and storm. The rich can work upon the very poverty which seeks relief against the tyranny of capital, to entrench themselves ; for the neediest of voters and legislators must naturally be the most easily moved by the golden favors the rich only can hold out.

But what could possess Breton to make this change? Was he rich enough? Absurd! who ever was rich enough? Perhaps there was some flaw somewhere, and this cunning lawyer knew all about it. They must not let themselves be fooled, so they listened with still quickened attention, and waded suspiciously into one after another of the big ledgers, for a few pages, to ferret out the secret.

" The gentlemen may ask," Mr. Giddings, the lawyer, had noticed the puzzled expression on their shrewd faces, " why Mr. Breton makes this offer. From the amount of stock we propose to issue, it ought to be clear enough," and he laid his fat finger in the palm of his left hand. " He proposes to keep just as big an interest here, as ever, but the plan is to make these mills, as they shall be extended, gen-

tlemen, as they shall be extended, the most stupen-
dous manufacturing enterprise in the country ; for
that there must be more capital, and you are invited
to join."

Philip had but little to say to the unwelcome visitors, whose carriages, of all varieties of elegance,
lined the road-side without. He moved about
among them, more like a stranger than the least
pretentious of them all.

" Ellingsworth, Mr. Ellingsworth," called Mr. Breton, " why, he was with me only last night. Can he
be sick ?"

Yes, sick with shame, and Philip thought how
quickly the flush of pride would fade out of his father's pleased face, if he knew—knew that his own son,
the heir of his millions, had been discarded at last
by the girl he had already taken into a daughter's
place in his heart. And it was this same man Philip
had defended and argued for, that had struck his
deadliest blows at the mills, and now thrust his knife
into the very home of the rich man. It would em-
bitter the father's life, when he came to know of the
broken heart his boy must bear forever—but he need
not know just yet.

Now and then the young man went out into the
hall for a clear view of the massive mills, and glanced
fearfully along their front, and listened. But the
roar of the machinery did not abate, and through the

jail-like windows he could see the tireless men and women forms stepping backward and forward, raising and lowering their hands at the tasks that had ushered in their cheerless youth, and were wearing out their tedious lives. Very likely there would be no trouble; could it be they had been influenced by his words? God forbid that any such responsibility should rest on him. Once, a man appeared at a door. Philip's heart stopped beating for an instant; he thought him the first of a long line that would now rush forth from their prison. But the man only stood listlessly a moment as if there was absolutely nothing of importance on his mind, and then went back. So Philip returned to the office.

"Is that Breton's son, that young man who looks so pale? He don't seem to take much interest in this business."

"I've always noticed business talent wears out in one generation. The father earns and saves for the son to spend."

"True for you," said a third, apparently of Irish birth. "Well, we won't want the boy's services when the old man dies."

"Hush, Breton is talking."

"And, gentlemen, I have never known a strike here, though I certainly don't pay any more wages than my neighbors." There was a slight noise of something falling outside and Philip hurried out.

The mill yard was as quiet as on Sunday; not a soul
in the whole village apparently who thought of a
strike but him. And whether he feared most an
outbreak or a day of peace, he could not have told.

"I wonder how the help will like the change,"
suggested a white-haired old gentleman, with a grim
smile.

"These corporations are the neatest device of the
century for a gagging machine. What the devil's the
use of the help grumbling, when there is nobody they
can find to blame, only a fiction of law. The overseers and the agent, and each particular stockholder
is, oh, awfully sorry, you know, but nobody can help
anything, that is unless they want to," the speaker
winked so slyly, they all had to laugh and wipe
their shining foreheads. "If a man or a crowd of
men are tormented by their help, why, there is the
shell of a corporation the law provides. A man can
creep into it, and even his own conscience cannot
logically prick him."

Philip was standing near the speaker, and was so
galled by his complacent enjoyment of his own un-
feeling philosophy as to venture to make a suggestion.

"Isn't it just possible, that this complaining you
wish to gag, has some occasion?"

A dozen craned their sleek wise necks, to stare
at the man who talked so wildly.

"Why, my kind-hearted young friend," replied the philosopher, glad of an excuse to vent his practical wisdom, "don't you see the poor will complain until the whole vast distance between us and them is bridged over. We have got to protect ourselves, you won't deny that. I climb to heights on another's body. Everybody knows life is only a fight—the weakest goes to the wall. The poor are the weakest in this case."

Could the mill-owner's son dispute such plain propositions? An odd silence pervaded the company. The gentlemen in the windows stopped talking to look at this curious young man, who seemed disposed to question the plainest axioms of his class. His father hitched uneasily in his chair and rustled a bundle of papers to attract Philip's attention. What had got into the boy?

But Philip had the boldness of desperation to-day. Everything seemed already lost, his future of happiness, his future of usefulness. From to-day he must be only a money lender, living on the big dividends saved out of the workmen's wages in his father's mills. And all the wealth of the Indies could not satisfy the hunger of his soul.

"But you don't strive to climb on my body. You have no feud as you describe with these other gentlemen. It is only on the half-starved, and wholly wronged creatures in the mill yard that we all climb together. We don't fight each other, we agree admirably, why shouldn't we, as we divide the wealth of the world between us, there is a great plenty of it since the lower classes don't come in for any. The fighting is only between our class and the laborers, and so far, even that has been only on our side; we push and stamp, they cringe and yield."

But of what possible account was his opinion. Mr. Breton rose to his feet, and all eyes were turned toward the mill-owner, on the course of whose ideas hung the fate of a whole village. The clock struck ten.

"Gentlemen, you pronounce yourselves satisfied," he waited. His lawyer smiled complacently, the paymaster and his clerks began piling up the books. "Well then, there are one or two formalities, my lawyer informs me—What is that noise?"

It was like a rising north wind, not a little like the breaking of the angry sea on a rock-bound shore. From the entrance to all the mills swarmed jostling human forms. A thousand heads turning at frequent intervals to catch courage from their numbers, gave an unpleasant snake like effect to the swaying columns which united, as they swept on toward the mill-yard gates. Philip Breton hurried back from the hall and threw open the office door. Within all was still as death. The complacent smile had died on the lawyer's lips, the clerks stood like statues, while the ruddy color slowly faded from his father's face, giving place to undefined dread of a danger that had elements no single arm could control. Kings and armies, before him, had trembled at the murmur of mobs, till they learned how short lived was the mad fury of the people, no matter how terrible their wrongs, till they learned how certain was the disunion which made patient victims so soon again out of the fierce avengers of blood.

" Do you ask what the noise is ?" cried Philip from the doorway. " It is a strike at last, see for yourselves."

The sight of the mill hands in open revolt, untouched by motives that commonly restrained them, at once awed Philip as one on shipboard when the waves suddenly toss high in ungovernable storms, and determined him to oppose their violence with his life if need be. The mill-yard gates were hastily unlocked by the frightened janitor, and as the first excited throngs, like a nation escaped out of bondage, swept through them, only one man stood calmly watching from the counting-room piazza. In the front rank ran some little children, whose faces, that should have been rosy in the first bloom of life, were pinched and wan, instead. Play-hours and merry sports were unknown to them. What their baby fingers could earn was the merest trifle, but it cost them the only hours that could ever be free from care. A number of them were deformed from a neglected infancy; they had to learn to be still because it hurt them to fall—tenderer lessons there was no time for. And now they must be driven forth with the rest to earn what they ate. Then came the girls, chattering, and nervously pulling their shawls about their shoulders, as if it were winter. One and all seemed to wear the plaid shawl—badge of their vocation—cold or warm, and there was the same dull yellow hue on their cheeks, the same lines of weariness on every face. Few of them looked well ; girls ought to be petted a little ; but the dreary monotony of their ill-paid work had frowned on their childhood as it cursed them now. And instead of resting while they might ripen into healthful, happy women and blessed mothers, their unknitted frames and soft muscles must work like their starving fathers and brothers. It is only the women of the rich, whom the sentiment of chivalry is for. In every eye was the dullness that comes when hope goes, and the vague delicious dreaming, the eternal privilege of girlhood, is broken rudely upon, when love has no more of its ideal glory, and all the beauty of purity and refinement is lost in the gross struggle for something to eat. The gentle poetical grace of womanhood was gone, those huddling awkward creatures were only weaker men.

But Mr. Breton had pushed his chair to one side

and was making his way through the group of his
friends with hardly a word. The rest tried to smile
but he was far too angry.

"Don't go," urged his lawyer, imperatively laying his hand on his shoulder, "don't think of it, you
can do no kind of good, and they will only insult
you."

"Insult me?" he repeated between his teeth.
Then he stopped, and suddenly faced about. He
frowned fiercely on the cautious business men, whom
he knew full well had decided to give him the lurch.
"If I had a pair of horses who behaved badly, they
are stronger than I, but I would whip them and
starve them till they forgot it." If he could subdue
his own rebellious factory hands, and turn them
back to their work like whipped beasts, he knew
these timid counselors would come back into his
office and put their names to his corporation scheme,
·if not— He bit his lip and pushed on out of the
door. And then his help had never dared think of
mutiny before; he had fancied they were afraid of
him. Five minutes more would prove whether they
were or not.

In a moment more he stood beside his son, who
watched, pale and stern, from the counting-room
piazza; behind him his lawyer whose face, deserted
by smiles at last, looked almost unfamiliar; and still
further back were a few of the boldest of his visitors.

"For God's sake—go inside," whispered Philip between his set teeth, "you will only make them angrier."

"Truckle to my own help, shall I ?" repeated his father in his harsh, grating mill tones.

The mill-owner threw back his head and shoulders, and looked commandingly at the crowd. He could not understand why they were not afraid of him. Had he not been the dispenser of bread, almost of life or death, to them for twenty years? They were a thousand, and he one, but for thirty years their fate had trembled in the balance of his will ; and was it any less so to-day ? They might be ever so numerous and strong ; the subtle machinery of the laws and the ingenuity of capital put them at his mercy. He frowned majestically on the women and children ; where would their dinners and suppers come from ? Where could they lay their foolish heads to-night if he chose to punish them ? But they only laughed in a novel sense of freedom as they hurried by to enjoy their whole holiday.

Then came the men, with the hard set look on their faces that should have warned the mill-owner this was not the moment for him to assert too boldly the sovereignty that had made their whole lives a barren waste. The word had been passed from lip to lip, that Mr. Breton was at the counting-room door, and very angry. But his son, who had shown him-

self their friend, and who had been too honest with
them to give them false counsel, stood with him, and
the men meant to show him the respect he deserved,
and march by in silence. Still, the seeds of old
wrongs and daily repeated privations had borne a
bitter fruit in every heart, and many a sullen look of
hate Philip saw on their faces.

"Stop, stop, I say?" shouted Mr. Breton. A
murmur ran through the crowd, and they stopped.
Philip saw the willingness of the halt ; it had irked
them to go by, without one word to relieve the universal sense of injustice that had seethed so long in
their breasts.

"You will do well to let them go in peace," muttered Philip, in a constrained voice, "the poor creatures will have to come back again when they get
hungry." But his father did not appear to hear
him. His face had flushed crimson, and he seemed
to have quite lost his self-command, as he shook his
fist at the sullen crowd that widened every moment.

"Do you think you can force me, you beggars?"
For a moment, admiration for his courage divided
the indignation of his strange audience, and the first
response was as much applause as anger.

"No!" he shouted, in a voice shrill with excitement. "You shall every one of you starve first. You
get more wages than you earn now. Do you know
what this strike will fetch you?"

His lawyer plucked at his sleeve; that man of
discretion did not like the expression on the faces
of the workmen nearest to the piazza.

" This is quite uncalled for, my dear Breton, and
not only that," he added, " but decidedly dan—"

But the excited proprietor shook off his arm, and
stepped forward trembling with impotent wrath.

" I will tell you," he cried, " I will cut your pay
down ten per cent more." A murmur started on the
outskirts of the crowd, and swelled into a roar at his
very feet, while the mass of ill clothed humanity
swayed tumultuously.

Philip saw that a catastrophe was imminent. The
excited workmen avoided his anxious eyes, and there
was a power of wrath in their slightly stooping attitude, like a panther before a spring. Their faces too,
were lit up with a fierce glare, like some long-caged
beast that has burst his bars. Injustice after all is
an uncertain foundation for riches, when it is thrilling human beings who suffer. He rushed boldly
forward to save his father from violence, could it be
he was absolutely blind to the peril in which he stood?
Mr. Breton's face had grown suddenly purple.

" I'll teach you to brave me. I'll starve your
obstinacy out of you, before one of you comes back
into my mill."

He threw up his hands in distress, reeled backward before their astonished eyes, and fell into the

arms of his son, a victim of his own passion. The
poor were avenged. God had taken judgment into
his own hands.

His friends bore his stricken form within, out of
the sight of the people. But he had tamed the mob
at last, though it took his life to do it. A hush as
chill as the breath of the death angel's wings, had
fallen upon them. They waited with the patience
of their class, they watched doctors come and at-
tendants hurry to and fro, but no one told them
what had happened. Nothing but glances of hate
were cast at them, till at last Philip Breton himself
with a new desolation in his face, came out alone
on the piazza. Some fancied he stood unsteadily as
if a vital prop had been taken away, others saw a
new force and dignity in his thin boyish face.

"My father did not finish his speech," he said,
with scathing satire in his voice, " I will finish it for
him." They would have borne all the reproach he
might have heaped upon them, but he only said,
"Will you go back to work," his voice began to
break as he added, "My father is dead, and I want
to take him home."

Not a man, woman or child but worked out their
tasks that day. Ezekiel Breton had triumphed.

CHAPTER XV.

A Holiday.

THE streets of the little village are alive with the people commonly shut up in the great mills out of sight. It was only one man dead, the world in which he moved crowded along, and if he had come back even so soon, he would have had to make a place for himself, as when he started first. Another man was born the minute he died, and the ranks were always kept full.

There was a holiday at last, and the people were the nearest they could get to holiday dress. The husbands and fathers had but few changes to make, their aprons, if they were fortunate enough to have them, were off, and their over-alls, their sleeves were rolled down, too, revealing the wear of storm and sun on the cheap stuff of which the clothes of the poor are made. But the young men had most of them some flashy color about their necks, and wore some threadbare black coat, with here and there a whole showy suit, bought regardless of the poverty that stared them in the face. The higher classes had taught them the lesson that a poor man can expect no consideration or respect anywhere, and each human creature, whose spirit is not all broken, will save his scant pennies to disguise in the livery of the prosperous the poverty that the world makes at once his misfortune and his disgrace. Most of the girls, too, had gilt or rubber jewelry in abundance, rich looking chains about their necks, and the most elaborate and massïve earrings. They wore flashing ribbons of the most startling colors, and for dresses cheap flimsy imitations of the most costly stuffs. They could manage to save enough by going without what reasonable regard for health or simplest foresight would require to strut about in this tawdry finery once a week, and win the favor and admiration they fancied never was accorded to beauty or virtue or sweetness, but to the affectation of lavish wealth.

All had gathered near the Breton mansion. The door was hung with black crape in voluminous folds, a melancholy hearse with plumes waving the insignia of woe was at the gate. But the faces of the multitude were happy, even gay, and the murmur of their voices had no cadence of sadness. But for one moment they were quiet. It was when eight bareheaded men, with awe on their faces, the awe of mortals in the presence of the grand mystery of death, came slowly out of the crape-hung door bearing between them the deposed lord of the house. Then appeared in the door the face of the heir,

young Philip, pale and grief-stricken, and an involuntary hum of greeting met him from the people*
who lined the roadside and hustled the carriages in
waiting. He was their hope, their trusted deliverer,
their friend who had seen how hard their lives were,
and had once promised to help them. His words
that night of the fire had sunk deep into their hearts,
they had been repeated from mouth to mouth, with
many an addition of an eager imagination. To be
sure, he had done but little to fulfill his promise, but
there were the fire escapes to bear witness to his
honesty, and his father, the one they were expected
to mourn for, was a hard man to move. Had the
young man not admitted in their meeting he was
too weak to help them? But now he was untrammeled, the unquestioned owner of the Breton Mills ;
his wish was the sole authority henceforth, and he
wished kindly to them ; his word the only law
throughout the great factory, and he had given his
word to help them. Not a soul but believed in the
dawn of a vague day of general happiness. Few had
clear ideas of the elements of their long wretchedness ; they thought everything was wrong in the
system under which the poor were so unhappy, and
the remedy that occurred to their minds was, of
course, to change everything. No more long hours,
no more scant pay, no more favoritism ; all should
have alike. No more strikes or conflicts or com-

plaints or bitterness, for there would be no hardships left.

No wonder, then, that Philip looked out on beaming joyous faces, on smiling lips and eyes that sent a glad welcome to his slight young form their warm fancies invested with such glory as a new prophet might sigh in vain for. But he stood behind his father's dead body—and they had slain him. So the god of their fond hopes ground his teeth at them. These people had cost him his father, and in sight of his unburied body they dared rejoice, and make of his funeral their gala day. The vulgarly dressed crowd of working people looked to his sorrowful eyes like a troop of murderers, who deserved not even common humanity. The glance of hate he gave their eager upturned faces boded but ill for their extravagant hopes. Then he threw himself into his carriage and resigned himself to solitary misery. His carriage moved a few feet and stopped.

His father had loved him, not because he was good or wise, but because he was his son. The village swarmed at this moment with people to bow humbly to him, to run at his beck, to listen when he cared to speak. His house,—ah, yes it was his now—was full of respectful mourners who would press his hand softly, and offer in lugubrious tones to do everything they could for him. Everybody seemed overflowing with consideration, but there was this or that present selfish motive for it all. His father had loved him without cause, only that he was his son, and his heart longed unutterably for the love of close natural ties. How terrible it is to be alone as he was, alone in the midst of a thousand willing servants, alone in the midst of a hundred eager friends. Then he thought of Bertha. At first it seemed a year since he had lost her, and he wondered with a dull ache in his heart where she could be after so long a time.

Then it seemed but an hour, so fresh was the wound in his heart. It was her place, that empty seat by his side, in this supreme moment of his desolation. She could comfort him in his loneliness, the most terrible crushing loneliness, that in the midst of a multitude. Perhaps he was weak, too weak for the stern requisitions of his destiny, perhaps there was not enough of the sturdy element in his character. He would rather have leaned on some other brave heart, than stand out alone before the world, better formed for the gentle graces of a friend than to wield undismayed the ponderous weapons of wealth and power. He would have been better to nurse the sick and comfort the fallen, than to be ordered to the front of the battle, where to be still is infamy, and to fight death to some pitied foe. And there was not one human being near or dear enough to him, to instil one spark of new courage into his heart, or brighten by one smile of love the darkening desolation that seemed to have settled over his life. If Bertha had only waited another day she could not have gone. She would have staid and learned again for very pity to love him, since she had forgot. If she had only waited another day! But no doubt the very weakness in him that cried out for her made him incapable of holding her love. It is hard to confess to oneself, his soul is too poor and small for the woman of his choice to love him; but that was the depth of humiliation Philip Breton had reached as he lay back on his carriage cushions. But at least he was generous to make an excuse, even at the moment of his greatest need, for the woman who had deserted him.

He heard voices from without. He had no interest in what any one in the world might say, he thought, but these were the first words that fell upon his ear.

"Sick is it? Well cheer up girl, the young boss will make it all right. Yer all tired out and ye never was fit for much anyhow."

"Will he give us doctors too?"

"Why not? he has 'em when he's sick. It's just as right we should, as works our best for him when we're well."

Philip was fairly startled into momentary forgetfulness of his sorrow. But the carriage moved along

a few feet and stopped again. Were the people mad? Was it his duty to keep a free hospital
and teach the sick to come whining to him for charity, when ill? Wouldn't it spoil them, to say nothing
from the business point of view? He began to sympathize more than ever with his father's perplexities,
and to feel that perhaps, after all, his solution of them
was the only practicable one. But he heard the rustle
of a woman's dress beside his carriage where it waited.

"Isn't it splendid to have a whole holiday?" said
a fresh girlish voice.

"This isn't the last, Molly," replied a man who
stood right against the carriage door. "They say
we're not to work but four days a week now."

Philip frowned very unpromisingly, but the girl
said,

"And how can we git along on much less wages?"

"Why the wages will be more instead of less. I
guess you don't understand."

Nor did Philip, but the carriage rolled along before the young man could explain, and stopped by
another group.

"Only eight hours a day and every hand will
get just the same; no more favoritism. Who told
me? why that's been the plan all along, only the
old man wouldn't agree. Now its goin' through,
though."

The other man laughed. "Well, I don't see how

the young boss is goin' to make the mill pay that fashion, but that's his lookout."

"Pay!" repeated the sanguine prophet. "Why those looms just turn off sheets of gold."

The horses started once more and Philip Breton sank back on his seat. The people had cost him his bride and his father. They had wrecked his life, and cast him on a shore of barren wastes, with never one fountain of hope for his famished soul. And here the thousand crushed, hitherto hopeless, creatures whose lives need not all be such wrecks as his, had fixed their longing eyes on his acts, which they expected to bring paradise to their doors, to banish all the evils that had cursed their firesides and untold generations before them. What could he do—what was there to do? If he were now some nobler specimen of manhood, such a one as Bertha might have loved; such a one as could be generous enough to forgive the suffering they had given him; or if, even now, he was wise as some men, and could see his way to help them, they might hope indeed. They had swallowed up his dream of love, so much sweeter and diviner than other men knew; they had killed his father, whom this moment they were following with heartless joy to his grave. And now, with stupid and yet pathetic trust, they looked to him to devote his fortune and himself to them, never questioning but a word of his,

a stroke of his pen, would let perpetual sunlight into
their lives.

That evening he sat alone in the little study in
the house that had been his father's. The house was
full of solemn-faced guests, but he would see none of
them. He had bowed his head on his folded arms
and tried to commune with the dead; his dead.
There were two. One his kind, tender father, whose
broad, florid face always brightened with a smile at
the coming of his son. His firm, assured step had
trod this very floor many hundred times, while he
devised his wonderful schemes which seemed fated to
succeed. He had filled the shelves along the walls
with their books; he had chosen the table on which
his broken son rested his head. The things he had
done remained, but he had gone; could it be, gone
where no prayers or cries could reach or touch him;
gone from the house he had built; gone from the
little room he best loved in it, dropping his
unfinished task into hands that were too weak to fulfill it; leaving his burden for shoulders too slight to
bear it. The other of his dead was a woman. He
saw her as if she yet lived. What there was in this
woman of all others that should have called forth
such tender raptures of love, he had never paused to
wonder. She was not brilliant as some women; her
lips, that he believed could have spoken so wonderfully if they had cared, were oftenest closed in society;

her eyes expressed to him the rarest of noble thoughts, and it was as if she deemed the common world unworthy, but that by and by she would speak. He had thought her heart spotless white, and the texture of her nature finer and sweeter than all other women. Every eye that saw her must admire the threads of fine spun gold she called her hair; her soft skin as delicate to the touch as a baby's lips; and the queenlike perfection of her form, a system of bold curves and lines of beauty melting into each other at their beginning and their end. But could there be a soul, to whom she was so much besides her beauty; for whom each phase of her thought or tone of her voice was just what seemed most fitting? And she too was gone; dead; where no prayers or cries of his could reach or touch her; dead and yet forever alive for him.

"Will you see a lady, sir?" It was Mary, whose manner was subdued suitably to the melancholy occasion. All these trappings and pretences provoked Philip strangely, as did the low voices of his guests and their drawn-down faces. He knew well enough they didn't care so much as all that. "She is very particular Mr. Phil—, I mean Mr. Breton."

Then he forgot his impatience in a strange thrilling thought. He rose to his feet and walked to the window without answering the girl. Could it be Bertha ·had felt his hunger for her, such as no

9

other creature could have for her presence? Was it
too unlikely that such pain as ached in his heart,
might have touched her? A throb of electricity goes
around the world; might not such longing as his
have reached her a few short miles away? The maid
began again.

"Will you see a —"

"Yes, yes, show her in." How wild he was to-
night. Why Bertha was married to the man she had
chosen, long ago; if she came back what comfort for
him? If she were not happy with this man after all;
oh, God save her from such a fate, since he had
paid such a price that she might be happy. God
forbid all his torment be for nothing. Philip was
rapidly walking the room. But supposing—and his
heart almost stopped beating at the thought—she
were not married and had come back to him after
all—what other woman could call on him now—what
then, could he forgive her?

The door opened and a heavily veiled woman
came in. She was too slight of form and not tall
enough for Bertha. The idea had been absurd, but
human beings never can believe miracles in their behalf quite impossible. So Philip was not required to
decide the terrible question he had asked himself.
Much as he had longed for that other woman who
had not one throb of pity in her heart for him, his
first feeling was of intense relief, when his visitor

laid back her veil and revealed the face of Jane Graves.

She looked a little agitated and hastened to speak. " I know you are surprised to see me, but I felt I must—"

" Do not distress yourself," he said gravely, recovering his self-possession. Was this his first visit of condolence, and so soon?

" It was about Miss Bertha," then she caught her breath and went on as if she were afraid he would interrupt her, he started so violently. " I know what a lover you are—if mine had only been like you;" she dropped her eyes and went on without looking at him, " but the girl you liked so much that you were blind to how mean she was, she never loved you; she never cared anything for you."

Philip had moved uneasily in his chair as she began, but now he sat still as death, with his eyes fixed, as if in some fatal charm, on the girl's face. She grew pale as she talked, all but one bright spot in either cheek.

" I could tell it when your name was spoken before her; women notice things like that—and when she expected you—and when she expected the other."

His eyes fell in shame, he wished a mountain might fall on him to shield his hurt face from even this poor girl's scrutiny. But she hurried on as if she took pleasure in his wincing nerves. " If you

could have seen how her face warmed at his coming.
and her voice, so cold to you, shook and stumbled
when she welcomed him.   And how her hands would
nestle like a kitten in his—at a look, you never saw
her like that, did you?   And there was no pillow so
soft, you would think, as his shoulder, and—"

"I cannot stand this," he cried, starting to his
feet.   "Do you think I am made of stone?"

"Wasn't it a pretty sight? I used to love to hang
out of my window to see it, or follow her out on her
Sunday walks.   Her kind of women make the biggest fools of themselves; so cold and lofty-like you
would think them angels; when all of a sudden they
lose their heads, and there's nothing too wild for them
to do for some man, till they get over it."   Her eyes
were all ablaze with hate, but Philip hung on the
scornful lips as if it were not poison he drank from
them.

"But she did not get over it," he faltered when
she stopped.   He raised his hands to cool his beating temples, his fingers were cold as ice.

"That is it, it lasted longer than I counted on.
I thought she'd come to her senses before she could
do anything rash, and then I supposed he wouldn't
leave the village and what he was doing here, just
yet."

"But why didn't you tell me?"

"What could you done, she cared nothing for

you. But I was doing the best I knew, if they hadn't been too quick for me. I was waiting till I thought she was just mad over the man. I never supposed they would be so quick," her bosom rose and fell as if it were hard for her to catch her breath. " I knew one thing was sure, and when it would hurt her the most I was going to have tried it. If I had only hurried." She rose sobbing violently, but she shed no tears. Philip had no consideration for her emotion.

" What was it, oh, why didn't you do it?" his form trembled as if he stood in a winter's blast, while drops of perspiration gathered on his forehead.

"I—I—hated so to—to break his heart, I—I knew he would—would never get over it. He ain't the kind that—"

" Curse him!" cried Philip, " what is he to me?"

" I was going to tell him that she was engaged to you. I knew he would never forgive her for deceiving him."

" And didn't he know it?"

" Ah, if he had, he was that honest—you don't know him. But I was too slow, and now, my God my God!" Then she rose to her feet and tied her veil tightly about her face and moved toward the door. But Philip Breton was there before her and held it against her.

. " Tell me first what you came here for to-night."
The answer came sharp as a knife.

" Because I wanted to make you hate that woman
too.   It made me mad that you should think her so
pure and good."

" But why should you hate her, I never could—
never."   His hand loosened on the door-knob and
he leaned back.   Jane Graves could have gone if she
would.

" And don't you hate her now?" she almost
screamed at him, " when I have told you how she
kissed and fondled him when she never had —-"

" Hush."

" Well I hate her, because she stole away my
lover.   May his love touch her yet to disgust ; may
his kisses turn bitter on her lips."   The door closed
after his visitor, and Philip glanced at the clock
which pointed to twelve.   Only half the night gone
then !   He sat down and dropped his head on his
folded arms again.

CHAPTER XVI.

What will They Fetch?

DAYS passed till they made weeks, and weeks till they made months, and no change came for the mills or for the lives of the creatures who worked within their grim walls, only the change from poor to more poor. Poverty, like riches, has the potent principle of reproduction. The bank account of the young proprietor was swelled by many thousands, but his account with the thousand tired, needy souls, who had looked to him for help in their distress, showed him more hopelessly in their debt every week.

They saw but little of the young mill-owner, and the village saw but little of him. It was said he was traveling from mill to mill studying up new methods of management, in and out of all kinds of shops, learning the special excellences of each. He wanted to sail closer to the wind, to stop all wastes and cut down surplus expense, they said. Many had predicted the Breton Mills would run down, but at least the first effect of the change was anything but retrograde. The wholesale dealers and the proprie-

tors of great commission houses rubbed their hands
with delight at the prospect of easy terms and fat
profits.   They received the thin-faced young man
into their offices much as the spider the historic fly.
Fortune smiles on the most unlucky occasionally as
when she sends such beardless boys as he, they
thought, with full power to trade with such shrewd
old business men as they.   But as they bowed the
quiet mill-owner out of their warehouses, and turned
back to congratulate themselves on their bargains,
not one of them all but came to wish it had been the
father instead they had made their contracts with.

He came into the branch city offices of the
Breton Mills like a mild-faced missionary, and the
clerks and pompous salesmen and dignified managers laughed in their sleeves at the good, peaceful
era that was coming.   But the small black eyes cut
a swath where they fell, and many a middle-man,
that had thought himself a vital element in the
success of the mill interests, found his services dis-
pensed with.   Only the very best salesmen and
traveling agents were retained, and those with a
new access of energy.   A dozen men, with fat beaming faces and portly frames, who had lived in lazy
contentment on excellent salaries they never took
any pains to earn, were suddenly out of a place.

The new proprietor was very unpopular in these
business circles.   The startled idlers only hated him

the more, because they had not respected him at
first. The free and easy dispensation expected did not
come. The young proprietor, who had been understood to be of liberal tendencies, seemed as anxious
to stop the leaks in his immense income as if every
leak did not support some man and his family in
comfort. One or two of the ousted ones came to
his hotel and told him how melancholy it would be
for them to lose the places they had had so long, and
then their families must be supported. He had but
one reply for them as he closed his audiences,

" Go to doing something useful, then."

His acquaintances saw new expressions on his
face—the open, boyish look had gone, and his
voice had new tones of decision; his step had
grown firmer and his eyes met a glance with a new
steadiness. Some said he was only plunging himself so deeply into business that he cared nothing
for, to make himself forget his bitter troubles.
Others thought he was developing exactly as his
father was, hard and close in business, but never the
jolly social soul among his equals. But either explanation was equally hopeless to the workmen in
the Breton Mills, who had counted on his easy generosity and business indifference to loosen the hard
bonds that held them down, and open up to them the
good things of the world they had longed for in vain
so long.

On one morning the three men who had been once on the fire escape committee, met in the doorway of number 2 mill, restored after the fire. They had left their work for a breath of fresh air.

"He is closer than his father; he scrimps and saves like a poor cuss trying to support a family on five dollars the week. What show is there for us?"

"Ye'll mind it's all jist as I told ye, Bill Rogers," suggested Graves, with the comfort of 'I told you so' left to him out of the general wreck. "Jist as I told ye that night more'n a six month ago in front of old Breton's. As soon as the lad feels his oats that's the last of his kind heart."

"The boy's had hard luck since then," said Rogers, handling his pipe out of old force of habit. "P'r'aps he's punishin' us for it. It seems so strange somehow his changin' all so sudden."

"'Taint that," said Graves, as he turned to go back to work, and then lingering a moment longer, "It is the natur of a man and crops out as sure as he gets his swing. There aint a one of us but would make a meaner rich man than him. It comes easy to be a labor reformer and radical as long as a fellow is poor, and it's just as easy for a man to talk beautiful if he aint looked to to do nothing. But it makes a man drunk, when he feels the reins in his hands and him nothin' but a man of the same stuff as the rest on us. Look at Curran now, how much better'n the rest is he? He deserted us at the most critical moment. Somethin' made him throw us up as if we had all of a sudden sickened on his stomach. We're poor stuff, all on us, boys. I never seen a finer feller than that Curran, but he's forgot all about the wrongs and rights he used to holler so purty about. There's no chance for us in any man's mercy; we must depend on ourselves."

At this very moment Philip Breton was pressing the little brass bell on his counting-room table. For an answer his paymaster came in with his pen, wet from the ink, in his hand.

" Do we pay our help enough? "

A thousand eager voices would have shouted a no to him that would have shaken the very foundations of stone, but Mr. Jennings, the paymaster, put his pen behind his ear, took it down, looked keenly at it, then in surprise at the young mill-owner.

"We can get a thousand as good for the same, if that is what you mean." Ah, what chance have the poor mills-people, when the young master chooses such advisers as this?

"No!" said Philip slowly. "It isn't exactly what I mean; can we raise the wages?"

" Can you, why yes, I suppose you can step right into the mills and give a hundred dollar bill to every hand. But you couldn't afford to do that way long, and I don't think it would do anybody any good. I

wouldn't assume to advise you, sir, but why not just
as well go up street and insist on paying a fancy
price for your flour."

"But don't they find it hard to live on what we
give them? and what a life it is at that," suggested
Philip sadly. Apparently he had not quite forgotten them.

"No doubt, no doubt!" repeated the paymaster
with the querulousness of his class, "but is there
any sense in putting in your or my fiat—you can't
make a ninety cent laborer worth a dollar and a
quarter by giving it to him. You insult him, and
damage business by making it all uncertain with the
gratuitous element."

"I see you don't believe in benevolence, my dear
Jennings," and Philip smiled curiously.

"Yes I do, for sick people and paupers, but if
you don't want to make paupers of everybody you
mustn't—"

"But I am not a pauper, and I never earned a
penny in my life till a few months ago" Philip's
eyes flashed at a sudden revelation.

"But, ah—but that is different. Drop that then.
To make our cloth, there are a number of expenses,
there is the mill and the machinery, the money
locked up in fabrics and material. These are fixed,
you don't think it your duty to pay extra prices for
raw material ; nor make a gratuity with every dol-

lar you spend on machinery, no matter how poor the man that sells to you. Now comes another element, Labor. That should be as fixed as the rest, and all calculations based on its market price. When you go to market with your cloth, you don't ask any gratuity, nor does the buyer claim any, the price is fixed better than the caprice of a moment could fix it. The element of labor enters into the cost, the difference between the cost and price is your profit. If labor stands you in its market price, your profit will reward your efforts, and it will pay you to keep up your mill. If you paid higher wages your profits would be small, you would give up your enterprise, and all would suffer."

"I didn't know you could be so eager. But supposing they tell me my profit is too large, that my labor pays me so well, I ought to make it up to them." The young proprietor was looking musingly out of the window where the autumn wind was chasing the russet leaves in savage glee. Mr. Jennings the paymaster had reached the door, but waited a moment to clinch his argument.

"Then if you lost money, your help ought to contribute. But it might not be at all their fault that you lost, any more than it is to their credit you succeed. Their labor in quantity and quality would be just the same. What reason in changing its valuation? No, I am sure there isn't but one way, to

measure the value of your labor as you do everything else, by what it will bring."

"Not quite everything," said Philip, but he said
it so low, the argumentative Jennings did not hear
it. All he heard was just as he was closing his door.

"Please send in the overseer of number 1
weave room."

It was but a few moments, during which Philip
did not move from his seat when the overseer came
in, stroking his apron deferentially.

"Mr. Bright, the men and girls complain; they
say they ought to be paid by the day instead of by
the piece."

"Which ones complain? The lazy ones, I 'guess.
Why surely Mr. Breton, it wouldn't be right to pay
the best weaver and the poorest the same."

"Why not?" asked Philip with unchanged features, watching the look of astonishment that shone
on the man's round fat face. "Why not, if we paid
them all the highest price?"

"Well sir, it wouldn't be a month before bad and
good would all be worth about the same, and that
as little as the poorest of them. It would be a poor
way to encourage them to be smart."

"Does Graves work in your room?"

"Yes, but he asked out for this mornin'—his—"

"Send him in if you can find him." Philip rose
to his feet now, and was walking the room impa-

tiently when John Graves slouched in. He turned
on him as if he was going to strike, but it was only
a question he hurled at him.

"What do you think ought to be changed in the
mill? Speak up now, and let me know your mind."

"I think we work too hard for our pay then,'
drawled the laborer, but his mind was in an unusually
excited condition.

" That is because the public want such goods as
ours so cheap."

" There's other things to cut on besides labor forever and ever. Oh, no, ye can't buy poor cotton, it
would show in the cloth, ye can't save on machinery,
it would spoil yer sales, but if we carders and weavers
and spinners be cut, it don't leave a mark on the
cloth. But it leaves deep gashes in our hearts and
joys, you be sure." Graves looked at the young
man to see if he might go on, but he could not read
his face. He hesitated a moment and then he continued,

" There aint a poor bent girl in the mill but
might live a life so happy it would make a strong
man cry to think of it. We are of more account than
your machinery. No beltin' or patent self-acting
springs could do our work ; it takes immortal souls,
and intellects in the image of God to do it. It's the
same sort of work you do, and compare what the two
of us gets. We aint paid till we gets, the weakest

of us, a taste of the sweet things in this world we
have longed for so long. I don't care what yer wise
book-men says." Was the young proprietor angry,
he stood so grave and still? What a change! Time
was when pity would have shone on every line of
his face. But he might have been a statue for all
appearance of melting in him now.

"I pay you the market price, as much as the
other mills."

Well, God have mercy on his poor children, if
Philip Breton could make that excuse! The man
sat down without an invitation, and leaned his
brawny elbows on the table.

"Now see here, you told me to speak my mind,
and I am a goin' to. We are poor; we aint got
nothin'; we can't lay back and wait for our price;
we want somethin' to eat to-day; we come to you
for work; we must have work, if it only earns us a
loaf of bread. Is it right, then, to value us at what
we can be got for? If we could haggle with ye, and
hang off the way a little ready cash lets a man do,
there might be some sense in it. But you never let
us get enough ahead for that; it's work or go hungry with us. The poorer we gets, the tighter ye
can squeeze us, and I sometimes wonder why ye
gives us as much as ye do; I s'pose a man might live
on a little less. And it's all business, as ye say."

Philip had seated himself, but he said nothing.

He had given the man the privilege of his tongue, and he did not seem disposed to stop him.

" Is the right price of a thing what a man'll give for it ? If they had it, men would give a million of dollars for a breath of air, when they're stifled. Would it be right to pump off the air, and then let it on at a million dollars a breathing? If you was drowning, you'd give a million to be saved if it was only to hold out a pole to yer. Is that a fair price for holdin' out a pole? We're starvin' unless we can get a bite to eat ; is it any more right to bargain with us for a life of hard work, for just enough to live on ? A man wants somethin' besides to eat ; he wants to send his children to school, to get a loafin' hour now and then, to make himself somethin' besides a brute, he wants—he wants some such things and chances as you have. Why, squire, we're all men together." The man's eyes looked across at Philip with a vague wistfulness, as if he was thinking of the beautiful possibilities of a life so far all drudgery and want.

" But what is there to do?" exclaimed Philip in an impatient tone, that put to flight all the workman's foolish fancies. The young man's heart seemed changed to flint. " You don't want to be objects of charity, do you ?"

John Graves straightened his arms along the table, then he stood up.

14

" Charity ! Well, no, not such charity as picks a creature up to-day as soft as a baby, and drops him to-morrow like a dog. But if payin' yer help enough of yer gains, so they can know what life is— if that is charity, as you call it, give it to us. Ye needn't be so precious, fraid of hurtin' the laboring classes, as they call 'em, by treatin' 'em too well. They're sinkin' every day lower and lower, and lots of fellows in specs, keep a warnin' you not to spoil 'em, not to hurt their pride, or break their spirit by givin' 'em nothin'. As if kindness ever hurt any human soul. Not that I would call it charity ; they earns every mite ye'll ever give 'em."

" But if the mills or employers don't make such gains as you seem to take for granted.—"

" If there aint money made, why, nobody can find no fault not to get big pay. All I mean is, when money is made, and that's pretty often, we ought to have some share in it."

" Don't go, John, I want to ask you—"

" I must, I asked out for to-day," and the door closed after the man. For quite a while after his last visitor had gone, Philip sat with his eyes fixed on the door-knob, in intense abstraction. Was he angry at the audacity of the common laborer ? was he wondering at the independence of speech and demeanor that lives in a race, long after the last semblance of real freedom is gone ? When he pushed

back his chair and rose to his feet, running his hands
through his hair, he made one exclamation :"

" How blind." But whom he meant, whether his
class or the laborers, did not appear from his tone or
from the bitter smile on his lips. That question was
a vital one for the factory village of Bretonville.
John Graves would have told in a moment that the
young proprietor meant no good to his help. The
man had had a glimmer of hope that Philip Breton
might only be waiting for an opportunity, but this
interview had dispelled it from his mind.

It was some little time afterwards that Philip left
his counting-room and made his way up the street.
He was dressed in somberest black, and his silk hat
was subdued with a wide band of crape. But his
dress was no more melancholy than his face. When
under pressure of business, one would not have noticed it so especially, but the instant he was thrown
back upon himself, his face became as sad and hopeless as the face of the most wretched laborer in his
mill. He was tasting the most bitter dregs in life, he
thought, what soul could be more crushed than his?
The time was, when it would have been impossible for
him to see a human creature suffer without a thrill
of sympathy ; it would have seemed a cruel and unnatural stroke of fortune, which it was for him to
prevent or cure. But he had learned better, he
thought. Suffering was common to all, there was no

good of trying to patch up this life or that, the terrible disease was forever at work. Conditions made but little difference, rich and poor, high and low, agonized together over some form of broken hope, some unsatisfied hunger.

The chapel door stood open, and he stopped and looked in. It was here Bertha and he were to have been married. And it would have been before this — but now.—He saw the place where they would have stood together. The church was empty and he walked softly in as if afraid of disturbing the ghosts of his dead hopes, who haunted yet, perhaps, the sacred spot they glorified in all the dreams of his early manhood. He walked wearily up the echoing aisle and threw himself into a seat. He bowed his head upon the back of the pew in front of him. Had he no shame to come to the rescue of his broken heart ; would he grieve forever over a woman that had become another man's wife ? She had called on the laws of the land for her protection ; he had no right to even think of her now. She was shut away from him forever, it was become a sin for him now to long for her, though she had been so nearly his own wife. There was no place in the world for unmated lovers like him. If she had not married that man.—How strange that he had heard nothing of that marriage, her note had not mentioned it and no one had spoken of it since. Why his belief in her purity was so absolute, he had not even thought to question it, and now it was like a guilty thing, that he permitted himself to entertain for a moment terrible fears. If she had never gone with him he might have been happy, but since she had gone with him, Philip would rather suffer as he did for all eternity than that she should not have married the man. What vengeance would be stern and relentless enough for him who had wrecked the noblest womanhood in the world, who had sullied a purity like an angel's, and insulted a sacred dignity like Bertha's? Oh, it could not be, no man on earth could have been so bold, so impious. How wild his imagination had become.

"Oh, I didn't know but it was young Breton and that Bertha Ellingsworth that was going to be married." Two graceless women had come in and seated themselves in a neighboring pew. He had been thinking so intensely till now an earthquake would hardly have disturbed him.

" That'll never be," giggled the other, " You don't say you didn't know she eloped with that Curran fellow? Though it's been kept pretty still."

" Do tell! " Philip shuddered. Why were creatures like these permitted to touch names like Bertha's? " Married another chap, eh, well young Breton never was much for looks anyhow."

" Married! " Philip started at her tone, " Who said she was married? The shoe's on the other foot.

She aint married at all; I know; don't handsome fellows like him has a wife in every town, such as they be, that proud minx is only one on 'em." How they rolled the shameful story, like a sweet morsel under their tongues, as if it relieved the blackness of their contemptible souls, that one woman more had singed her angel wings in the pitiless flame of disgrace.

Philip had struggled to his feet. The women blushed like fire and tried to look unconscious, but he did not even glance at them as he moved down the aisle. He could not see very well; was the chapel full as it seemed? and was that an usher in white kids who was coming toward him and saying,

" Just one minute more; the bridal couple are just coming in ? "

Bolt upright he sat where he had been guided, and saw as in a dream a white phantom of a woman it seemed, and a black shadow of a man go by. " Married ; who said she was married ? ah it was horrible ! Perhaps they two those women fiends, and the one who had told the knowing one of them, were all that knew the shameful secret. Would it do any good to pray them for the mercy of God to keep it, would money hire a woman to keep a disgrace that had fallen on a fair sister's name ? "

" Aren't you going to salute the bride ? " smiled an acquaintance. " This is the marriage of Labor and

Capital at last." He had perpetrated his witticism a dozen times at least, and this was the first who had not laughed. Jane Graves and Silas Ellingsworth, Bertha's father—were they mad, or was he?

"I am ill," he muttered incoherently, as he pushed his way almost roughly out.

CHAPTER XVII.

Tea for an Old Woman.

THE terrible seeds of suspicion sown in Philip Breton's mind bore the bitterest fruits through the dreary winter months. No effort of his will, nor course of reasoning, could comfort him. For a moment he might find relief—but his torment would only return afresh. Humanity are slow to believe good of fellow-creatures, but nothing is too bad to be true. He thought it might have calmed him to have been assured even of the worst; he believed that then he might despise the woman he had elevated to the highest pinnacle of his ideal temple of woman-hood, if she had made so little of the most sacred gift of God. But it would have been a violence to his feelings, he could not endure to inquire of those who must know. Her father knew, but his smiling face revealed nothing and his very reserve was peopled with horrors for Philip. His wife Jane must know too, but he could not bear to think of the malicious pleasure she would take in detailing the shameful story'to him. She would sate her hate in his misery. But if it were not a shameful story—still he could not form his lips to ask, the humiliation of such a question from him, a discarded lover, about her at whose feet he had been proud to sit, shocked him into silence. He even dreaded lest they might speak to him, but it had been months since he had heard Bertha's name once breathed.

It was the morning of a day at the very close of winter that the operatives in the Breton Mills gathered in astonished groups before a number of white posters in the entrances. They were printed in the largest and plainest of type but the people read them as if they were in some foreign language. And the ideas called up seemed common-place enough, but it was only after reading them over and over and an exhaustive interchange of explanations, that the groups broke up with looks of surprised satisfaction on their faces. This was what they read :

"The paymaster or his clerks will be in the south office Monday and Thursday evenings. Any of the help needing coal or groceries can obtain them of him at cost hereafter. Those who cannot pay cash will be advanced goods on account of unpaid wages due them."

But long and cruel experience of the selfish principles, of which they are victims, has created a deep feeling of distrust in the poorer classes. Their bitter complaints against hardships that seemed intolerable have been silenced so long by the catch words of "business," "political economy," "competition," "supply and demand," that they have grown to accept the melancholy view that there is no honesty but policy, no fairness but necessity, no pretence of either but has some business trick for its motive. So as the mill hands scattered to their work they grew suspicious again. The smile of satisfaction that had lit up their faces at first gave place to a smile of cunning, as each for himself devised some possible profit to the wealthy mill-owner in this fair looking scheme of benevolence.

"He don't mean nobody else shall cheat us anyhow," suggested Bill Rogers, incautiously.

"You always was a fool, Bill Rogers," drawled John Graves. "The whole thing's as plain as daylight, and I tell ye the lad's shrewd, too, he beats the old man. He sees a big chance in keeping store for his help; they'll all have to trade with him, you bet."

"But don't the posters say that everything's to go for cost?"

"Yes, for what they'll cost you. I'd rather see his profit and loss account than trust his word." John Graves had on a better coat and hat than had ever fallen to his lot before, but apparently his prosperity had not turned him into an aristocrat. His daughter might have married young Breton himself, he had learned his lessons in too terrible a school to forget them.

"I thought now 'twould be a big savin'. Why I s'pose there aint a store hardly but makes two thousand dollars right straight out of our poor pay. If that was divided back amongst the customers 'twould be quite a help. I see the rest on ye looks kind o' sour, but I don't see for the life of me why 'taint a big thing for us. It aint right to make us support all these store-keepers, they don't make or raise the stuff we eats, they only clips their livin' off of it 'fore we gets what we pays for." Two or three men stopped, as they went by, to see Bill Rogers make a speech, and the girls giggled and looked over their shoulders. Rogers was the picture of awkwardness as he tried to scrape up a little pile of dust with his great boot.

"It's such innocent cusses as you just encourage the upper crust to press down on us. Yer right, the store-keepers will lose their livin' if we all buy of Breton, but he will just be so much the richer. He aint satisfied with grindin' us, he wants all the good things he can get his greedy eyes on."

Friday evening the walls of the south office, as it was called, were lined with merchandise, such as is the first necessity of existence. On the floor were barrels of flour and sugar, and baskets of eggs and potatoes ; brooms and pails, oil and molasses barrels on tap, crockery and lamps and cutlery showed out of glass doors, and chests of tea and coffee and boxes of all conceivable sizes and patterns packed the shelves. The paymaster stood behind his new desk with a distressed look on his face, as if his life had suddenly become a burden to him, and his clerks stood about the room with most disgusted expressions on their countenances and in their very attitude for the new occupation that had been assigned them. Every two or three minutes the mill-owner looked in to see how much trade was doing, and then resumed his nervous walk along the hall. Now he turned into his office and made as if he would sit down, but would go out again and walk instead to the piazza door and look up the street and calculate how many of the patches of particular blackness he could make out in the distance were operatives in his mills hastening to buy at his new store. But strange enough, the trade on this, his opening night, was very light. A great many came in and stared about, and asked prices. But when the impatient clerks wanted to sell them a gallon of this fabulously cheap and yet first brand oil, or a quart of the molasses almost for nothing, or a pound of these delicious crackers for a mere pittance, most of them shied off like a skittish horse. A few made purchases and betrayed astonishment, in spite of themselves, at how much they got for their money, and though the rest looked at them for remarkable curiosities of enterprise, the buyers hugged their bundles as if they were afraid of losing such rare acquisitions, and went out in high glee.

At nine o'clock the paymaster and his clerks came into the proprietor's office, and took the chairs he motioned them to, in significant silence. They apparently had something unpleasant on their minds, and were not judicious enough to see that Philip Breton was fretted and dangerous. They might have seen from the way he closed his lips, and the fact that he forgot his usual smile, that it was a poor time for any.—

"Well gentlemen—" he did not even wait for them to begin. "I suppose you don't like your new employment." There was time for them to smooth matters over even now, but—

"Well, that's what we came in to say," began Jennings, who had seen Philip grow up from a boy, and had no terror of him, any more than a keeper of a young lion which he handled when a whelp. "Our business is book-keeping, and selling a pound of tea to an old woman don't come easy."

"You would like me to give up my plan, would you?" The black eyes of the young proprietor rested curiously on them. His tone was smooth so far.

"I don't think it will amount to anything; you can't sell all your stuff, and some will spoil on your hands."

"That will be a part of the cost just as freight is. I don't expect to save the cost, that would be impossible, but the profit, I believe it is my duty to save my poor help."

"I suppose our extra work will be a part of the cost too—"

"I consider that is paid for already. It would save them something if I had to hire help even," Philip went on slowly, "but you see my special advantage is that my help is salaried already, salaried abundantly."

His meaning dawned on the paymaster and his two clerks, and their faces flushed like sunrise.

"And do you expect us to turn ourselves into petty shop-keepers twice a week, for nothing," exclaimed Jennings, and the two clerks looked indignant remonstrance.

"Call it shop-keepers if you like. I should prefer, if I were you, to consider I was acting as almoner to the poor. It is only when a man makes a gain out of small dealings, that he need be ashamed; kindness in little things, generosity in the smallest things even, is always noble." Philip's eyes danced with sarcastic humor. "I wouldn't humiliate you gentlemen, I appreciate your sensitiveness, I wouldn't think of letting you make a penny out of the old women who want a pound of tea."

"I resign!" cried the paymaster rising, "to take effect immediately."

" I resign ! " echoed the insulted clerks, " to take effect to-night."

Well well, mused Philip, I suppose they will stay around a day or two more. Now I am sure I paid them too much.

"Good evening, Mr. Breton, we just called at your house, we wanted a little—a—friendly talk, you know."

The three grocery-men of Bretonville filed in with melancholy visages distorted in a frantic attempt at a smile, appropriate of course to the friendly talk that was coming.

" We are sure," began the one of them that was a deacon in one of the village churches.

" I have no patience for any long preamble," interrupted Philip, " say right out what you have to say."

" Is this the way you help the poor then," snapped one of the shop-keepers, much as he would reproach a delinquent debtor. Philip looked at them in silence for a moment. " And so I shall take away your means of livelihood, shall I ? " he said at last thoughtfully.

" Yes," urged the deacon plaintively. " No doubt the young man had not calculated so far as to see the consequence of his benevolence to such worthy members of society."

" And if I made a free gift to the poor in the village of all the necessaries of life, it would wrong you too, would it?"

"Well, you put in queer, but I suppose we would have to go to doing something else for a living." The deacon laughed uneasily. Philip rose to dismiss them.

"I can't see any sense in your laying a tribute on every mouthful a poor man wants to eat. You don't put in one stroke of work to produce the food. Why should the poor have to contribute of the little they have to support you? If the race of middle-men who stand between the people and what the world has for them, were blotted out poverty would turn into comparative comfort."

"But how can you dispense with us?"

"I think the experiment is worth trying, at least."

CHAPTER XVIII.

The New Stock Company.

THE dry goods dealers and the butchers had no kind of sympathy for the villainous grocerymen. Their extortions were positively outrageous, and it was good enough for them that the customers forsook their stores. It did these virtuous merchants great good to see the change in the condition of the poor, their relief from imposition produced ; they could buy so much better clothes, and need haggle so little over the difference of a few pennies more or less in price. And it was remarkable how much more meat they could buy ; why it quite shocked the generous hearted butchers, to find how many families there had been even in this prosperous village who ate meat but once or twice a week. How pleasant and profitable it was to be able to satisfy their wants, and to see their own trade well nigh doubling in a month because there was so much saved on groceries. But imagine the disgust of the dry goods merchants and butchers, when word was brought to their blighted homes that branches had been opened in the mill stores to cover the varieties of business

15

on which they had fattened for so many years. What expletives of scorn and contempt were terrible enough to express their disapproval of the quondam butcher boy, Philip Breton had installed over his ridiculous meat market, where tender juicy steaks and ribs were sold so cheap almost the poorest creature in Bretonville could hope for them. And then the ex-dry-goods clerk who worked making cloth in the day time, and now sold it two evenings in a week under the new paymaster's supervision was a subject for endless mirth, only that the selling prices were as low as the village merchants could buy at. A general hegira became necessary of the village shopkeepers. Eight men with their indignant wives and shrewd eyed children, shook the dust of the ungrateful village from their feet, and journeyed westward where there yet remained towns and cities perhaps that had not learned to get along without their sort.

The results of Philip Breton's plan were very remarkable in the little world that revolved about him. Instead of raising the wages, he had devised a way to make the same wages go a great deal farther. It amounted to raising the wages of his help twenty per cent., and all it cost him was the interest on the small capital locked up in stock. It amounted to dividing up among the poor of Bretonville all the money which went for the rent of eight stores, with the price of the time of as many clerks, and the support in comparative wealth, of eight proprietors. Philip did not have to watch his experiments in fear and trembling, lest nobody should buy ; the mill-stores were fairly swarming with delighted purchasers the nights when opened, and the fame of them traveled hundreds of miles. The example was followed by other mill-owners in the neighborhood, but with the disinterested principle left out. Other proprietors had two methods of reaping a profit out of store-keeping. One set of them took advantage of the cheaper cost of living, to cut down the wages of their help, on the generally accepted axiom, that wages should be at the lowest point which can sustain life. The other set charged a profit on the goods sold, and managed to get back again nearly a quarter part of the wages of their help before a month could pass. But the Breton system varied not to the right hand nor the left a hair's breadth, and the crushing weight of poverty was lifted a little from a thousand human creatures who, for the first time, saw the power of great wealth exerted in their favor.

The people seemed grateful at first, but the proverbial ingratitude of their class asserted itself at last. It had cost the proprietor but little, and after all was a mere ingenious arrangement to make the poor wages he gave them quiet their loud complaints. It was only a makeshift, it was no reform. The mill-owner had no confidants, but from all signs, he had tried his only innovation. He seemed to grow closer every day, more watchful over losses, more stringent on expenses.

One evening he called a meeting of his help, and the old market-hall was packed from door to platform. Reporters were planted by their tables, to catch every word of the mysterious proceedings. Representatives from all the factories in the country elbowed the crowd for their three feet of standing room, eager to learn some new device for making money out of their help as good as the other. But the great audience was strangely silent; they knew not what to expect. Perhaps the economical mill-owner was going to announce a new reduction in their wages, everybody said he was reducing everywhere. Perhaps he had some new plan to help them. But the feeling in their hearts was more of fear than hope, and it was a look of piteous terror, almost, that they cast at the slight form in black, that came forward on the platform. They reminded Philip of a flock of frightened sheep that had never had a shepherd. Then he thought of a great army massed before the smoking cannonmouth, an army that had never had a general. He saw they feared him.

"This village is happier than it was a few months ago. I have tried to fulfill a little of my

promise to you." A murmur of applause swept
through the crowd like a summer breeze through a
grove of pines, and then it was still again. " But all
I have done so far, is to keep others from wronging
you. I have been for a long time trying to think of
some way to make your lives more fair for you, and
yet be fair to myself and my class. I have been cutting
on expenses to make the whole business machinery as
economical as I knew; at last I am ready to take you
into my confidence and make you a proposal."

There was a stir in the great audience, as if every
man changed his position at the same moment, so
as to be sure not to lose one precious word of the
new gospel.

" I cannot feel that I ought to give you anything. And I cannot see that it would be reasonable to pay more wages than others pay, that is,
than you have now."

A hush had fallen upon the people like death.
There was no hope for them then. Still the speaker
went on.

" But if your labor is profitable to me, so that I
can pay you your price, and pay my other expenses,
and pay me for the time I give to the business what
such service as I do is paid elsewhere, and then have
something besides—"

The reporters dropped their pens in astonishment;
was the man mad?

"I am disposed to think that you have earned a share in it." He paused to catch his breath, and one could have heard a pin fall in that crowded room. "My capital should be allowed for too. In a word I propose to divide the profits of my mill, after all expenses are paid, into two equal parts hereafter, one for labor, yours and mine, and one for the interest on my money. The part which belongs to labor will be distributed according to the worth of each one's year's work. The one that earns the largest year's pay will have the largest per cent of that dividend. We shall all be stockholders together, each with a share large or small according to the value of his work."

The building trembled with the roar of applause that went up, and it was several moments before Philip could make himself heard again. He had thought there was nothing left in his life, with love gone out of it, but as he stood that moment with the glad shouts of the poor ringing in his ears, and felt he had led them out of bondage, his heart thrilled with a proud joy that was almost ecstasy. Right or wrong his wealth had brought him a happiness that made even a life like his worth living; had conferred on him a glorious sense of the dignity of manhood which lifted him as on wings.

But they must listen while he explained the terms of his plan more fully. He motioned to a dozen boys and took a printed sheet of paper from the pile of similar sheets which he ordered distributed among the workmen. He then read aloud the following from the paper in his hand.

The first dividend will be distributed August 1st for the year ending July 1st. The surplus is $200,000. $100,000 is set apart as the allowance for capital invested, which leaves $100,000, to be distributed to the labor in proportion to the wages or salary earned by each. The whole amount of wages and salaries earned in the mills was about $360,000. Therefore the rate per cent of dividend is about $27\frac{7}{10}$ to be calculated on the wages or salary of each man, woman and child as shown by the paymaster's book for the past year. For example, the man whom the pay-roll shows to have earned $300 for his year's work, will receive $27\frac{7}{10}$ per cent on $300 in addition, or about $83.10 as his dividend. The paymaster, who received a salary of $2,000, will receive about $554, and as manager worth a salary of $5,000, I shall receive more than twice the dividend of the paymaster. Certain restrictions will be imposed. 1st. Only one-half of the annual dividend will be in cash, for it would hurt the interests of the mill to withdraw so much from the business. The other half will be in stock, which will draw dividends as the rest of the capital. 2d. Stock cannot be transferred only to operatives, but will be redeemed at the counting-

room, after notice, when holders leave the mills, as
stock will yield dividends only while holders work in
the mills.   Holders of stock may hold meetings and
choose a committee to examine the books of the company, before the annual distribution of dividends."

When Philip Breton sat down a noisy hum of
voices followed, as the people read and commented
upon the prospectus.   The figures looked anything
but dull to them, the bright possibilities that came
up before their imaginations as they read, were such
as no gentle cadence of poetry could have given
them.   Apparently they would never have tired of
reading the wonderful words of hope and good cheer
over and over, only that the outer door swung open,
and a tall man's form entered.   Philip Breton from
the platform saw it, and the pride sickened on his
heart.   The crowd about the door passed the whisper
around, and it was hardly one short minute when the
building shook again with cheers, as they shouted
the name of —" Curran."

Yes, it was he who pushed his way well into
the room and then stopped and took one of the
printed sheets as if he were unconscious of their
cheering and read till his face that had looked so
stern and terrible softened like a child.   Then he
mounted a settee for his platform and uncovered
his head with a new grace that became him as
well as his strength.   The old bitterness had gone

from his lips, it had given place to a touching sadness that sobered every face that was turned toward him.

"He means to deal well by you, he wants to make you shareholders in your work." Philip had risen excitedly to his feet. The sight of the man who had been with Bertha, who came perhaps but this instant from the woman he had wronged so terribly, was at first almost maddening to him. Ah, how grand and beautiful he was. with his deep mighty chest and shoulders, and his limbs like pillars of some temple. There were no laws for such men as he; the holiest and purest of women love to make themselves base and common things to win smiles from his proud eyes, and men forget their vengeance, and only remember how small and mean they seem before him. But who could look at his melancholy face and the calm dignity that rested upon him always, and believe he could be vile? Only perhaps nothing was vile or low to him, and even sin was glorified in his eyes when it suited his caprice to sin.

Philip had come to the very edge of the platform and beckoned a friend to him. "Do you see the man talking, the man with the auburn hair curling about his neck, no don't look yet," his voice was husky with excitement. "Get behind him while he is talking and stop him before he goes out. I must see him and speak with him; I would rather ten thou-

sand dollars than lose him. Quick now." As Philip
sat down again and watched his friend trying to
make his way through the close packed crowd he
heard Curran's voice again. What was there changed
in it? It had lost its old ring, there was a queer
drag in it sometimes, and when he used to raise his
voice till every nerve tingled for sympathy he seemed
now to let it fall and his long sonorous sentences
died down at the end like a muffled bell.

"If others were like him," he was saying, "the
reform I would die for would come soon, would be
upon us. It is so much easier for the rich and the
mighty to give us our own, than for us to wait till
the slow pulse of the millions of the oppressed
beats quick with resolution so that we will take
them."

How slow his friend moved. Philip actually hated
the people who were too stupid to get out of his
messenger's way.

Had Curran finished, was this all that was left of
his eloquence? Yes, he was stepping down and
moving toward the door. His friend was almost there,
the man must not escape thus, and plunge again with
the woman whose life he had blasted into the ob-
scurity he seemed to love. Philip leaped to his feet
and almost shouted to the people. All turned their
faces expectantly toward him, Curran with the rest
his pale worn face. Philip's friend was come almost

to him now. If Curran could only be detained for
one moment more.

" It will of course be for the interest of all of you,"
he knew he was talking weakly, but it was no matter,
"to earn the most wages you can, to lose the fewest
days, to turn off the most piece work." Of course,
he spoke too stupidly, Curran turned on his heel and
moved toward the door. Almost instantly then,
Philip Breton gave a sudden short bow to the audience and disappeared back of the platform. He
bounded down the narrow stairs, four at a time, and
rushed around to the front of the building like one
mad to stare for a moment in the faces of the escaping crowd. Then, wilder than ever at the thought
that Curran might have gone out among the first, he
ran back and forth after one group and another, but
all in vain. Then he forced himself to stop and think,
and forthwith made inquiries for Curran's boarding
place. He reached the place at last and ran breathlessly up the stairs. In another moment he would
know the truth if it killed him to bear it. He must
remove the poisonous shadow of suspicion that was
polluting all the holiest precincts of his nature.
Certainty was better far, for the nerves can brace
themselves against the clearly defined features of
ever so hideous a monster; far better certainly than
this crawling slimy terror that made him ashamed of
a manhood that could cherish it. He dared ask

Curran for the truth, he did not shrink from it. If the man were innocent he might strike him down for the insult to the purity of his wife. Philip thought such atonement would seem just and proper. But if he were guilty, ah, if Bertha was guilty through him what death was terrible enough for his penalty!

A portly woman, with the unmistakable expression of the expectant boarding mistress on her face and in her attitude, met the pale-faced young man at the top of the stairs. She did not recognize the proprietor of the Breton Mills, in his slight form; she would have looked for a man of lofty stature and commanding mien, and not a mere lad whom nobody would glance twice at on the street.

"Where is Curran? I—I want him."

"Why, he's just gone, he drove off to Lewiston."

"To Lewiston? are you sure?" Why this must be some important personage after all, he was so peremptory. Poor people can bully, but there is a shame-facedness or an over-affectation of authority that betrays them, their self-consciousness lets the whole secret out.

"Either Lewiston or Raleigh, I can't tell, really, sir, shall I get you a carriage, Mr.—Mr.?"

"Two horses and a buggy, a driver too. Tell them it is for Mr. Breton, and," he shouted after the woman, "if they give me a poor horse, he will be dead before they ever see him again."

It seemed an hour before the horses drew up before the boarding-house door, and another hour before they had left the village behind. Then the little patience Philip had forsook him; he caught the reins from the astonished driver, and at the threatening snap of his whip, the horses broke into a wild gallop. But he did not attempt to restrain their plunges; if they fancied they were running away, all the better; if he was hurled down this or that high bank, the fate was better than to live in such agonizing suspense. But the hostler had no inclination for a violent death; he dared not touch the reins, for fear an incautious pull might send them to instant destruction, but all that words could do, he attempted. All respect of persons forsook him, and he heaped all the curses and profane abuse in his vocabulary on this mad driver who made so little of common prudence. But as Philip did not even seem to hear him, but only urged the panting horses the faster, the hostler finally relapsed into silence, and only held on to his seat with both hands, while great drops of perspiration started out on his forehead.

It was a little past nine o'clock the next morning, that Philip Breton, pale from a sleepless night, knocked at a low studded door in an ill-ventilated tenement house, where they told him Curran lived. Within was Bertha, the high-bred woman, wonted to the costliest luxuries of wealth. And she was willing, then, to live in such squalor as this to be with the man she loved. Could change have been cruel enough to have touched her? Perhaps an infant hung hungrily on her bosom, and Curran, fallen back into his vulgar traditions, lounged in red flannel shirt sleeves in her presence. Could he bear the sight? But she might be alone; his heart beat faster with terror and hope. She would lift her sweet eyes pleasantly to him—so easy it is for women to forget the agony they have caused. She would hold out her shapely hand to him, but it would be stained and worn from hardships. Should he fall at her feet? Would he be able to remember she was another's—dead to him?

He knocked again, possibly no one was at home.

"Come in." It was a man's voice.

As Philip opened the door he saw the man he sought, by the window. He was eagerly looking up and down the street, as if waiting for some sign. There was no guilty fear or shame in the calm face that was turned to his visitor.

"Breton." He gave him his hand with hearty good-will. "Somehow I could not speak last night, but you have begun a noble work. Why, I had rather feel the proud satisfaction you must have, I would rather be in your place than the greatest man in the whole world."

Philip was afraid to look about him ; perhaps Bertha had no wish to speak to him, or else she was not here ; there was no atmosphere of a woman's love and care in the place, somehow. But Curran went on in his quick, eager way, " The rich men have the most glorious privilege ever men had ; the world is ripe for such work as you have done. Each man of wealth can let the fountains of light and joy into the lives of a village in some way which shall make his name blessed forever. Instead of that, whole generations of us have to break ourselves in pieces in the effort to wear away their rock. We fail, as the wretched two thousand creatures who strike here to-day, will fail, to gain one privilege more for ourselves, but our children may profit from our sacrifices, perhaps, or their children. Anything is better than spiritless, eternal submission."

Philip released his hand from the man's clasp and turned to look about him. No woman's shawl hung on the rack. No baby's shoes or toys. A man's rude hands had set the chairs in an awkward row. A man's hands made the comfortless looking bed that stood in one corner. There was no soft scent of perfume, such as Bertha would have left behind her if she had but lately gone. Why, Bertha could never have breathed for a moment there. Love can do much, but it cannot make a woman over.

" Where is your wife?" he said, in a low, breathless voice. " Bertha."

The eager look faded from Curran's face, and his
blue eyes grew troubled. For an instant he did not
answer, but stood with folded arms gazing out into
the street.

"What is a wife?" he said at last, "A woman
who loves a man and lives in his love, who pines in
his absence and listens to the coming of his footsteps, as the sweetest music in the world to her; to
whom all the gifts of life would be nothing without
him; to whom poverty and disgrace would lose
their hatefulness if he shared them. A wife is a
sweetheart, a hundred times tenderer and happier." His voice grew bitter and hard for a moment as he added, " No, I have no wife, Bertha has
left me."

He heard a shout, and a score of hurrying forms
rushed by his window. He turned from the window
in a sudden passion of excitement.

" The strike has begun. What pity do the rich
deserve? Even their women are taught only to
break honest men's hearts. They are beautiful as
the angels of heaven and cruel and pitiless as the
angels of hell."

"But wait," cried Philip, catching him by the
arm. Curran had not yet spoken the words he
wanted to protect her name from the insult of

another suspicious thought. But a shout rolled up from the street, and another and another in quick succession. Curran shook him off and, catching his hat from the table, sprang down the stairs.

CHAPTER XIX.

Why Couldn't She Wait?

IT was the same room, and yet it was not. The walls were papered as they used to be and there was the same round baize-covered table. The table however, was not now in the centre of the room which it was designed for, but stood awkwardly in a corner. The great morocco-bound volume called, " The Dresden Gallery" was not on the table. Mrs. Ellingsworth had no taste for that class of art. But there was the same bookrack, only now it was packed with bloated looking novels, cheap in binding and in paper. Not but that Mrs. Ellingsworth had abundance of money at her command, but it unfortunately happened that such books as she cared for were of a class which few people bought if they could afford better. Higher up in the corner hung that inexcusable invention, a triangular bracket, whose three shelves were littered with the ugly rubbish called bric-a-brac.

Naturally enough the portrait of the first Mrs. Ellingsworth had disappeared from the wall, but it certainly was a little cruel to replace it by a vulga

print, entitled in glaring letters, "Kathrina, or My
Meditation of Thee shall be Sweet." Of course a
man must submit to let his wife furnish her own
parlor according to her taste or lack of taste, and so
it was that Mr. Ellingsworth saw his delightfully
comfortable and aristocratic old chairs and sofas
packed into the attic. The new upholstery was exquisite in material, and brilliant in tint, but unfortunately was out of harmony with the wall paper or
the carpet. The new mistress might change the
arrangement of her new furniture as often as she
pleased, it seemed continually out of place. It
seemed incapable of taking on a domestic tone, as
much as if its price tags had never been removed.

The new maid who showed Philip Breton into
Mrs. Ellingsworth's parlor was not nearly as pretty
as her predecessor in office, but he was too much
absorbed with his delicate errand to take any notice
of her. Bertha was alone somewhere, deserted, un-
protected, something must be done for her. It was
a strange place to seek pity for her, in the woman's
bosom which he had seen heaving in hate of her,
but a magnanimous heart is wont to count on the
generosity of others. Philip could not imagine a
creature so hard and cruel, but that he could move
her by explaining how poverty and desolation might
that moment be the portion of the loveliest woman
in the world. For the three days following his

interview with Curran, waking and sleeping, he had seen an endless panorama of all the woes and sufferings imagination could picture, and in every scene the pale tired face of Bertha, friendless and alone, with her great blue eyes almost speaking in their hunted appealing look. He might tell himself she was nothing to him, that she had deserved all she could ever suffer, it did not satisfy him. If such a woman as she did not deserve happiness, still he would have her have it. It seemed the depth of unmanliness for him to let her suffer for her fault. But what was it to him, had she not a father? It was more than uncalled for, for him to espouse her cause as if she needed a knight; it was ridiculous for him to volunteer to be her knight. And still he could think of nothing but her, he could do no business, he could complete no plans, till at last in desperation he had come to her father's house. The maid had said Mr. Ellingsworth was not in, and so he was left to appeal to the womanly tenderness of his wife. At least she would know more than he of what had happened.

He had dreaded to come, for fear of reminiscences that would be called up in Bertha's parlor. He had thought each familiar object here would give him a pang, but now he looked about the room in a sort of daze. However much Mr. Ellingsworth might regret the change, Philip was very thankful for it. He felt that he could not have borne that

the sweet associations of the room where he had
been so happy, poor fool, should all cry shame to
him. It was very fitting, he thought, that the very
place where he had known the holiest of love's illu-
sions, should be transformed.

He rose suddenly from the satin-covered sofa,
and looked wonderingly at a woman's form in the
doorway. Could this be the poor little factory girl,
this fashionably dressed woman, with a train like a
queen? He had stupidly enough expected to find her
in the same old calico dress, perhaps with the dingy,
plaid shawl about her shoulders. Wonted, as he was,
to the usages of good society, he could not disguise
the surprise in his eyes.

But the girl was not so sensitive as to be annoyed.
Had not she kept him waiting while she dressed, on
purpose to enjoy a triumph? And now she was
quite pleased at the plain evidence of it. She
smiled rather consciously as she extended her jew-
elled little hand to him.

"Why haven't you called before?" Her voice
had lost the desperate or sullen tone he remembered in it of old, but he was not sure he liked it
any better. He bowed, like any gentleman, as he
touched her hand, and noticed the great gold bracelets on her slim wrists. Philip was unpleasantly
reminded of manacles, and then the massive chain
around her neck, with a huge locket shaped like a

padlock, had suggestions, too, of a sort, he fancied, the girl would hardly have liked if she had thought of them.   He glanced at her olive cheeks, and the slightly oblique eyes, and the voluptuous fullness of her form.   How could an American village have produced so perfect an odalisque?

"I did not wish to interrupt your honeymoon." He seated himself again.

She was looking oddly at him, as if curious whether he had forgotten her indiscreet visit, when she had told him of her own broken heart.

Philip suddenly met her eyes as she sat oppo-site him.   "The truth is, Mrs. Ellingsworth, I have hardly been in the mood for polite calls of late.   I suppose you understand."

"How should I?" She elevated her dark brows rather unpleasantly as if to dismiss, once for all, any further confidences with him.   Philip smiled, in spite of himself, at her tactics, when she tried to look unconcernedly out of the window.

"Do you know where Bertha is?" he asked, simply.

A sudden flash of color lit up her cheeks.   "I hate the very name of her," she exclaimed, as she rose as if to leave him.   She was not yet wonted to the customs of her new rank.

"Don't go," he urged, "I am so anxious to know where she is.   No doubt you have cause to be

angry with her," Philip did not notice the growing
passion in the girl's eyes, " but you surely would
not have her starve to death, or suffer and die
alone."

"Perhaps not," Jane meant to smile, but she
only produced the effect of showing the cruel white
of her teeth. " Hasn't she got—" the word stuck in
her throat, " him ?"

"Why, didn't you know," cried Philip breathlessly, "she has left him ? She is alone somewhere,
for all we know, in want; think of it, and she too
proud to—"

" Left her—husband ?"

" If he was her husband, I didn't know," he hurried on, as if afraid of the answer that would come,
" I never heard, you know, and I didn't like to ask."

She had seated herself on the pink satin beside
him and caught his hands as she bent toward him to
read his thoughts before he spoke.

" Did you hear they were not married ? " she almost hissed at him.

"Why yes, that is—" he looked away in his shame.
" It was told about the village, but you know better
of course." He tried to laugh, then he grew sober
again. " How vile of them to whisper it, and it was
vile of me to let even the taint of a fear into my
mind."

But she did not answer him yes or no. Her eyes

had grown preternaturally large, and there was a happiness in them as if she looked right into the gates of heaven. All the common expressions were gone from her face. One could read there now nothing but purity and sweetness such as make up the substance of dreams of love.

"And he is alone, oh, where is he, I must know, I must go to him. It cannot be true." The angelic look flitted, the exquisite drooping at the corners of her mouth was gone.

"If you have dared to lie to me." Philip was perfectly astonished at the sudden change in her face and voice. Her black eyes blazed ungovernable passion into his, the quick transition from the height of blissful hope to the depths of despair, seemed to bear her over the line of her humanity. "Tell me, have you lied to make a show of me?"

She trembled for an instant, like a wild creature before a spring, then she clutched with her hot supple fingers at his throat, magnificent as a tigress and in every motion a perfect terrible grace. Philip threw her from him as he would some untamed animal; it was hard to remember her womanhood then.

She sat where he had left her, as if just awoke from a terrible night-mare, her fingers parted and curved and moving spasmodically as if she yet held him by the throat. Then she buried her face in the cushion in a flood of tears.

" I didn't know what I was doing," she sobbed.
" Don't remember it, I was mad." She rose trem-
blingly to her feet and came forward covering her
face with her hands. She might have been an abused
child, so gentle and sweet she seemed. She took
down her hands from her face; what man could be so
cold and hard as to stand against such eyes as hers
looking through their tears ?

But she was alone.

CHAPTER XX.

A Radical.

"OH, my God, my God, why couldn't I have waited!"

She tore the gold chain from her neck and cast it on the floor. Her husband had given it to her, and she hated him at this moment and the proud name he had put upon her. She had rather one smile of that other than all these empty golden favors.

"I am sick of their soft ways and their lying tongues," she moaned, "Why didn't I wait." Jane Ellingsworth began to walk rapidly about the room, wrenching the great gold bands about her wrists, unconscious that she chafed and bruised the skin.

"I might have known God would not deny him to me, I wanted him so much. Oh, my love, my darling, I would have fought for you, I would have starved for you. It would have been sweet with you—and I could not wait one year. I might have known it would come, but I could not wait." She drove her nails into her flesh as she clasped them in her anguish. She panted for breath, her rich silk dress seemed to suffocate her, and the perfumed air was too heavy and dead, it seemed to strangle her.

"He is free, he would have opened his arms to me. He may be coming now to ask me to go with him. He could never have loved that cold, bloodless creature. Ah, how I could have loved him. I would have taught him that a woman can love."

She unclasped her hands and let them fall gently to her side, and her convulsed face took on a new soft tenderness. "I would go with you," she murmured. "A hungry heart cannot feed on such things as these. Oh, but he would not have me, a low creature who has sold herself, he would not have me. He would despise me, he would not even look at me, as if a woman can be as strong as a man."

She fell back in one of the satin covered chairs she had bought with her husband's money, and cried and sobbed till the salt fountains dried up. It was then, while she sat silent and tearless, looking at her bruised wrists and at the wounds her nails had made, that she heard a familiar delicate tread in the hall. It was as well Mr. Ellingsworth did not catch the expression on her set, weary face as his tall, shapely form appeared in the doorway. He seemed to her fancy that moment the most terrible monster in the world, this elegant figure of a man, whose disposition was the very essence of refinement, and she dropped her eyes to the carpet as he came toward her with his eternal smile.

" All alone, Jennie ? Why you have dropped your chain, here it is on the floor."

" Oh, thank you," but she shuddered in spite of herself as he seated himself near her and warmed her hands fondly between his own soft, white palms.

" My little girl," he began.

Yes, she was his, his and no other's, his every day and hour of her life, for hadn't he bought her, and what better title was there than that by purchase ? She raised her eyes and made them rest on his fine, smooth shaven face. She had never noticed before a certain cold and cruel light in his eyes, as if he could enjoy keenly the torture of a living soul, or that beside the sensual lines of his finely chiseled mouth there was a suggestion of an exquisite brutality on the thin lips. She trembled before him. If he knew.

" I have a favor to ask of you." He looked admiringly at her as he spoke. Mr. Ellingsworth never tired of the rich, oriental type of his wife's beauty ; if Bertha's mother had been like her there need never have been any unpleasant stories in the community on her score. And Jane was lovelier than ever to-day with this peculiar brilliancy in her eyes and the bright red spot on either dark cheek. She didn't know how to furnish her parlor very well but he had never yet been sorry he married her. And she seemed to understand so well how to manage him, never too fond, always a little on her guard, like a judicious artist, who will not let even the most ardent admirers come too near his canvas.

" It is about Bertha," he continued, not seeming to notice her start. " She has left that fellow. I haven't troubled you before, but she has been alone up in Vineboro for a good many months. I think best she should come home now. It will be in better taste—"

Mr. Ellingsworth rose to his feet at a rumbling noise, and stepped to the window. When he came back the color had faded from Jane's cheeks, and her small mouth closed very tight. Her hands were trembling violently, but she had hid them in the folds of her dress, so her husband could not see her intense excitement. Her heart was beating loudly; her old madness seemed coming upon her again, but this man's cold smiling face subdued her.

" When is she coming? "

" I didn't know but that was the carriage; well I suppose she may be here," he glanced at his gold-faced watch, " perhaps in an hour or two."

The girl's lips quivered, she almost broke into a passion of angry words—the hate that seethed in her heart for that woman was almost bubbling forth its bitterness. But the cool assurance on her husband's face, as his keen pitiless eyes seemed to search out all the secrets of her soul, cowed the woman. She rose and moved as one in a dream, toward the door.

"I must get things ready then." And so this was what her gentle-voiced husband called asking a favor of her. She did not love him, but she feared him, now, as she remembered her secret. She would obey his nod as if she were his dog, she would study the signs on his placid face. He had never had anything but smiles and kind speeches for her, but she would have sunk into the very earth at his feet, rather than that he should open his mysterious armory of instruments of deadly torture for the soul.

"Well, well, I thought she would make more fuss."

The afternoon sun was well down on his last stretch when Philip Breton came back from his factory, and up the street towards Mr. Ellingsworth's house. There was some one with him, a man so tall and slight that the weight of his head, which was quite large, seemed to bow him. It was an old gentleman to judge from the wrinkles on his face, he had hardly enough hair to show whether it was grey or only flaxen.

"You have done splendidly, my boy!" It was an old acquaintance of Philip's he had used to talk philosophy with at college, one of those benevolent-minded gentlemen who are so optimistic that they have to go to boys for sympathy. "Splendidly," he repeated, "only why stop just where you are? If every mill-owner would do in his mill what you have done, it would be a grand thing for this world. But they won't. Now you have started beautifully, but there is too much business to your plan."

Philip smiled argumentatively. It was like his boyhood returned to hear the old man's mellow tones.

"But, Mr. Philbrick, an honest business man can do more good than a dozen impracticable philanthropists like you."

"But think of the things that business principles never can regard. Your help work ten weary hours a day, all their poor lives; business demands that, doesn't it? Well, I say that is where benevolence must come in. It is terrible to be shut up as they are; it kills body, mind, and soul; business principles never can save them," said the old gentleman, turning his kindly eyes on the young mill-owner, " philanthropy, I don't care what you call it, some gentle spirit of love ought to lift the burden that crushes the life and hope out of them, contrary to business principles, higher than business principles."

As Mr. Philbrick finished, a close carriage rolled by them and stopped a little beyond, where a gentleman and lady stood to welcome the visitor.

"Your reforms," answered Philip, after a moment's thought, "should be founded on business principles. Then the force of the business instinct will carry them out. Otherwise—" he lifted his hat to Mrs. Ellingsworth, but she did not seem to notice him; her eyes were fixed on her husband, who was in the act of handing a lady out of the carriage. The lady wore a traveling suit of a blue shade. Her face was hid as she stepped down, showing the white feather in the back of her hat, and a few strands of golden hair below. Then she raised her face as the carriage rolled away, and a wild, sweet thrill of pain shot through Philip's heart, while every nerve in his body tingled, like finely tuned stringed instruments, trembling in sympathy with a resounding chord. His feet refused to take him away, while his hungry eyes devoured Bertha's beauty, for it was no other than she come back—his lost darling found again. His heart warmed, as he looked, into a divine glow; how cold it had been, and so long; a great burden of weariness seemed lifted from him; it was as if, after a dreary old age, the sweet peace of childhood was born in him again.

For the moment he forgot everything that had come between them, as in the bright, perfumed morning, a child forgets the dreary night just past. But the long night had changed her; the exquisite roundness of her face and form had gone; even her grand blue eyes seemed faded like her cheeks, once so rich in their sunset glow. And he only yearned over her the more tenderly—the new element of pity seemed only wanting before to glorify his love into a religion. He longed to rush to her, putting away her father, who had no caresses for her, and his wife, who was darting flashes of hate at the unwelcome guest. He would enfold her in his arms. She would be glad for them at last ; such love as his made the closest kin in the world. He took a step toward her, but no one saw him.

The eyes of the two women met. Their wills met and struggled for the mastery in that moment. Undisguised hate was in one face, lofty contempt in the other. There had been one gentle, wistful expression in Bertha's face as she first alighted, but there was no trace of it now. She had drawn herself up to her full height, so that the other woman seemed like a child before her, and her hand, as it fell to her side, opened outward in a gesture of disdain for the creature her father had chosen for his wife. It was hardly a second before her rare lips parted ; they at least had not changed. Jane winced for fear of some bitter taunt. She had learned how terrible a blow well-trained tongues can give, but the words were only some polite commonplace, the tone—well, it caused Mr. Ellingsworth to glance critically at his wife. She seemed vulgar in his eyes

17

for the first time. Jane tried to brazen it out, but her face only took on an expression of pugnacious insignificance.

"What was it you were saying?" resumed Mr. Philbrick as Philip overtook him.

"I had forgotten."

"Speaking of business?" suggested the other, and then continued himself, not displeased at an extra turn. "Business I say is heartless and cruel as death. It is pitiless, and pity is the noblest of emotions, it is ungenerous, it is unfair, we have had enough of it when it grinds so terribly."

Mr. Philbrick thought his tirade would surely fetch an enthusiastic retort; but Philip only walked on by his side in silence, he seemed intent on some beautiful masses of clouds just behind the sun as he sped his way to the west.

"Can't afford it, can't afford it," went on the old gentleman, gesticulating with his forefinger, " that is what you would say, I presume ; of course you can't if the upper classes waste the wealth they do. I tell you there is no sense nor excuse for a man spending ten and twenty and fifty thousand dollars a year ; why it is a good workman in your mill who earns ten thousand dollars in a life-time, adding all his days' wages together. There ought to be more fairness about these things. Such men as you, Philip Breton, get too much,—more than any reasonable creature could want, now you ought to go right to work and distribute your surplus, I mean your real surplus, back where it came from, among the poor. It don't take but very little money to buy what can make a life comfortable and complete. The rich are always complaining that they don't enjoy life more than the middle classes ; but they manage to waste what would make a thousand wretched homes happy without one pang of conscience."

" But what do you want me to do ? " asked Philip in astonishment.

The old gentleman's face was flushed with enthusiasm.

" Why I want you to take hold, and begin to make things equal, by paying back your surplus in one form or another. Give them better homes to live in, shorten their hours so they can have a little existence besides drudgery, pay them better wages."

Philip looked distressed and doubtful. He had thought the subject over carefully and believed he had done a great deal already for his poor. His philanthropic friend would turn the whole world topsey-turvey.

" Why, you know what the books say,—that giving so much would spoil all the spirit and patience of the working classes."

" Mere arguments devised to soothe the consciences of the rich,"explained Mr. Philbrick with a grand

air. " Though there is such a thing as unwise benevolence, encouraging paupers and beggars : but a man
who works every day of his life isn't a beggar. Your
father made a good investment that brings you in
say a quarter million a year. That is rather above
what you pay your best workman ; but it doesn't hurt
your manliness any, my boy. The poorest-paid hand
in your factory works a great deal harder than you ;
you needn't be afraid of degrading his manhood till
he gets a quarter million."

" But wouldn't they hang off on their oars unless they had to struggle for a livelihood ? "

" My dear Philip, you wouldn't think it necessary
to starve a horse, and hang a bag of oats just before
his nose to make him go. Better feed him the oats,
and a healthy animal likes to go. Do you lie off on
your oars? You could afford it a thousand times better
than they. Give them a chance for hope and ambition
and it will produce the best work ever known. Who
lives here ? "

He stopped in front of a graceful little cottage
through whose open windows one could see into
cheerful well furnished rooms. A row of maple
saplings had been lately set in front, and plenty of
green shrubs and ample vines gave the place a most
charming air.

" John Graves, one of my workmen. His daughter married rich, and it is her husband's money has

worked a remarkable transformation." Philip was very glad to change the subject. "John's wife was sick,—supposed to be a life invalid. See that lady-like woman watering the hanging pot, that is she. Ellingsworth's money made the change. As for Graves himself, he used to be bowed almost like a cripple ; he was as melancholy as an undertaker, and he had reason to be, poor fellow. He used to pull a great slouch hat down over his face to hide as much as he could of himself. Well, you wouldn't know him now, he is as respectable-looking man as one often sees, and they say he works as hard as ever."

"He isn't degraded any, then ? " asked Mr. Philbrick slyly, as they walked on again, " by his good fortune."

Philip frowned. Mr. Philbrick ought to appreciate the difference between the boy and the man a little better.

" I cannot carry out your proposal, it isn't in my line. I am a business man and must work in character. I actually feel as if I had made quite a step, for me."

" A step !" cried his companion, eagerly reaching out to clasp his hand, "A stride, only I want you to go clear to the goal."

" I am too slow for you," smiled Philip, sadly, as he shook his head. " What I have attempted seems enough for one life-work. I don't want to risk it

all by a new experiment.   Here we are at my house,
won't you come in?"

They stood at the gate.   The front door stood
invitingly open, showing the broad oaken staircase,
and still beyond, the table set for the evening meal.

" Not to-night, thank you."   Mr. Philbrick shook
his hand for parting but did not seem quite ready
to go.

" Tea is all ready," urged Philip, " and I am quite
alone."

" Oh no, my train leaves," he made an excuse to
look at his watch, " in half an hour."   Still he hesitated.

At last he laid his hand gently on Philip's arm.

" You are young and have probably a long life
of usefulness before you.   But a man can never
tell."   Philip looked in surprise at him.   " You may
change your mind, or give up your work; if you
should want to, just let me know, I would like to
buy you out and run things on my plan."

" But you are not rich enough.   You probably
know the valuation of the Breton Mills," answered
Philip, a little proudly.

" I could pay you something, and you wouldn't
drive too hard a bargain.   You would be glad, perhaps, to contribute in that way."

Philip burst into a hearty laugh ; his honest old
friend was losing his wits.   Give up his factory and

his own scheme, that was his only hope in life! But
Mr. Philbrick did not smile. He seemed actually
serious and awaiting an answer.

"Well, I will give you the first chance when I
want to sell."

The old gentleman's earnestness sobered Philip
in spite of himself. He was sorry he had laughed.
Perhaps he had been mocking his own destiny. The
philanthropist's proposal began to affect him as a
death's head at a feast. He was afraid he could not
forget it. Did his friend know him better than he
knew himself? Did he see elements of weakness in
his character that would be sure to wreck his beautiful hopes?

Philip walked slowly up to his door; once he
turned and looked after the bent but still vigorous
figure of the bad prophet. No doubt he was already
planning how to revolutionize the whole management of the mill.

"I will never speak with him again," he muttered.

Then he looked back at his house again. It was
in that very doorway, open as it was now, that
Bertha had stood and kissed her hand to him the
last time she had been at his home. That was
when his chief thoughts of life were as a wedding
journey—that was before the first cloud had dimmed
his sunlight. And now she had returned. She had

shamed her father's house and her mother's pure
memory. She had shamed him who had been her
lover since childhood, and all for a man she did not
love enough to stay with him. Still he could not
help that first tumultuous throb of his heart, the
unreasoning wave of joy that had swept over him at
the very sight of her changed, tired face. She had
done her worst to spoil his life, to drive peace and
happiness from his soul, but that pure, steady glow
in his heart, ah, it was love yet.

Philip's heart was very full of bitterness, the fruit
of his love instead of peace. He stopped midway
to his door, and plucked a rose, slowly tore out its
blushing petals and let the summer breeze carry them
away.

The great work for the poor he had commenced
would have made him the happiest man in the world,
if she could have shared his enthusiasm with him.
His was the disposition even and sweet, just the one
to get the most contentment out of his life, but loneliness was terrible to him.

"Perhaps it is better so," he said aloud, as he
crushed the fragment of the flower in his hand. No
doubt he was light and weak, and it was only under
the pressure of a great burden, that he could accomplish anything. That gave him intensity. And
then Bertha might have weakened his purpose if he
formed one, not sympathizing with him, and it had

not been her wont to sympathize with him. His very devotion to her might have made him waver, or for very happiness he might not have thought of anything but his·bride. If a man has a great work to do it is better to be alone. Two souls never can have but a single thought, and the least friction might delay his progress; the least discouragement might hinder his footsteps on the mountain, bringing glad tidings to the wretched.

All that peril had been saved him. Curran had proved a better friend to the people than he thought, even when he deserted them, in breaking in upon Philip Breton's idle dream of love.

Perhaps it was from Bertha's shame had sprung all the good that blessed a thousand hopeless lives.

Philip shuddered as he went up the broad stone steps to his silent house. It seemed infamous to associate the thought of shame with the woman whose beautiful high-bred face he had looked into again to-day. And Bertha was in the very village with him; the great outside world had given her back safe. He need not tremble for her any more, for her father's arm protected her.

He looked across the fields where he could see one gable of the house that held her, almost hidden by overshadowing trees. Perhaps she was in her room, this moment weeping bitter tears for the sweet rare life she had lost by her madness.

He passed his hand over his eyes.

"Must she suffer forever—for what she has repented of, and the streams of despair flow always
through her heart, washed whiter than snow?"

He walked into his home, and through the echoing hall and stood in the door of his dining-room.
There were sideboards and chairs enough to provide
for a party—the table glittered with its massive
plate, and glistened with exquisite china, but only
one seat was placed.

A piteous look of loneliness was in his face, but he
only muttered through his closed lips,

"Nothing can ever be blotted out.   She cannot
be forgiven."

CHAPTER XXI.

Very Odd.

"A MAN of wealth like Philip Breton owes especial duties to the community. He may very easily be guilty of criminal remissness, for the tranquillity of the masses depends very much on the firmness of the higher classes. It is not for him to say, I may do what I will with my own. The great danger of the world to-day is from the discontent of the poor; the people are impregnated with new fatal principles, which threaten the bulwarks of centuries. Now it seems to us Mr. Breton's new scheme encourages the spirit of uneasiness among the working classes; he may think he gives them enough; their wants and complaints will always keep just ahead of the favors granted them. They will grow bolder at signs of weakness, and he will soon find that they have passed beyond his power of restraint."

Philip laid down the morning's paper on his office table. What a stir his innovation had caused; how many vested rights he seemed to be outraging, how many terrible dangers he tempted. Could it be, one single act of justice put everything awry, and that his neighbor had a right to require him to sin for the comfort of his class?

His paymaster put his head inside the door ; he looked anything but self-possessed.   The mill-owner started nervously—was the crash at hand?

"Some gentlemen to see you, sir—"

"Show them in, of course."

Were they going to take him by storm. Three of the wealthiest manufacturers in the state walked in and shook his hand, then came three agents of large corporations, and lastly, Giddings, the attorney. They talked of the tariff and the president's policy, and the money market.   At last the attorney cleared his throat, and an impressive silence followed.   One gentleman took up the newspaper and became suddenly very much absorbed in its contents; another opened his penknife, and began to pare his finger-nails very carefully.   But how Giddings had changed; not alone in his dress which had become threadbare and untidy, but in his face which had grown abnormally red, at least in spots, as if he had become dissipated and bankrupt at the same time.   Well, he would make a very respectable fee out of this day's work to mitigate his bankruptcy perhaps, but to intensify his dissipation.

"But we had a more especial errand here to-day," began the attorney with a propitiatory smile. "The truth is, Mr. Breton, your benevolence is playing the deuce with all these gentlemen. Their help have grown uneasy and fault-finding, and we have lost the old argument that we are doing the best we can for them, for they can point to you who are doing better."

"What do you wish me to do?" asked Philip, in a queer tone, as he pushed back his chair and braced one knee on the table.

The lawyer glanced triumphantly around among his clients. Old Giddings hadn't lost his brains yet, if he did drink a bit too much sometimes. They ought to have called him in before; the boy wasn't obstinate if a little diplomacy was used.

"My dear sir, we wouldn't presume to dictate, I express your feelings, do I not, gentlemen?"

"Entirely so," assented the gentleman with the newspaper. "Certainly," remarked the guest who was still paring his nails.

"But we really feel," resumed the lawyer, smoothly, "as if you ought to retrace your steps, and stand with the rest of us. We ought to present a bold and unbroken front to the enemy."

"The enemy?" repeated Philip, doubtfully.

"Oh! that is, the laboring classes, of course."

"But what reason could I give for retracing my steps?" asked the young man modestly enough. "The people in my mills are so delighted with their new dignity and profit as stockholders in the busi-

ness, that I ought to have a very good explanation
to give them for such a proceeding as you suggest.
They take a new interest in their work. The dividend the poor creatures get is very small, but it
seems enough to change the very look in their
faces."

"Ahem! why," Giddings wasn't getting along
as well now. He was more disposed to think the
young mill-owner a conceited puppy. One or two
of the wealthy and important clients frowned un-
favorably on their indiscreet attorney, who had let
in, indeed fairly invited this irrelevant talk.

"You ask how to explain the change to them.
Well, tell your help times are hard, and there won't
be any surplus next year, dismiss the committee
who will want to fumble over your books. Explanations—they couldn't understand accounts or business secrets cannot be exposed." Giddings smiled
shrewdly. "It is easy enough to fool them; the
difficulty comes when you try to improve their condition; regular cattle, you can drive them, but it is
the deuce of a job to lead them."

The gentleman with the newspaper threw it
down very abruptly.

"Why, Breton, you are giving us all away, and
your policy is suicidal besides. How are we going
to get rich on half profits? We can take what we
choose—what fools we would be to give up our ad-

vantage! Of course I am sorry for the poor folks, but I don't care to make myself poor too. You can't expect a man to risk his money for a five per cent rate of interest."

"Very true, not when they can get twelve or twenty, but we would all invest money at five per cent, rather than get nothing for it. We tax the world too much to keep us rich."

The man with the penknife shut it with an emphatic click. "Our skilled work, as managers, deserves big rewards. What would the work of your thousand help be worth without your guiding?"

"Or," added Philip with a smile, "what good would my guiding be, without their hands? They are equally important in their place, equally entitled to a share in the profits produced out of the dead capital by our united efforts." Then he rose suddenly to his feet. "I would like to show you through my mill."

The visitors looked at each other queerly, but one after another stood up in response to his invitation, and in a moment more were following him towards the factory.

He led them first into the room where the cotton was emptied out of the great bales and torn by revolving knives into the finest shreds, while steam fans carried off every particle of dirt or waste. The room was hot and the air full of dust and bits of

floating cotton. The four or five men that tended
the grand machines, fairly shone with the perspiration, and their shirts were open at the neck for freer
breath. The rattling machinery overwhelmed all
ordinary tones of voice, and the men had learned to
be silent ; so from long habit their faces had acquired
something of the expression of the dumb. Thence
Philip conducted his guests to the room where the
rolls of cotton were still further cleansed, where one
boy had the care of a long row of frames. They followed the cotton to the human-like mules as they
were called, which twisted the thread all ready for
weaving, and then to the looms whose angry clatter
was like the rebellious voices of ten thousand sprites,
forced to do the work of men without reward. A
girl or a man more rarely had charge of five or six of
the looms each ; they had all the same look of deaf
and dumb mutes ; quite shut out as they were from
the human social life from the dawn to the setting
sun. The dull, cheerless routine of their life was not
changed ; under the new system the terrible roar and
rattle of the machinery was no softer than of old, but
there was no face in all that great factory, but that
had a happier, brighter look than of old, not a bending form but seemed to have a new spring and vitality. All the men and girls and even the little
children wore better clothes, and looked much cleaner
than they used, and perhaps it was partly this which

heightened their self-respect, so that they showed no
disposition to avoid the eyes of their distinguished
visitors. The sullen expression which is so familiar
on the faces in great factories was gone. Their young
master had planted a little seed of hope in every soul
of them all, and its first slight sprouting had given
them that pride in their work which marks the distinction between slaves and freemen.

" A little more money for each one, that makes
all the difference," said Philip as he conducted his
guests out into the open air, where they could hear
each other's voices again. Seven cold faces met his
pleasant glance.

" But a little for each," suggested one of the gentlemen, "means a pretty good lump out of you.
There isn't enough to go around. It's my opinion it
isn't possible for only a few to have much chance in
this world. The world is too poor. There isn't
enough to go around."

" Not if everybody asked to live as he does,"
thought Philip, " and earn as little." But he said
nothing: he led them to his tenement-houses and
showed them the signs of a new ambition after taste
and comfort and even refinement. It appeared in
very little things, in particulars one would hardly
notice, perhaps a new door mat on the step or a cloth
curtain instead of a paper one, sometimes a rosebush
in the front yard. But it was a change which makes

18

a house over into a home ; the men and women in
the Breton Mills suddenly had homes, and one would
think these gentlemen of uncounted wealth envied
their new blessings, from their frowning brows.
Then Philip showed them the village schools fairly
crowded with the children of the poor; most of
them old enough to earn a few dollars a month in
the mill.   They seemed strangely ignorant for their
age ; the simplest lessons were hard for them, and
yet there was hardly a face of them but had a
certain shrewd unchild-like look; they had borne
the crushing burdens of life too soon poor little
things.

   " Isn't it worth while to enable the mill people to
send their children to school ? " urged Philip eagerly.
" They used to have to grind every pound of work
out of their puny little forms to keep the wolf from
the door.   It was a terrible sight to me, gentlemen—
the torturing of the soft muscles and weak little
limbs, which stunted and deformed their bodies, and
dwarfed their unshaped minds and hearts.   Nothing
can excuse a system that requires such sacrifices as
that ; better burn our mills and go back to savage
life if we cannot pity these babies."

   " But education only makes the poor more uneasy," remarked one of his portly visitors.   " I
believe it does them more harm than good."   Philip
looked indignation at the speaker, whose round face

was of a soft pink, from high living and rare wines of fabulous prices.

"You are right, if all the good you count is to run your mills forever at starvation prices."

Then he showed them his factory stores, and as he explained his system in full to them he saw they were interested at last. All vestiges of scowls were gone, and their eyes snapped delight as they asked the most minute questions. Philip was well pleased. If they would adopt, in their own mills, even so much as this, it would be a step. So he told them where he bought his groceries and goods of all sorts, and the excellent terms he could make. He explained how little additional help it required to carry on the stores and the immense saving to his poor of the cost of living. He showed them, too, by his books, how many of the evils of the credit system were obviated by the simple method of letting those who desired, draw provisions against their unpaid month's wages.

The pink-faced gentleman turned smilingly to his companions, "We must certainly try this at home; we are very much obliged, Mr. Breton."

"I hope your help will appreciate the change," smiled Philip.

"Ahem—well it isn't so much that—ahem—but if we can lower the cost of living so much—ahem—

we think labor ought to be cheaper, eh, gentlemen ?
Wages can be cut down."

Philip bit his lip and turned his face away to
hide his intense chagrin. He had only put new
weapons in their hands to fight the "enemy." Was
it possible that every progress in science and each
successful invention which the world rejoices over
only sweeps into the coffers of the rich more and
more of the wealth the poor have earned.

"Well, Mr. Breton," said the pink-faced gentleman, as the guests prepared to go, "we cannot but
hope our visit may not prove in vain for you. You
will come round in good time. You must have
some of your father's blood in you, ha, ha, ha."

But Philip was in no laughing mood. "No, but
you or your children will see the right clearer. We
are only a few, after all, compared with the millions
held in bondage, yes, bondage for want of a few dollars ; they ought to have some chance. You say
there isn't enough wealth to go around, but give
them a chance and they will produce enough to
make every creature on the earth comfortable and
contented. Their arms are strong and their wills
good if they have a spark of hope, and there is certainly work enough." Philip looked around at the
seven politely surprised faces, and nipped his enthusiasm in the bud. The only reply they had for him
was a

"Good afternoon, Mr. Breton."

It was an hour later that Philip pushed back his chair from the office table preparatory to going home. He did not acknowledge to himself a certain sweet excitement that affected him as he rose to his feet, much less the cause of it; and he laid it to ordinary masculine vanity that he paused a moment before a mirror before he went out.

It was not the same face he used to see in the glass. His black moustache had grown heavy and completely hid his rather unartistic upper lip, but it was not that had changed him so much. His forehead had some new lines in it and there was, somehow, a firmer look about the corners of his mouth; the youth and freshness that had lasted for twenty-six summers had given place on the twenty-seventh. There was a self poise and suggestion of reserved force in him now that stood for some very rapid development of character. The mirth and gayety seemed gone out of him; he fancied now he was the sort of man would make the young straighten their laughing faces when they saw him. He was certainly immensely more entertaining before. If a woman did not like him then she would not be likely to love him now. Women like to be amused, and the humor seemed all crushed out of him. And yet there are women who, when it comes to falling in love, don't seem to choose the men who please them most; as

likely as not the rudest of all their lovers, possibly
the one who would disdain to amuse them, and who,
from appearances, would be the one least likely to
make a home happy.

As Philip went up the hill, his quick eyes caught
a glimpse of a woman's dress by Mr. Ellingsworth's
gate, and in a few steps more he could see it was the
shade of blue Bertha loved. Why might it not be
Bertha, why not, only that he was so eager it should
be? He hurried as much as he dared—how strongly
his heart was beating. She might turn any moment
and go into the house. He tried to think of what
he could say to her if it was she, he—

Yes it was Bertha, her face was turned away,
showing him only the perfect Greek profile, and the
uncovered coils of her wonderful golden hair. Her
hand rested on the gate as she looked off on the
hills. How grand her thoughts must be to harmonize
with the superb dignity of her face. Philip felt
guilty at disturbing her, but it had been so long. He
came quite near, so near that the magnetic thrill of
her presence touched him more deeply, more tenderly
he thought, than of old, but she had not turned. He
saw the path of care-born lines across her forehead,
that had been smooth as marble; there was a faded
look on her cheeks, less full than they used to be, and
their exquisite color less evenly spread, her hand was
whiter and showed its blue veins almost painfully.

His heart ached over her, his proud Bertha, why could not God have spared her, he would rather have died and saved her the care and suffering that had stricken her loveliness. Then she turned at the sound of footsteps, and a great wave of tenderness swept over his soul. He looked at her so eagerly, so gently that it seemed her face might soften a little, but it did not, nor was there any mark of startled surprise at his coming so suddenly upon her.

"It is you, Philip," even her voice was changed, there was a new hardness in it. She reached out her cold white hand to him.

For a moment he did not speak. It seemed as if his heart would break, there was such a stress upon it. And then he was afraid she might be ashamed before him, ashamed of the terrible injustice she had done him, ashamed of the blot that had touched her name. But whatever she might have felt, there was no sign of any emotion on her impassive face.

"And you are the mill-owner now," she said. "How odd it seems." She smiled graciously, but still he could not speak. He could only look down at the thin blue-veined hand he held, and keep back the sob that trembled on his lips for his lost love.

And that smile and such words as those were all she had for him at last. He had to look away for strength to speak. He must think of some commonplace, that would not startle her repose. Ah!

there was the doorway where she had given him the first ardent caress of his life the last time he had talked with her, the night she forsook him. Did she remember, he wondered? He looked back at the cold beautiful eyes, and the amused smile yet lingering on her lips.

"Yes, it does seem very odd."

CHAPTER XXII.

Out, Damned Spot.

PHILIP dipped his pen in the ink-stand. He was sitting in his study at home, later into the afternoon than usual. Nothing unimportant could have detained him so long from his factory, and besides, there was a look of unusual solemnity on his face. Philip Breton had just written his will. It was a very elaborate instrument, prepared from memoranda of the ablest lawyer in the state. A moment ago he had signed it, and the names of the witnesses were not dry yet. He had been uneasy for a long time, that the destiny of the thousand creatures who worked in his mill, and of their successors forever, should hang on so feeble a thread as a human life, which might snap before he could give spontaneous energy to the plans that now only lived in his brain. He wrote in large, plain letters, across the back of the paper, "The Last Will and Testament of Philip Breton." Then he read the whole instrument over again—the magna charta of Bretonville. How glad the village would be when his will came to be known—when it was found that the mill-owner had not been satisfied with what he could do in his lifetime, but had placed his benevolence on a perpetual footing, to reach back his hand from his grave, to shower blessings on the laboring poor God had committed to his charge. Some men had wives and children to work for, to defend, to hope for. If he had been happy, and blessed with love and kisses, he might have been like the rest, never listening to the groans of his poor under burdens too heavy for them to bear. His heart would, perhaps, have been too full of the little wants and trivial discomforts of his own circle, his mind too busy with plans for the future of his sons, while a thousand dreary hopeless lives wore themselves out in the struggle for their scant bread, with never one pitiful thought from him.

Philip Breton was relieved, now that he had made his will. He folded it carefully, and put it in his inner breast pocket. Perhaps, he thought sadly enough, if he should die this moment, it would be better for Bretonville, for his will might waver while he lived ; he might not be able to sustain his high tone, but once dead, nothing could be changed ; the words that an idle stroke of his pen could make null and void, when once his hand became rigid in death, would leap forth from the written page into potent everlasting life. Suddenly he remembered another occasion when he had sat at this very table,

he had been interrupted by the servant bringing
him a letter—no, it was a note from Bertha. And
he had been very happy, fancying the shadow had
now gone from his life. He had opened this very
table-drawer, when the maid had tapped at the door ;
he was searching for something at the time. Oh ! it
was one of Bertha's pictures, and it must be here
still. In a moment more he was unclasping a morocco case, then gazing with such tenderness as one
has for the dead, on the delicately tinted oval of
Bertha's beautiful face, in porcelain. The great blue
eyes seemed to look surprise and reproach at him.
It had been taken long ago, before so much as a
dream of sin had tainted the holy innocence of her
girlhood.

Philip closed his lips very tightly; he longed
unutterably for her lost innocence ; he hungered so
desperately for the maidenly purity that looked out
of these startled eyes. If she had died then, he
might have cherished her memory ; oh what had he
done that he should be punished so terribly? Then
the memories of the day when the picture was taken,
came rushing back upon him.

They two had been sitting in her garden on the
afternoon of a summer day. It was two, three,
almost four years ago, but he could see the bloom-
ing roses and hear the drowsy hum of the bees as if
it were yesterday. He had been reading a love-poem

to her; that was as near as he dared come to love-making; sometimes letting his voice soften and tremble a little over the tenderer passages. He was but a timid lover, and Bertha so royally cold. Suddenly glancing at her, he saw she was overcome with the heat, and had fallen asleep leaning her shapely head back against the rough bark of the tree. Her fingers loosely clasped in her sloping lap suggested perfect repose; the girlish bosom rose and fell with her still breathing and there was an exquisite pout on her lips as if vaguely mutinous against the hardness of her pillow. His heart was beating violently as he laid aside his book, and seated himself on the bench by her side. But he dared not profane the vestal purity of such sleep as her's; he devoured her face with his eyes but did not steal one kiss from the red lips, though there was such a sweet mute invitation on them. But he put his arm about her, and drew her toward him as gently as if she were a sleeping infant, and made her head rest on his shoulder. Then he looked down the red-tinged cheeks, like the woods in autumn's tenderest mood, swept by her long golden eye-lashes, and tried to fancy she was awake though her eyes were closed, and that she was willing her head should rest on his breast and her hair like fine threads of twisted Roman gold kiss his burning face.

But she moved in her slumber, and then her star-like eyes opened and looked mute astonishment into his eager face. For one startled moment, she did not move, and in sudden boldness from the liberty he had already taken, he poured his passionate declarations into her ears, covering her hair and her forehead and then her cool white hands with kisses.

"You frighten me, Philip." Her quick startled tones as she rose to her feet yet rung in his ears. She looked at him as if half of a mind to run away. "I don't understand you," she said reproachfully. The porcelain picture is just as she was then.

"Why Bertha!" He had risen too ; but she drew back from him. "I love you ; I want you for my wife."

How coldly she had looked at his flushed, excited face. He thought it was the supreme moment in his life ; but it seemed to be nothing to her.

"Is that all? Why I thought you were mad."

Ah, and the same madness burned in his soul this moment ; time could not wear it out ; shame, outrage, desolation could not kill it. He rose to his feet and pushed the tinted porcelain away from him.

"But the woman is spotted with shame, her purity that you worshipped has been dragged in the dust." He paced the room like a caged lion ; he was only a gentle-hearted man, caught in a dilemma, with only a choice of agonies, out of all the beauty and

love in the world. But had she not left the man
who had degraded her, had she not repented her
folly ? And after all he had not loved her because
her acts had always pleased him, but because—because her nature made harmonies that stirred his
soul to sweetest accord. She had made a mistake,
ah, a cruel mistake. What then? Men err griev-
ously and are forgiven. Women are weaker, whose
glory is their gentleness. When they err, shall their
lives be trampled out of them by the nail-shod boots
of their lords and masters ; shall shame and infamy
be fed to their quivering lips forever? Rather let
some man's constant love gather his frightened darling to his bosom and soothe every memory of reproach out of her bruised heart.

Philip arose to go out and his face was lighted
up with a new holy joy. But it was only for a
moment and then a great shadow passed over his
features.

But this woman cared nothing for him. She
never could have loved him. He remembered his
last meeting with her at her father's gate, how his
whole nature had been racked with conflicting waves
of emotion, with fear lest her superb pride should
be wounded—with longing to draw her to his throbbing heart, and with the bitter flood of memories
that almost caught away his breath. And she was
as cold as a woman of marble, with never a softening

expression in her queenly eyes, as if a blessed past of mutual love and peace had ever been between them—not one smile of joy that she met him. "I will wait," he said, but as he spoke he took his hat and went out.

Mrs. Silas Ellingsworth was all smiles and grace as Philip entered her parlor, and as she shook hands with him, lingered as cordially over the greeting as if she had quite forgotten her pretty fingers had ever been on his throat. She made him take a seat and began to make conversation with him, as if she supposed he had called to see her. But suddenly she affected to be struck with an idea.

"Oh, I know why you are not more talkative, you didn't come to see me at all." She stepped to the door. "Susan, call Miss Ellingsworth."

"Miss." Then there was no longer any room for doubt. Philip shrank at the blow she gave him. He had thought all uncertainty was gone long ago, but he found that up to this very instant he had cherished a spark of hope that Bertha had a right to the name of the man she had fled with. And she was "Miss" still. His hostess was saying something, but he did not hear it, there was such a deathly faintness about his heart.

Then there came a step in the hall, and his familiar thrill of tenderness at her coming, which seemed, at this moment, like a flash of lightning on

the face of one's beloved dead. She lingered an
instant on the threshold, an old habit of hers that
gave him time to step forward and meet her.

Mrs. Ellingsworth had risen, too, and was waiting
to speak. It was only tenderness in Philip Breton's
eyes as he took both Bertha's hands so gently, but
she said,

"Am I very much changed then?" and a pained
look flitted across her face. Philip did not answer
her for a moment, he was so distressed at her inter-
pretation of the love that made his sight misty as
he gazed at her.

"Well, I suppose I am in the way," remarked
the mistress of the house, with inbred vulgarity.
She was smiling sweetly, but women's smiles do not
always signify amiability. "I suppose," she added,
letting her skirts touch her two guests as she passed
out, "you want to talk over old times with Miss
Ellingsworth."

It was the last terrible assurance; Philip winced
again at the heartless blow, but not so much as a flush
passed over Bertha's cold face. She accepted the name
without even a shade of silent denial on her calm
features, though it was the badge of shame for her.

"Oh no," but he dared not look her in the face
for fear she should see his anxious pity for her.
"You have been ill, perhaps, but I always thought
you the loveliest woman in the world."

She smiled as she let him lead her to a seat, " You always said that." Then she glanced sadly into the mirror. " But it is more pleasant to hear now, for I know I am not pretty any longer."

Could she understand that the change that had come over her radiant beauty only changed his love to make it deeper? Could she not see the new intensity of yearning in his eyes as he raised them to her face again? He longed to draw her into his arms and kiss her tired face into eternal smiles. His love had been refined into a new divineness ; a love capable of all sacrifices for her ; that asked no price but would pour itself in an eternal flood against her dull indifference, if it must be ; a love more pain than joy, of unutterable yearnings for what he believed she could never have for him ; a love that had a fountain more exhaustless than any woman's kisses ; that would seem to grow on her unresponsiveness, that welled up the mightier for her coldness, content if hereafter it might throw a little brightness on the path her snowy feet should tread, content if she would but let him warm her cold heart with his burning love.

" Are you glad to be at home?" he asked gently.

" Do you call this home, with my servant its mistress?" For a moment it was Bertha as she used to be, her anger curling her red lips and flashing new fire into her tired eyes.

19

" Does she insult you ? " Then Philip bit his lip, but apparently he was far more sensitive than she.

" It is insult enough that she is my father's wife. She cannot go beyond that."

" Shall you stay here always ? " asked Philip stupidly enough.

" I suppose so, where else is there ? "

A wild impulse touched him, he loved her and she needed love, had he not waited long enough ? But a sudden fear came into his mind and chilled his hope like a frozen fountain. She might have a child —how strange he had never thought of it before. Ah, it would be a strong love could endure that, a baby to hang on her bosom and take her kisses, a baby with Curran's face. No, he could never bear that, anything better than that. Her sin he could forgive ; though it must linger forever in his memory he would bury it beneath more blessed experiences. His love should hallow her, he would kiss away Curran's caresses from her lips. But if there were a child—

Philip started violently and looked at the door ; he fancied he heard a sound like the pattering of infant feet. In a moment Bertha would catch to her arms her child and Curran's and half smother it with a mother's kisses.

" Isn't that a child's voice ? " he cried, rising to his feet and his eyes rested on her in a new pitiful reproach. He thought she started strangely, as if a mother's instincts stirred in her bosom.

" Oh no, it is only Jane, I mean Mrs. Ellingsworth. What an innocent little laugh she has."

A child, with sweet winning ways, is a strange thing to hate, a lovely little rosebud to blossom no one knows how faultlessly by and by. But Philip thought he would hate her child—Bertha's child, perhaps with his darling's star-like eyes ; ah, was it not Curran's too, the symbol of her shame? As he walked home in the twilight he saw in each toddling baby in the doorways and windows, an image of his own materialized fear and horror. Philip looked back from the hill on which stood his home, to the village his father had built up. Those massive mills with their thousands of looms were his ; those long rows of white houses, each one of which held a family rich in possibilities of virtue and hope, they all were his, and the new element of brightness and thrift, that had made the whole village a nursery of comfort and happiness, was his work. Behind him was the great stone mansion with its arched gothic windows green with clustering woodbine, it was his too. How powerless he thought all that wealth and material power can do to solve one of the terrible problems a heart makes for itself.

Moodily he walked to his stables, in a kind of vague longing for companionship, and threw open the doors. Four horses stood in their stalls within, noble looking creatures all of them. They turned their stately heads toward the sound of their master's feet, they returned his love with love. One of them whinnied welcome and laid back his ears as his master came into the stall beside him.

"Poor fellow, good boy," Philip patted his white neck affectionately. "You would do what you could for me, wouldn't you, Joe. I know you would, old fellow." He laid his cheek against the animal's velvet nose. "But you couldn't go fast enough to get me out of this trouble, not if you died to do it."

CHAPTER XXIII.

No Barrier.

SENSITIVENESS is a very unfortunate quality in a life where no object is molded in accordance with the strict rules of art, where there is no character but has a repulsive spot in it, no history but with its dark page. The happy man is neither too enthusiastic over the virtues of his acquaintance, which may be accidental or merely a pretty optical delusion, or too stern and unrelenting towards a sin, which he fancies might have been a virtue under different conditions. But Philip Breton had fallen out with life. The great world seemed to jar him as it rolled ; each hour had revealed unguessed means of suffering, and even the beams of genial sunlight had daggers for him. He only wondered why all mankind did not prefer to die, instead of this foolish laughing and affecting to be happy ; he had looked on life as a mechanism of satanic ingenuity for torment in which each man is made to arrange his own rack and then stretch his tired body upon it in sweet hope of love and peace.

Yet it is hard for a man to understand that his

fate may be pure unalloyed pain; he is ever smiling
through his tears and trying to awake from his despair as if it were but a dream of disordered fancy.
So as the next morning came, and Philip Breton
threw open his door to go out into the sweet-scented
September air he felt happier than for many weeks;
the peace that came over him seemed to leave no
place for cruel distrust and unrelenting pride. He
even reproached himself for his ungenerousness of
yesterday; the world of nature left no unsightly
wounds and breaks in the whole dominion. Gaping
graves are soon covered with green grass and wild
flowers; life springs quickly out of death, and apparent ruin is soon forgotten in renewed magnificence.
Why should he then let two lives be wrecked for one
wrong act in the past—forever past?

He swung down his walk in a new buoyancy; he
believed he had passed through the cloud, and come
out into the clear light of reason. And only last
night he had been so far from hope. It was all his
own arrogance, setting himself up to be the judge of
another's life, when he could not know the mood that
had swayed her, or the temptations she had striven
with. But he did know she was as pure in heart as
the day; he did know the exquisite balance of her nature, that charmed him of old—charmed him still.
What folly for him to linger over a past she had laid
aside, and that left her as lovely in his eyes as ever.

But at his gate a carriage rolled slowly by him. It contained a bridal couple, and he stopped to smile at them. The girl's face had no culture in it, but was sweet, and had the innocence of childhood. That ungainly fellow, who now wore his first broadcloth suit, at whom she looked so fondly, was the only lover she had ever known. She had no secrets from him, no past his jealous eyes might not scan without a pang. Her soul was open to him. No whisper to her shame could ever reach his insulted ears. Her life was commonplace, but no blot was on it, no guilty thought had ever left its trail across her heart. The rough lad, who was bold enough to put his arm about her waist in broad daylight, could pour his foolish love-making into her eager ears without stint. There was no theme he must avoid with her, no page in her life he must not cut.

And were there so few spotless women in the world, that Philip Breton could not have one to fold to his heart ; to sit at his table ; to brighten his home? His peace was gone so soon, he suddenly hated the genial sunlight, with its eternal smile, and the smell of roses seemed to strangle him.

It was that same day toward evening, that he met the village policeman leading along an unwilling prisoner. It was a woman whose hair was disheveled, and her thin, faded cheeks tear-stained.

She had been powdered and rouged, but there was
nothing only pitiableness in her appearance now.
It was plain enough to see that shame was the portion of her life, plain enough to have gathered a
crowd of boys at her heels, whose coarse jokes and
insults made the creature hang her head. Philip
stopped, and the crowd drew closer to hear a moral
lecture. "Will you try and live an honest life, if
you are let go this time?"

The woman looked up quickly at the kind,
troubled face of the young man. She laid her hand
on his arm in her eagerness, and the crowd laughed.
She began to tell her story; true or false, it was
enough to break a man's heart, but she rolled it off
her tongue glibly. She had told it a thousand times,
as an excuse for her past, to call out a little sympathy,
which reaches to all classes but hers. The policeman
would have stopped her, but though he interrupted
her a dozen times, and the crowd glared insultingly at
her poor hunted face, and jeered and laughed at the
saddest turns of her old, old story, she did not stop
till she had finished it. The young mill-owner had
grown pale and his face twitched nervously as she
talked ; his eyes did not leave her faded face, nor did
he open his lips till she was done. He was about to
speak, but the policeman broke in roughly,

"There's no use, squire ; when they've got
started there's no savin' 'em."

" Please give me one chance," pleaded the harsh, grating tones of the lost woman. " If I had a little money to start me, I—"

Philip had opened his pocket book, and her greedy eyes were devouring the rolls of bills within.

He handed her a few dollars.

" Better let her go this time."

He shuddered and walked on. He would rather half his wealth he thought, than have met this fallen woman just now. She had started in his brain such a terrible current of thought. She had suggested such comparisons. He was afraid he could never forget her; that Bertha and this bedraggled, painted creature would be forever associated in his thoughts. He would rather half his wealth than have seen her.

After his tea that evening he had flung himself wearily on a sofa, the mad whirl of horrible thoughts and fears that day had made him almost sick. He wished he might sleep, and never wake, since waking meant renewed agony, and renewed horrors of a morbid fancy. And he slept and dreamed; he stood in the church with his bride, and the minister was pronouncing them man and wife. A warm glow of happiness was about his heart at last, after his long waiting. All his fears and shame seemed things of the past; he seemed to be looking back with wonder at his own misgivings. But suddenly his blood was congealing, he tried to cry out to stop the fatal words, for his bride was the rouged creature he had saved from jail, and the same jeering crowd of loafers were pointing their soiled fingers at him.

He leaped to his feet, the perspiration standing in great drops on his forehead, and found it had become quite dark as he had slept. His great house was as still as death ; that was always so, but it oppressed him intolerably now, and he caught his hat from the table and hurried out to his stables between sleeping and waking. In a few moments he had saddled and bridled Joe, the white horse, and had mounted him. He was in just the mood for a wild ride, but still he had to wait, a gentleman stopped him as he turned out of his drive-way.

" No, I won't come in, I see you are just going for a ride," said his acquaintance. " By the way, I suppose you are going to Low's wedding to-morrow."

" I hate weddings," answered Philip, whipping his boot and then pulling his horse in when he started. He was thinking of his dream.

" Oh, but this bride is such an excellent girl. Such a wife as you ought to have, Breton. Cæsar's wife you know, must be above suspicion, ha, ha—Well, I see your horse is impatient. I won't keep you, ta, ta."

" Fool," muttered Philip as his horse bounded

down the street. He rode past Mr. Ellingsworth's house, and looked up at Bertha's window; his eyes turned up to its dim light, though he swore to himself he would not look. He galloped by, and the words of the young fop echoed in his ears, " Cæsar's wife must be above suspicion." Clack, clank, went his horse's hoofs, but what were they saying; to Philip's ears, it seemed to be " Cæsar's wife, Cæsar's wife "—clack, clank, " must be," clack, clank, " above suspicion."

And the world was full of beautiful women, whose lives were as sweet and pure as an unsullied rose. Ah, he could never bear, never, that his wife should be pointed at with smiles of derision.

" Good-bye, Bertha, good-bye, my darling, you must reap what you have sowed; cruel is it? So is life and nature cruel, the hand put in the fire must surely burn. Unmagnanimous; must a man then put a soiled lily in his bosom?

But he stopped his horse so suddenly the animal had to plant his feet to keep from falling. He loved the soiled lily, loved it more than all the fresh roses. All other women might as well never have been born for him ; this woman he would have died for. Could he not protect her from evil tongues; if she were trampled could he not lift her into his bosom; if she were insulted could he not put his man's heart and strength between her and shame? A sudden revul-

sion of feeling passed over him; he blessed the fop
who had driven his disordered fancy so far that reaction came; the devils and fiends that had tormented him so long seemed vanquished; they had
disguised themselves in the raiment of angels of light
and purity; they had prated virtue and holiness to
him, but this moment he saw they were cowards and
liars all. He would hurry to his darling, throw
himself at her feet, her past should be buried, her life
should begin with his happiness to-night.

"You want to marry Bertha? I supposed you
were acquainted with her past."

It was in Mr. Ellingsworth's room, where he sat
in dressing-gown and slippers, well back in his easy
chair. He was looking at Philip Breton very curiously. He had really fancied he understood human
nature before.

"I suppose I am," answered Philip, simply.

"Well, I know more of it than I wish I did. She
ran away with a beggar, and she has come back. I
dislike unpleasant memories, so I avoid unpleasant
information. You know her—her—her relations
with Curran, yes, well," and the gentleman shrugged
his slight shoulders, "no doubt you know what you
are doing, you run your own risks."

"Risks?"

"Understand me, I asked but two questions,—
have you left Curran forever? do you want to come

home? I had heard she had never been married.
Jane has heard it. I feared it. Do you wonder I did
not ask, not caring for a disagreeable certainty?
Well, do your own questioning. I suppose the fact
of her keeping her maiden name shows something."

What if she should find she was indeed married
after all, when he had at last decided he could not
live without her; when he had at last made up his
mind that he must have her if he took a burden of
life-long shame into his soul with her? That would
be a wretched freak for fortune to play with him;
but how foolish he was, did not her name prove
that she was unmarried?

" But I hate so to harrow up her memories," said
Philip, in an unsteady voice; " to make her confess
her shame before me. I should think that would
be a father's duty."

" Can it be, my dear Philip," remarked Mr. Ellingsworth, with his own brilliant smile, " that you know
me so little as to expect me to perform an unpleasant duty. There are people that love them—that
never seem so much in their element as when engaged in some act of self-sacrifice. You must really
excuse me."

When Philip went down into the parlor, Bertha
was sitting there alone, and his fate seemed thrust
upon him. Before he had time to dread breaking
the subject to her he stood at the back of her chair,

looking down on her thin, white fingers moving over
her embroidery work.   He laid his hand very gently
on her shoulder.   Ah, it was less round than it used
to be.   She was good enough to keep her eyes fixed
on her work.   There was no shade of heightened
color on her cheeks, nor did she quicken her
breathing.

"Bertha," he began, in a low, sweet voice, " I
am going to ask you something."   Still she did not
look up.

"If, at some time before you died, a man whom
you liked came and asked you to marry him," he
spoke very slowly, "is there any reason why you
must say no?"

Not one flush or nervous tremor.   She threaded
her needle again with the red worsted.   "What do
you mean by reason?"

"I mean," he said, in forced calm, "is there any
barrier which the laws make to prevent you from
marrying him?"   How lovely she looked to him as
he waited, how had he ever hesitated when he
thought she was free?   Since he had, of late, begun
to dream of marriage, he had thought only of the
barrier of her shame ; he had not thought that there
might be a barrier more impregnable.   But it came
over him all the more terribly now.   That would explain her lack of shame, her unbroken pride, that
would be more consistent with his lifelong idea of

her, that she had preserved her honor and, alas, was already married and cut forever away from him. That would save her purity that he had thought sullied. No fingers of scorn could ever be pointed at her. No, but she would be lost to him forever. God forgive him, then, if he would rather have her dishonored, insulted, degraded, than lose her. Would she never answer? She laid down her needle and turned her face up toward him. He trembled like a child as he watched her lips part; in a moment his fate would be decided; it was terrible that his happiness could come only through her shame, and her honor meant a life of despair and loneliness for him, but so it seemed to him now.

"There is no barrier," she said.

"Thank God," he whispered; the strain was removed; she had established her own disgrace with her own lips, without a drooping of her eyes, without a quiver of her lips. Ah, but he suffered in his very hope; it wounded him that he must rejoice in her shame; it was almost as if he had caused it. He bent low over her shoulder, in another moment he would have told her of the unchanging passion— of his love, all the bounds of his nature were broken down now; his whole soul seemed dissolving in ineffable tenderness for this cold woman into whose calm beautiful eyes he looked so hungrily.

"Like embroidery, don't you, Mr. Breton?"

Mrs. Ellingsworth flashed her small black eyes in delight. Philip started back in ill-concealed dismay, but Bertha's face changed not one shade of expression as she rose magnificently to her feet and swept from the room.

The lady of the house looked unpleasantly after her.

"Isn't it funny she don't seem to like me? Do you suppose it is that Curran scrape has put her so much above me?"

Philip glanced savagely at her : he could almost have struck her, without thinking of her womanhood, there was such a snake-like look in the glistening black eyes. One might as well reproach a wild creature of the forest for following out its instincts; but after a moment he said :

"Mrs. Ellingsworth forgets she is a lady."

But she was beautiful, if not a lady, her hot blood lighting up her round olive cheeks as if it were liquid fire and her curled lips glowing like a perfect rose just bursting into bloom. No man could look at her now and not feel a mad soulless fascination for her, a fascination the greater because mixed with revulsion. She was a perfect type of the womanhood that can madden a man with passion, without tenderness, that can wreck his life, banish every noble hope or ideal from his soul and feed him nothing but dead-sea fruit.

" It's strange what makes a lady," she answered him in growing excitement. " Your Bertha is one no matter what vileness she sinks to, but I can't whisper one rude word."

She came close to him and put her burning fingers on his hand. " Your horse loves you better than that woman ; she will torture you to death, let her alone." Then she sprang away from him and walked backward and forward clasping and unclasping her clinging fingers in her old habit. " Oh, I hate her, I hate her, but what good is it ? I would dash myself to pieces to break her, but I could not. She steals my lover and then leaves him ; she comes back disgraced in the eyes of her own father, but she does not feel it. And now comes her lover with his riches and offers everything to her. She deserves nothing but she gets everything." She would have raved on but Philip Breton walked slowly out of the room. Nothing could ever move him now ; he preferred the woman she maligned to all the other hopes or possessions in the world.

CHAPTER XXIV.

A Race with the Cars.

IT was the next afternoon, as Philip Breton was unhitching Joe from the post, that he had occasion to doff his hat to Mrs. Ellingsworth, driving by with her husband. They made a very pretty picture of marital bliss; perhaps they were all the happier because neither of them had souls. Philip had been intending to go to his factory, there was some business he ought to attend to, but the sudden assurance that Bertha was alone, made his heart give a great bound. What better time than now to tell her of his unaltered love, to win her promise to let him make her happy? So his business was postponed, and he rang the bell at Mr. Ellingsworth's, instead.

" Not in?" he repeated after the servant in dismay. Would his luck never change? Had she been frightened at his manner the night before, and gone away to avoid his unpleasant suit?"

" But she isn't far away," and the girl smiled at the disappointment that had come over his face.

" I guess, now, you will find her in the garden; or I will call her if you say."

" No, don't call her," and Philip hurried out to the garden. What more fitting place for what he had to say, if he could find his voice for the great lump in his throat. He ought to be very eloquent to persuade her, to answer all her objections, to assure her that it was not pity that moved him, for she would resent that, but love—a love that craved her above all the world.

She looked up from her embroidery, at the sound of his footsteps, and smiled. Her beauty might all go, as its first bloom and freshness had gone, and her cheeks fade like the autumn leaves whose glowing tints they had once worn; her golden hair might whiten with age, he knew it would make no difference in his love. She wore the same dress she had worn in that other garden scene. She had grown thin and gone back to the dresses of her girlhood. It was a light blue silk, open low in the neck, filled in with nestling folds of lace. The sunbeams made their way through the low hanging trees, and with them came the breath of the roses, and the humming of the bees, just as on that other day.

Philip seated himself on the bench beside her, and tried to make his voice calm as he said,

" Do you remember when you last wore this dress ?"

Would she be frightened at the intensity of gentleness in his voice ?

But she smiled as frankly at him as if he were her brother, " Oh, yes."

He put his hand on her arm, cool as if love and passion were forever outside her experience. "Bertha, I love you more now than then. I will not frighten you with my vehemence ; I have learned to conquer myself, I will cherish you as a child, but, oh, Bertha, I want you near me."

The woman did not draw away from him. She was looking with a changed expression at his eager face—the face of the lover whom no coldness could chill, who returned again after her desertion of him, whom no shame could alter. He had stirred something like admiration in her at last. A tinge of delicate color rose from her neck among the folds of lace, and mounted to the roots of her golden hair. It was the first time he had ever moved her.

" And you love me as much now as that day I fell asleep on your shoulder—ages ago, it must have been ?" Then her great blue eyes drooped under the intensity of love that looked from his face—a love beyond her power to understand.

He gathered her hands in his. " As much and more—a deeper, purer, gentler love, that will protect you against its own very vehemence—that would rather make sacrifices for you than joys for itself."

" Take me then," and she let him draw her head on his breast, where she felt the throbbing growing mightier and mightier, though he only pressed his lips upon her cool forehead. Then she drew back ; she did not look in his face, which had a great light in it, perhaps she was ashamed that she had nothing to give him, ashamed that her heart was so cold under the rapture that looked out of his eyes.

" But Philip, you must not hurry me too much. I am slow, and this is so sudden, I would as soon thought of an earthquake." Then she glanced wonderingly at him, as if to make sure. " Ah, Philip, you deserve a better love than mine." But he caught her hand to his lips and held it there, while he covered it with kisses.

" I would rather the flower you wear in your bosom, than any woman in the world besides you. I learned to love with you, Bertha."

But she took her hand away uneasily. " But you won't hurry me will you, Philip ? " How could she ask him to wait much longer, " for if you will—"

" Oh, no—I will give you a whole week." He laughed, and then grew suddenly very sober. " Haven't I given you long enough ? "

" I must take a little journey first," and her eyes appeared to avoid his. A sudden tide of jealousy swept over him. Had she deserved his trust ?

"I will go with you. It shall be our wedding journey."

She flushed nervously—"Oh, no, not yet."

Where could she be going? To one last interview with Curran, perhaps, and he felt that he could not bear one thought of him should ever cross her soul again. How short a time it took to spoil his happiness. The glow had left his heart, the light had gone out of his eyes, all in a moment. Is misery then the only thing that can last?

"Only this once," she said. "You shall go with me always then."

His mood melted and in a moment he was kneeling before her. "Oh, Bertha, be fair with me—for you hold me in the hollow of your hand. Do not fail me now when you have seemed so near me."

She put her hand on his bowed head, perhaps some sweet word trembled on her lips. He hungered for it, and when she did not speak, he looked up into the face of his bride. She had seemed so far from him, a world could not have parted them more, but he was at her feet, and she had promised to be his wife.

"My dear Philip, excuse me, but you are crushing my embroidery." So he was, he was kneeling on it in his fond idolatry, as if a piece of worsted work were of no account. He found his feet, and cast a pathetic glance at the square of canvas before he stooped to pick it up. It was strange indeed that he should have been so carried away in his passionate ardor as not to notice what he was kneeling on.

"I hope I have not ruined your work," he said simply. No, he had only rumpled it a little, and he would have been willing to purchase all the canvas and worsted in two cities, rather than have missed the tender word he thought was on her lips.

It was several hours later and Philip still sat in his office. He was doing his best to attend to his correspondence, but such a mist of joy floated before his eyes he could hardly see. He had accomplished almost nothing and finally pushed away the pile of papers—to-morrow might do for them, his heart was too full of joy for work. He had surely waited and suffered enough to win a few hours' respite. But the door swung slowly on its hinges and a tall massive figure stood on the threshold. Philip tried to smile, but his smile froze on his lips ; he seemed powerless to move from his chair ; his dreams of happiness faded away ; his fate had come. The man in the doorway was Curran.

The man was as noble looking as ever. A more haggard expression was on his face, there were deep hollows beneath his eyes, but the marks of care and suffering only gave a more admirable dignity to his bearing. In the first terrible moment Philip Breton had not the first shadow of a doubt that Curran had

come to claim Bertha.   Perhaps he would offer her
marriage at last.

But the man threw himself into a chair in silence.
Philip did not even utter a greeting.   If he wished
to tempt his darling away to new shame he would
have to fight for her.   Oh, Philip would die for her
honor, now that he was warned.

"Well, I have got through planning strikes ; the
one you saw started failed like the rest.   I have
learned what cowardly stuff the souls of the poor
are made of."   Curran spoke in bitterest contempt.
"That is another of the luxuries of wealth—you
can afford to be brave and noble.   You can stand
by your principles.   A poor man can't afford it.   He
sees everything the heart longs for, even to a woman's
love, bought with money, and his family starving.
Can we blame him for abandoning eternal principles,
to escape the pangs of hunger a week longer ?   If
the poor would stand firm they must win, but they
grow hungry.   Bah, what can they do."

Philip heard but little that he said ; he was trembling for Bertha.   He, himself, felt the man's resistless magnetism.   Bertha had yielded to it once, why
might she not again ?   She must not see him or her
proud womanhood would go down into the dust at
his feet a second time, and at the thrilling tones of
his voice she would follow him forth to new disgrace.

"You are fighting to win money, and you find

you must have money before you can fight. Is that it?"

"We are not fighting to win money," replied Curran, rising nervously from his chair and coming up to where Philip sat, "but the rights of humanity, and it is the grandest battle man ever sharpened his sword for." He seemed to flash lightnings from his magnificent eyes. "It is nobler than all the revolutions and reformations, this emancipation of the world from its bondage. Where are your prophets and your poets? Why are they not arousing the spirit of the great armies of fighting men? When was there ever a cause like this to die for? Where are our martyrs? The wave will come and sweep all mankind with it, when our cries and prayers have knocked at the gates of heaven long enough. It is only in times of great excitement that great changes come,—excitement that makes small things seem small, that disdains to consider the violet that claims a right to blossom undisturbed in the path of the army marching on to the salvation of the race."

"Shall you wait till then?" Philip rose to go out. The strain of the man's presence was intolerable; such hate burned in his heart for him, and yet he seemed so grand and noble above all other men.

"Wait? no, I have wasted precious time enough and" he caught his breath, "I have been punished for it. But I shall pursue different methods. We have the ballot, the poorest man has it. That is the lever for us to move the world with. We are a majority. If we want a thing what hinders us from having it? The laws have reduced us to a condition of abject slavery; the laws shall restore us our birth-right. But we must be united, we must agree in what we will seek, and that is my work now. To-day I have consulted the poor of Bretonville; they must help their less fortunate brethren. To-night I go to the westward where my district is. I shall spread a knowledge of the precise laws we need and of the precise means suitable to enact them. Peace-ably, slowly but surely the world will be revolution-ized."

"When are you going?" Philip dared not look him in the face as he waited for his answer; he was afraid his hate would show on his face, his hate for the man who stood between his life and happiness.

Curran glanced at the office clock. "At six o'clock, why it is but half an hour before my train goes, and I have an errand to do. Good-bye. Why you aren't too proud to shake hands! I don't sup-pose I shall ever come back, there is nothing to keep me, not now, God forgive her." He turned back for a last word. "I hope no woman will ever break your heart, somehow a man don't get over it and your high-bred women are as cruel as the grave."

The six o'clock train was just drawing up to the

depot platform when Mr. Ellingsworth's carriage
stopped on the other side, and a heavily veiled lady
alighted.

" Why, Bertha, you must not go on this train,
not for worlds." Philip was almost beside himself
with distress, " not for worlds," he repeated. This
was the train Curran was going on. Should he
trust his lamb in the lion's mouth ? He fancied Curran catching a glimpse of her form, and coming to sit
with her ; he would pour a torrent of tender words
into her ear, her heart that was cold to all the world
besides would glow again for him, again she would
be lost to the lover of her youth, again shame and
sin would lay their evil tainted hands upon her.

But where was Curran, if he was indeed going on
this train, the bell was ringing, the conductor had
given his warning? If Curran was to stay might not
Bertha better go.

" Quick, then if you want to go, the train is just
starting," he cried as he led her across the depot.

" But I don't want to go unless you wish, not
to-night," answered Bertha with charming docility.
Philip looked around. He did not see his arch enemy
and hers.

" But I do wish it, quick. Good-bye, my darling."
The steam escaped in great puffs from the piston
box, the train started, Philip gave a great sigh of
relief. If they had met on the platform, if at the last

moment, just before the train had started, Curran had leaped aboard—why even now, the train had not cleared the platform, he might come now! Philip looked about him; thank God, he was alone.

But he thought he heard a shout, yes, a man was running from the tenement houses at the top of his speed, and waving his hat. It was Curran and he was gaining on the train; the lumbering cars seemed to crawl and he came like the wind. It seemed but an instant more that he dashed across the depot and up the track. All was lost, no, was the man gaining? Still, there was but a rod between him and the rear platform, one more effort and he would be aboard. No it was two rods, four rods—the man had lost and sat down beside the track to catch his breath, while the train went faster and faster till it was out of sight.

CHAPTER XXV.

Woman's Sympathy.

BERTHA has returned, never to leave her lover again, in safety, and still faithful to him ; his fears were unfounded, his suspicions rebuked. It was only last evening that he had looked into her beautiful eyes once more, and it was to-day, she had told him he might come. It was a great day for Philip for another reason, for he was to break ground this morning for a new mill, whose walls and foundations would be cemented in love and justice. In the mill-yard a hundred laborers waited with their spades over their shoulders, and with them the young mill-owner, grasping a spade like the rest. At the contractor's word the iron glistened in the sunlight, and in an instant more, a hundred and one spades struck earth. Ten thousand eager workmen all over the land were waiting on the undertaking ; each night ten thousand anxious tongues will ask how many feet the new walls have risen that day ; will reproach the masons if they are slow, will bless them if they work mightily.

The looms in the Breton Mills are still to-day,

the great water-wheel is unharnessed from the myriad belts, while the men and women and children gathered around the great parallelogram marked out by the engineers for the foundation of the new mill. It was their mill, too, and the face of the poorest creature of them all, reflected a little of the blessed hope which was making life over for them. Not a voice was heard, for the moment all eyes were fixed on the bending forms. Philip Breton's slight form was bent, too, as he drove his spade deep into the stubborn sod. Every laborer stayed his hand for the moment, till the young master threw up the first earth. Then a cheer broke from each brawny throat, and every spade at once lifted its burden of green turf.

The hundred laborers bent again to their task, and the frightened daisies trembled on their green stems, but Philip, spade in hand, had mounted the steps of the nearest mill, and now looked down kindly on the operatives who gathered expectantly about him.

" I mean that not one injustice shall ever desecrate these new walls. I mean the new mill shall be a temple of co-operation. I believe the world is just entering on a new epoch, more glorious than any before, because blessings that have been confined to the few, comforts that have comforted only the few, leisure and amusement, even, that has cheered only

the few, shall be universal ; that each hand that tills
the earth shall share in its bountiful harvests which
now pack the storehouses of a few in senseless pro-
fusion; that each hand that weaves our cloth shall
share in its profits according to his worth. It isn't
because the world is so poor that you have been
poor so long, but because its wealth is wasted. But
be patient ; violence only destroys, it does not build
up, and every particle of wealth destroyed leaves so
much less of your heritage. We will not work any
more to-day ; it shall be a holiday to be kept sacred
in our memories, as an inspiration to more faithful
labor, and more honest, contented lives."

For a moment no one moved, till he leaned his
spade against the wall, and started to come down.
Then a murmur ran through the crowd till it
swelled to a cheer, and as he made his way out, he
had to clasp a thousand dingy hands, reached out to
the young master, in token of the love and trust of
a thousand brightened lives.

His destiny that had frowned so long and so
terribly, smiled at last. As if by a miracle, his life,
that had seemed so dreary and barren, was become
a path of flowers. All dangers were averted, all
evils turned into blessings, and it was so short a
time ago that he saw no spark of joy in life. It had
been like a day when the clouds had shut away the
sun, and settled gloomily over the earth for a storm.

A shadow creeps into every human face, darkness
cowers in every home, the birds flutter in terror
from tree to tree, or nestle fearfully in their retreats.
The very brooks moan instead of babbling. Then,
suddenly the summer sun burns through the clouds
which scatter to their caves beneath the hills; the
rippling rivers glisten and sparkle like rarest jewels,
and the birds break forth in song as they mount in
ecstasy towards the sunlight. Not a human thing
but brightens into sudden gladness. So short a time
ago he thought life only a dull cheerless struggle,
that he rose in the morning heavy and disheartened,
that he lay down at night, careless if he slept forever. But suddenly the world looked like an
enchanted palace to Philip Breton, and his life
seemed as perfect as a day in paradise.

It was at three o'clock that he was to go to
Bertha, and it was only two when he was ready and
waiting in his study for this last slow hour between
him and happiness, to slip away. He looked up the
street and down again, but the streets were quite
deserted; he might have fancied the world all gone
to sleep, only he heard the roar of the waters going
over the dam. There were a thousand creatures
whose hands could never rest idle unless he chose
to grant them a holiday. Poor souls, he had done
something for them, but how little it was after all;
how many weary centuries would roll by before, by

such slow processes as his, the millions would have the heritage he had spoken of to them. Could it be Philbrick was right—that the terrible injustice the working classes suffered ought to be rectified in great acts of benevolence? Then he glanced at the clock. If he had not heard its loud ticking he would have been willing to swear the hands must have stopped. He picked up a newspaper and tried to interest himself in it. What a child he was, to be sure, not to know how to wait. Did he imagine there would be nothing more for him to wait for, after to-day? His eyes glanced impatiently down the pages. There seemed to be absolutely nothing in the paper at all; he must stop his subscription ; he might as well write to the publishers now, it would take up a little of his surplus time. But what was this odd-looking advertisement in such very black type.

Divorces obtained without trouble or publicity, for any cause desired. Address, in strictest confidence, John T. Giddings, No. 4 Errick Square, Lockout.

"Well, well," soliloquized Philip, after reading the card a second time, " our corporation counsel is come down pretty low, getting bogus divorces for a livelihood."

Then he glanced at his watch; he was out of temper with the pretty little clock. Perhaps allowing fifteen minutes for the distance to Bertha's house he might not be very much too early.

21

Philip found Bertha standing, she generally preferred to sit, and she wore an anxious look he had never seen on her face before. He thought to make her laugh.

"I suppose Mrs. Ellingsworth will not miss her chance to spoil our *tete-à-tete.*"

"She is not in town," and Bertha turned to the window again. "She went yesterday. Do you know whether she has any relatives in—in Vineboro?"

"Why that is where you—" Philip bit his lip, "no, I didn't know that she had."

He came up to where she stood, and, when she did not speak again, he tried to take her hand. But she drew away from his touch with a gesture of impatience.

"I am in no mood for foolishness." It seemed foolishness to her, then! There was a pang of pain about his heart, and then a thought struck him.

"You are not afraid of her, are you?"

She drew herself up to her full height in her old superb arrogance, and her lips curled in scorn.

"I will be afraid of no one. If I owe no one a duty I need not be afraid." She seemed to be gathering force for an instant, while her cold eyes rested on the face of the man who loved her so nobly. "I must take back my promise; I cannot marry you."

" Do you owe me nothing now then?" he pleaded in a startled voice.

" Perhaps so—yes I think I ought not to make you miserable."

" Then do not leave me; do not kill me, Bertha, after letting me hope." He had seized her hand again, but she would not let him draw her to him.

" But I should make you miserable." She dropped her eyes before his. " You would not like— like—"

" I will take all the blame then," he put his arm about her and this time she did not repel him. " I call God to witness you will not be responsible; I will forgive you everything, my darling." She was in his arms but still she held back her face from him.

" And you won't blame me; whatever happens?"

" No, oh, never." The color came back into his face; his triumphant heart sent the hot blood through every vein and artery.

" And you will remember I warned you?"

" Yes," he whispered, " and will remind you of it when you have made me the happiest man in the world. But we won't wait till Jane comes back; we will be married to-morrow."

" Oh no." Her smile was very beautiful and sweet but as cold as the river of death.

" The day after, then. Say the day after to-morrow, before anything has time to happen."

He saw her lips were forming for a ". no," but he kissed it away; and another and another, till she broke away from him with a laugh.

"Well yes, then; but you will be sorry for it to the end of your life." He made her put on her hat after tea and they went across the fields to the village cemetery.

He had stirred her by his enthusiasm to an unwonted pitch, but now she had become colder than ever and very silent. It seemed as if she were sorry for what she had promised and Philip was afraid each moment she would open her lips and take it all back. He talked very eagerly to her all the way to take up her mind, telling her all the plans he had made and how gloriously they seemed to be succeeding. She did not make much response to what he said, but he was only too glad that she did not repeat the words she had met him with in the afternoon. At last they stood by a massive pillar of granite; not broken to signify an incomplete life work, but perfect in symmetry and finished in outline. Bertha could make out in the deepening twilight the name of "Ezekiel Breton" cut deep into the everlasting stone.

"I wish my father had seen things a little differently, and could have laid the foundations of all the mills in justice and charity. He could not see that we are all men together, and the wants he had the workmen suffered too. He did what he thought was right, as do so many thousand men to-day, whose every breath means, a harder burden for the poor."

" What is the use of considering the poor? They have no gratitude, and then they are made differently from us; they have their place; let them be content with it. Your father was right."

How cold and hard her voice was, and he had seen her so enthusiastic over the wrongs of the poor.

" But they ought to have a chance to enjoy a little more of what they earn, there are so many of them." But she made no answer, and Philip's heart sank with the conviction that he must carry out his great work as he had begun it, alone. He had counted so much on her sympathy; he had felt sure of it, and he was so lonely among the grand ideas he had summoned into his soul, but perhaps it was not best for him ; a man never knows.

" My father would have been very happy to have seen us married before he died," he said gently at last, and then flushed crimson in the darkness at what he had said. There were so many subjects he must never touch, so many thoughts he must never put into words, would he ever remember them all ?

It was quite dark when he bade Bertha good-night at her gate. He had kept her hand for a moment after she would have gone, in the thrilling indulgence of the sense of possession. His heart was very full,

his hope was almost blossoming into reality, at last,
when it had seemed blighted once into despair. Only
two more days, and all the storms that might rage
could never separate them, but must only make her
dear white arms cling the closer to him. Why had
she not said to-morrow? it was almost too much to
hope that God would hold back all his thunderbolts
and all the myriad messengers of evil for two days.
The wonderful fate that had brought her back as
from death to him, that had saved her so strangely
from another meeting with the man whose voice
would melt her will, and madden her brain a second
time, made him the more afraid now. The tide
would turn, perhaps to-morrow, perhaps to-night, and
carry his darling out to sea and dash him into pieces
on the rocks.

But how cold and firm her hand was. Ah, how
glad he would have been for one little tremor in it.

" Bertha ? " he said almost piteously, " have you
nothing else for me to-night."

" I think it is all you should ask, if I don't take
back my promise." Then she seemed to be musing
for an instant. " I am sorry you like me so much,
what is there about me—"

" How are the mighty fallen." It was Mr. Ellingsworth's voice, as that gentleman sauntered toward
the two young people.

" There is something in this newspaper I have

marked for you. One of our old friends found his
level at last—Must you go this minute. Well, good
night."

It was a long time before Philip could get to sleep
that night in his great quiet house. There were so
many tender thoughts and memories, now coming
out in clear relief in his brain, now grouped with
others, and again lost in a vague sense of delight.
He remembered Bertha's attitudes and her move-
ments; he imagined how much more kindly she
might have meant than she had said, and he blessed
her that she had yielded to his prayers when he so
nearly had lost her forever. But what could she
have been afraid of, how could Jane Ellingsworth
harm her; what was there in her history worse than
he knew? Poor little girl, could there be anything
more terrible than what he had forgiven? How far
she was from knowing how wonderful a thing love
can be? Well, he might as well look at Ellingsworth's newspaper now as any time, he was not able
to sleep apparently. Who could it be had found his
level at last? Philip struck a match and lit the gas.
Then he fumbled in his pockets and finding the
newspaper at last, unfolded it, looking for the marked
paragraph. It was not in the editorials, nor in the
locals. Philip turned the inner pages out, nor in the
political news. It couldn't be an advertisement,
yes—it was this.

Divorces obtained without trouble or publicity for any cause desired. Address in strictest confidence, John T. Giddings, No. 4 Errick Square, Lockout.

" The idea," laughed Philip to himself, " of my getting up to read his card in another paper. I hope I shall never hear of him again now."

CHAPTER XXVI.

What are We waiting for?

THE bay span were tossing their heads impatiently at the gate, and still the young bridegroom delayed in his house. It was the evening he was to be married, and when he entered the arched doorway again, Bertha would be with him. So he must make one final tour of his home, to see if there was any last finishing stroke of work necessary to make it worthy of his beautiful bride. He found all his servants, the new graceful maid to wait upon the door, the portly butler to wait upon the table, and all; and instructed them carefully in their duties. The intricate domestic mechanism must work with not one jar or rattle to disturb the new mistress. He went into the drawing-room and looked about him. The grand piano that had been closed and locked so long was open, and music placed on the rack as if it were but yesterday that Bertha had sat before it. He remembered how her round white arm had out-dazzled the ivory key-board, the last time he had seen her here. The chintz covers had been removed from the furniture, whose blue damask upholstery

seemed fairly smiling with delight to have escaped
from its mask.   In the embrasure of the window
looking out to the street where the three laborers
had stood the evening our story commences, lay a
little volume of exquisite engravings as if some ad-
mirer had just put it down.   Philip glanced at the
page where it was open.   It was a Magdalene, and a
shadow passed over his face at the suggestion.   He
turned a few leaves, and spread the volume open
again, this time it was " Marguerita."   Impatiently
he closed the book which seemed to have no beautiful picture but it would insult his bride.   Then he
went out and crossed the broad hall into the library.

This room he had completely changed since his
father's death, and when his house became a home
again he could begin to enjoy it.   The modern iron
grate was taken away, and a great old fashioned fireplace had been made for burning logs of wood instead of little blocks of coal.   The andirons were two
bronze dragons who looked deadliest hate at each
other across the fireplace.   Above the mantel as
broad as the chimney, was an oblong recess, faced
with bronze panels, and on each the head of one of
the heroes of literature, in bas-relief.   Below each
head was an open volume showing the title-page of
his greatest work, and a keen eye could read written
in everlasting bronze the first few lines.   In the space

at the bottom of the recess, just inside the mantel was a censer of exquisite workmanship in yellow bronze. The furnishing of the room was of the strictest simplicity, the floor and the tables and chairs were of inlaid natural woods. Not one inch of upholstery could be found. On the walls hung paintings of the spots most famous in literature. Besides the books that filled the cases, there was a great standing portfolio, full of all the choicest engravings necessary for a school of art. And sculpture had a symbol in a bust of the first Napoleon, who seemed mighty enough even in marble to make the kings of all Christendom tremble again. Philip felt satisfied with the shrine he had built; the very air of the place seemed of finer quality than outside.

He had not made the slightest change in the study—his father's room—where he had learned too to fight out his spiritual battles. It would be a profanation to alter one feature of the room; it should be always as it was the day Ezekiel Breton died. Philip opened the door and looked in for a moment, then with a full heart he made his way up the oaken stairs. The room he next entered was furnished in the shade of blue that Bertha loved best, the silk upholstered lounge that made one drowsy to look at it, the sleepy-hollow easy chair, the dressing table and toilet-set. Over the windows hung lambrequins of a darker tint, softened again, however, in the flowing curtains below. Even the drop-lamp had a blue porcelain shade so that no such thing as white light should ever enter Bertha's boudoir. Philip imagined her sitting in the easy chair lifting her eyes wonderingly to him, her husband, who never grew tired of telling her she was beautiful ; or he pictured her asleep on the lounge one white hand by her side, the other beneath her cheek. How much of his thoughts were vague dreaming? Could it be she was at last to be his ; lighting the gloomy old house with the radiance of her presence? All his other life faded in his memory, in the brightness of his joy in her. It seemed a small thing to him that he had lifted a thousand lives into a new plane of existence— that he had given hope to a thousand desperate hearts—compared with the hope of making this one woman happy and of living in her smiles.

But he suddenly started from his fond revery, and passed into another room, all as white as some cave in a mountain of snow. The mantel was of marble, the curtains cloud-like masses of snowy lace ; and even the upholstery of the chairs, and the carpet was white damask. His heart beat fast as he stood for a moment in the chamber, then he went softly out and locked the door behind him, so that no foot should cross its sacred threshold till its mistress came.

It was to be a very quiet wedding—no guests, no

cards, no banquet. The shortest and simplest form that could make a man and woman one was enough. But the hour was past, and yet there was no wedding; the bride, all dressed, waited to be called from her room; the young bridegroom paced to and fro across the parlor floor. There was no minister.

The clock struck the half hour. It was half past eight. Mr. Ellingsworth sat in the parlor, reading the evening paper in unbroken tranquillity. Philip was wondering where Jane could be; whether she was indeed preparing a terrible blow for the white bosom of his bride. What could she do? it was only Bertha's nervousness that made her afraid. Why, for his part, he had every reason to be pleased with the state of affairs, for if Bertha had not been frightened, she would not have consented to such a sudden marriage.

"Ah! I think I hear the carriage," remarked Mr. Ellingsworth, laying aside his paper with a little yawn.

"From which direction?" asked Philip, listening eagerly, while the feverish blood rushed into his face.

Mr. Ellingsworth went to the window. "Why, from both directions. It sounds to me like two carriages. I will go out and see."

Philip hurried to the window and raised it, but it was pitch-dark; he could see nothing. Who could be in that second carriage? He waited to be

called, but no one came for him. He heard the
doors open and shut, and indistinguishable voices,
but no one called him. Then he made his way out
into the hall, in vague terror. He thought of his
bride waiting up stairs, and set his teeth for the
worst. No earthly power, no vileness of calumny,
no shameful disclosures should move him. His
bride waited for him, ready to be his when he called
for her. Ah! he would not shame her, though all
hell hissed at her. But how fanciful he was; he
could hear the mild mannered minister talking in his
polite tones. He caught his complacent laugh.
Thank God for it. Nothing could have happened.
He walked along the hall; the voices came from the
dining-room; there was the minister's laugh again.
He pushed open the door and went in.

The minister rose, with the especial deference for
wealth that marks many of the priests of God, and
gave the young man's hand an affectionate squeeze.
"No doubt Mr. Breton is ready. It is the bride-
grooms who should always be impatient. I believe
I am right, am I not, Mrs. Ellingsworth?"

Mrs. Ellingsworth—Philip started violently and
the color left his face. She had returned in time
then.

"Not always," she smiled strangely and reached
out her hand to Philip. It was but a woman's hand
small and velvety, but he touched it as if there were

a dagger in its white palm.   He knew by the look
of evil triumph in her face, that she had not been
away for nothing.   Could it be there was anything
worse than he had forgiven already—some page of
Bertha's life so black no depth of love could cover
it?   A deathly faintness was upon him.

"I have brought two visitors," she went on;
showing the tips of her white teeth in a beautiful
smile.

To be sure, there sat a portly woman with the
slightly elevated chin of a certain variety of the sex
when on its dignity.   But Jane said "two "—where
was the other?   Ah, the other was in the woman's
lap.   It was a baby.   Mr. Ellingsworth had a very
peculiar expression on his face to-night, as if his wife
was disappointing him.   It was rather of a dangerous look if Jane had understood it.   She was offend-
ing his elegant tastes extremely by bringing to his
house a vulgar fussy old woman and her baby whom
she, no doubt, had picked up on the railroad cars.
Philip stood nervously fumbling his watch chain, and
waiting for a blow to fall on him, he did not know
whence.

It was a little baby's hand that caught at Philip's
arm, and he turned to look into its great star-like
blue eyes.   He had seen that same marvelous tint in
cheeks before, and a cold horror of recognition
darted through his soul.   He tried to lift his spell-

bound eyes, and they rested instead on the face of Jane Ellingsworth, which was lit up with a fiendish exultation as she held the child up to him.

" What—not kiss the baby ? " she laughed gayly, " Such a pretty baby, too, why it really has com. plexion and eyes like Bertha's." She did not cease to look at his shrinking face. " But its mouth and chin—" Something made him look at the baby's features as she mentioned them, and then he shuddered ; it was too horrible, " are more like somebody else I know." Her small flashing black eyes seemed burning their way to his very brain. " Who is it ? " She bent toward him so that her hot lips seemed almost to kiss his ear. " Curran " she whispered. Could he not tear himself away from her poisonous breath. " Not so strange though ? " She let the baby put its chubby hands into his hair, though she saw every touch was a thrust through the quivering fibres of his heart. She fancied he did not understand, he was so still and silent. " Not so strange that a child should look like its— father."

Had the young bridegroom forgotten all about his wedding and the beautiful woman up stairs wondering why she was not called ? It seemed so, for he sat down, and they foisted the pretty baby on him, and his face wore a ghastly smile as he looked at it. Once, at an expression in the little face, he caught it to his lips, but as suddenly he thrust the child into the nurse's lap, and rose to his feet.

" What are we waiting for?" His face was like marble for firmness, and it seemed as dead.

Jane drew him quickly into the hall. " You are not going to marry the mother of that—"

" Hush," and her woman's soul quailed at the look he bent on her. " If you dare to whisper a word to Bertha, or show her that child—"

" I thought you would thank me," whispered the false lips. She saw it was all in vain—her journey to Vineboro. She had followed Bertha's tracks like a bloodhound, and had found her fatherless child in a stranger's home, learning to forget its high-bred mother. Now surely she must suffer repulse and disdain as the poor factory girl had suffered it—in her very wedding dress. For the sight of this baby face would chill the most ardent love that ever burned in a bridegroom's heart.—But no. This man's love was deeper than the sentiment and vanity that commonly makes the chief part of what is absurdly called passion. His faith was so sublime, shame was ashamed before it.

His face had lighted up at her words. "Oh I will thank you a thou—a thousand times if you will send that woman and the child away."

He had taken her hands. " Jane, for God's sake do it."

22

He would have given her a fortune, but she had sold herself once, and her price was enough. He could only pray to her in all the phrases of entreaty the agonies of life have taught mankind.

"They shall leave the house at once," she said at last as she turned to go back into the room. He thought his prayers had moved her. But she knew her plot had failed; she had wrung his heart but his will was unmoved. She made a virtue of her necessity. Philip would be grateful to her forever, but there would be something else, perhaps. Such hate as hers could not be turned aside by so feeble a thing as pity.

"How pale you are, Philip. Are you afraid?" and Bertha smiled royally on him as she took his arm, and they passed up the hall.

"I am the happiest man in the world," and he tried to smile as his hand closed over her fingers like an iron vise, it was so cold and strong.

But how sad he was, as if an exquisite piece of sculpture that he loved had fallen from a great height and been shivered into a thousand fragments. The hope and joy of his life seemed slipping away from him. That little child's face hung between him and the bride who was promising to be faithful— if she only had been faithful to him; its baby hands seemed to shield her bosom from him, its quavering cries to reproach him for daring to kiss its mother.

So small and sweet a baby, but its face seemed threatening him, its infant form linked indissolubly a past he had hoped he might forget with a present and future he had foolishly thought had a great store of happiness for him.

The minister had taken his seat. Was he really married to the golden-haired woman whose hand he held so tightly? Was this the moment he had dreamed of as marking his entrance into a new ideal life? Had he said everything correctly? He could not remember, but he did not want any mistake made about this at least. Oh yes, it was now he was to kiss his wife. He held her to his heart an instant. This was his wife, but joy was dead behind his dry, feverish lips, and his smile, meant to cheer her, was as if some terrible pain was gnawing every moment at his heart. But Bertha appeared to notice nothing wrong.

The train which bore away the bridal pair had not traveled a great many miles, when something caused Philip to look in the seat behind them. There sat the portly woman with her chin at last depressed in slumber, and the baby with Bertha's eyes and Curran's mouth. One of Bertha's coils of hair had become loosened, and a braid of golden hair hung over the back of the seat as she let her head rest on her husband's shoulder. Bertha's eyes were closed drowsily, the nurse in the seat behind nodded in her dreams, but the child reached out its baby hands to play with its mother's golden tresses. The young husband watched the child's lips forming again and again one word, " mamma," the wife fell asleep and dreamed she was the happiest woman in the world, while beneath her head every throb of the man's heart was an ache.

CHAPTER XXVII.

One Short Hour.

IT was a week later that the Breton barouche came over the brow of the hill toward Mr. Ellingsworth's house. The bay span never stepped so proudly, and certainly the gold-plated trimmings on their harness never glittered so brightly before. As the carriage had passed through the lower village the factory girls had all rushed to the windows to see the master and his bride, and for the moment the laborers on the foundations of the new mill stopped their work in one accord, and were all eyes till the bridal couple were out of sight. Philip's face was fairly radiant with hope and love, and he could not teach his eyes to look anywhere but at Bertha. She glanced idly on either side, at the white-gloved coachman on his high seat, or at the prancing horses, anywhere but into the earnest tender face, which might have been a constant reproach to her calm indifference.

Clearly enough, the clouds that had settled so gloomily about his wedding night had lifted ; his love and the sweet reality of his present life and his new sense of duty toward the woman who now called him husband, all helped him to put away her past, even to its most terrible incident, and his healthful mental nature was rapidly building up a new life which should have no taint in it. Philip Breton made a noble lover. Perhaps it was because he was not a great man. He was not so wise but that he believed in the reality of the sunbeams poets make their love songs of. He had many holy aspirations, he caught now and then glimpses of ideal beauty and truth. In some vague way he fancied all these were realized in Bertha. In her he loved all the harmonies. In her he worshipped purity and charity and all the graces.

As for Bertha, she continually found new surprises in his gentleness and in his devotion—surprises partly because she forgot them each time. She really wished he were not so devoted. She wished he did not make her feel as if she were forever posing in tableaux. She thought him inclined to be foolish, because he did not seem keen-eyed enough to see her most obvious faults, not magnanimous enough herself to understand that he looked at her through a halo of glory his love had put about her. In spite of herself he could see something beautiful and good in everything she could do or say.

"We are just passing my home," she said a little petulantly, "can't you see anything but me?"

" This is not your home now, my dear." He corrected her very gently. As he glanced into the windows of the parlor where they had been married, Jane Ellingsworth's dark face looked out at them, cruel and malevolent. Philip started forward in his seat. Why, no, he must have been wrong, the face in the window was wreathed in the most charming smiles. She even kissed her fingers to the bridal pair and let a sheet of paper she had been holding flutter to the floor in her child-like enthusiasm. Bertha nodded coldly, Philip lifted his silk hat, and the carriage passed on out of sight.

Philip was too wise to weary his wife just now by showing her all the changes in his home, which would delight her so much, later. He knew by her drooping step, as she walked along the hall, that she was tired and would appreciate rest above all things. So he took her first to her own little sitting room, which he called her boudoir. He had rather expected a little lighting up of her eyes, perhaps some pretty exclamation of pleasure. Possibly he had made an absurd artistic blunder. Could it be he had got the wrong shade of blue after all? She only threw off her bonnet and sat down in the least inviting of the chairs without seeming to care to look about her at all.

" You must be tired, Bertha," said Philip at last, trying to hide the disappointment that made his heart swell so oddly. "Won't you sit in the easy chair? I am sure you will like it, though perhaps you would rather lie down."

"Oh, no, I am not tired," she said carelessly, without turning her eyes to look at him where he stood, restlessly playing with the window curtains. He pulled roughly at them, he longed that moment to ruin the beauty that had failed to please her. He could not see where the fault was; the carpet was as thick and soft as a bed of violets, the light seemed delicate almost as some perfume, but Bertha did not seem to care for anything he had devised for her. He bit his lip to keep down the inner pain. She was going to speak; if she would only criticise, he would change everything again to win a smile of approval from her. She might at least understand how much he had tried to please her.

"Where does that door open?"

"I will show you if you are not tired," yet he dreaded to take her into that room, and see her as cold and indifferent as she was now. He felt it would break his heart.

She rose to her feet, and looked in curiosity at him as he took a key from his breast pocket, and turned it in the lock. "Is it your treasure chamber?"

"Yes," he whispered, and threw open the door, and stood back for her to enter. The room seemed as pure and white as if a thousand angels brooded over it with their snowy wings. Peace and holy rapture seemed breathing from the very walls, and the young bride felt a new timidity steal over her heart. She was awed indescribably in the temple of love he had made for her. Poor soul! would there be but one true worshiper? "Come," she said, and she smiled more sweetly than he had ever seen her. She held her hand out toward him, as he lingered on the threshold.

He came and took her hand, and then put his arm about her as she stood in exquisite pensiveness, struggling to take in the meaning of the place. She had cast her eyes down on the carpet, which seemed like the driven snow, sparkling with hail-drops. The solemn beauty of her chamber subdued her like a child.

"You would not dare to kiss me here, Philip," she said at last in a voice so gentle and thrilling, it seemed to his throbbing heart as if a new soul had been born within her. "It is so pure and—"

But he drew her unresisting form into his arms, and kissed her full cool lips again and again, and she did not stir on his shoulder, but her great blue eyes looked a startled reproach at his ardor.

"There is no place too pure for the kisses I have for you."

There will never be an hour in Philip Breton's

after life, when he shall not look back to this moment, as worth all the agony, as the acme of his being—when the cup of his happiness was full.   And
who should overturn it ? Why should he not hold it to
his ever thirsty lips forever, the well-spring of his love
bubbling and sparkling forever within ? Might not
the world stand still awhile ? Must it jostle him from
his unwearying rapture, and push him on and on
into the barren desert of failure which awaits all
mankind at last ?

The dinner bell tinkled invitingly, and the master and mistress of the house came down together.
At the door of the dining-room stood the man
servant, salver in hand, and the silk skirts of the
lady of the house swept against him as she passed
in.   Philip frowned fiercely at him, for the usually
most well behaved and respectful waiter seemed to
forget all his duties in staring with brazen impudence
in the beautiful face of his master's wife.   Philip
grew pale with anger, but Bertha only gave a glance
of lofty contempt at the fellow's smooth face and
white apron.

" Your servants are not well behaved, my dear
Philip."

In a moment more they were alone, and Philip
forgot his wrath in the new picture of his wife across
his table.   His old lonely days were ended, no more
solitary feastings.   Bertha was always to brighten

his house and his table for him. The satyr or bronze
on the mantel that had scowled on his desolation,
seemed actually smiling now. The portraits around
the green tinted walls had seemed to his imagination, as he had sat down so many times to his richly
furnished table, like guests at a funeral, or again, as
if morosely curious how a man could violate all the
principles of hospitality by dining alone. Now, he
fancied they had taken on a more genial, compan-
ionable expression. To be sure the sun poured in
through the open blinds in unusual brightness, but
it was the light in Bertha's blue eyes that changed
everything for him. It was the beginning of his own
home ; this woman who seemed too lovely to be
other than a caller for an hour, had come to stay,
to sit with him as she did now, whenever he break-
fasted or dined or supped—always. The world
might heap wrongs and outrage on him, his factories burn and his wealth dissolve—she whose presence in itself was a perfect existence to him, had
come to him to stay forever.

Bertha's face was bent over the table studying
the odd device on her napkin ring. The sunlight
flickered in her golden hair as tenderly as if it were
giving her kisses of welcome. So she would sit
before him always. But the sudden creaking of a
man's boot made him look up. The waiter had
come in almost noiselessly and stood at the side-

board carving a bird for their second course.　Philip
was glad he had not said one of the hundred caressing words that had come to his lips, he remembered
the look on the fellow's face at the door.　But how
slow he was at his carving ; was the canvas-back so
tough, then ?

Ugh—there was a glass in the side-board, and
Philip happened to glance into it.　The man held
the knife and fork in his hands, but he was not carving at all, but was still staring at Bertha's bent beautiful face in the mirror, with his evil swine-like eyes.
He seemed to be studying her features as if to recall
some association—oh, he had succeeded, a hideous
grin distorted his mouth, and whole face, when Philip
rose and pushed back his chair.　His servant recognized her, apparently she had played some very in-
harmonious part in some previous scene he had wit-
nessed.　And he was but one of the world she had
disgraced herself before.　What could his evil eyes
have seen—which miserable page in this lovely
woman's history, that her husband was trying to blot
out of memory?　If he could forgive her, might not
the rest ?　Must she be subject to insult in her own
home?　Was he not powerful enough to protect her
against the shame of such looks as this fellow gave
her ?

He had stepped to the side-board and touched
his servant on the shoulder, and beckoned him to

the door. The malicious grin had hardly time to vanish from the frightened face.

" Go ! " the words came hissing from his master's lips, " and if I ever see your face again, or if you ever breathe a word against the woman I have made my wife—" The man slunk up stairs like a whipped dog.

" Why, I didn't notice you had been out," said Bertha in mild surprise as Philip re-entered the dining-room, " were you ill ? how pale you are."

But she did not rise in her solicitude and come to him. Instead, he came to her, and bent very gently over her, and tried to kiss away the lines of care on her white forehead, which he had never caused. He did his best to smile gayly, and succeeded well enough to deceive her.

" I will be your servant to-day," he said, " with no profane eyes to look on."

Then he shook off his unhappiness by sheer force of will, and began to talk lover's nonsense to the cold mistress of his home, in more perfect abandon than ever, even in the exuberance of his youth. He must be happy while he could, he dared not stop talking, lest he should think too much. But she only looked at him in far off surprise, with now and then a curious, not quite pleased smile, at his absurdities. At last, all too soon, she arose.

" I must go and dress, and try and look a little

prettier, for to-day at least." She touched his
shoulder kindly as she passed out into the hall, leaving him sitting still at table.

It was only then that he discovered a letter that
had been concealed by a plate. But what did he
care for business to-day? Still it might serve to pass
a little of the time, till his wife should return. How
the thought of her warmed his heart. In a few moments the door behind him would open, and he
would turn to see her graceful form on the threshold. She would be dressed in some new color, or
perhaps in black that gave her the air of a de-
throned queen. By this time she must have thought
of some kind thing to say to him, but first it
would be,

" Sitting at table yet ? " Then he would rise and
draw her jeweled hand through his arm and show her
through her whole home. She would be so delighted
with the library ; he was sure everything there would
please her exquisite taste. He had never enjoyed the
room, though it was so perfect ; there had been something dreary to him in its classic simplicity. But
now everything would be changed. Then he would
lead her to the drawing-room, and would make her
sit down again before the long-silent piano, which
had given out not one tone of music since her white
fingers had last caressed its glistening keys. And
she would play and sing for him while he dreamed

of the new rare life of beauty and peace that was to be his henceforth.

He glanced at the face of the envelope; but it was not for a moment more, that the mist of joy cleared from before his eyes enough to read the words stamped on its upper corner.

" John T. Giddings, Attorney at Law," and beneath in smaller type, " Divorces procured without trouble or publicity for any cause desired." What was he or his business to Philip Breton? He tore open the envelope impatiently; probably a begging letter. He unfolded the sheet he found within. At the top in big letters the attorney's name and address; and below the advertisement about divorces again. Philip frowned and began to read what the man had written to him.

" DEAR SIR :—I understand you will have just returned from your *wedding* journey when this reaches you. I am sorry to interrupt your bliss but it will be very important for you to call upon me immediately upon your receipt of this communication. You may wonder how my advertisement about *Divorces* which your observant eyes will have detected at the top of this page can concern you. If you call on me at once I will be able to explain that and several other points of interest to you. Very truly yours,

JOHN T. GIDDINGS.

Philip spread the letter open on the table cloth
before him, and read it again and more carefully.
He seemed very slow to take its meaning. Then he
folded it very accurately and put it in his pocket-
book. He rose to his feet and rang the bell for the
maid. How cool he was; he showed no sign of
having received a terrible blow, unless it was by
passing his hand wearily across his forehead once or
twice.

The clearest feeling he was conscious of was a
nervous anxiety lest Bertha should come in upon
him just now; and when the door opened he started
violently. But it was only the maid who had answered his summons.

"Tell your mistress," his voice was very low but
it sounded firm enough, "tell your mistress I am
called away to Lockout. I shall be back by tea
time, at six, I suppose. Can you find my hat for
me, Jane, I mean Annie. Thank you." He pulled
it well over his eyes, and walked along the hall and
opened the door. He did not like to glance up the
oaken staircase, for fear he might see Bertha. He
dreaded to look in her face just now. The maid
stood waiting.

"Tell your mistress that I am called—oh, I told
you, did I?"

CHAPTER XXVIII.

A Legal Distinction.

"AH, Mr. Breton, yes, yes, I was sure you would come."

The lawyer pulled two chairs together near his office table. John T. Giddings had changed a great deal since the time when he undertook to engineer the corporation scheme. Apparently he was going down hill very fast, without brakes. His eyes wore a glassy look, as if he had just waked from a drunken sleep, the smooth roundness of his cheeks was gone, his lower jaw was strongly marked, and his nose seemed drawn out and sharpened to give the effect of a bird of prey. Philip glanced significantly about the room. The lawyer followed his eyes and laughed.

"Changed some aren't we—all, lack of money. Actually, you have no idea how ten dollars even would furbish up this old table and polish this floor. Times aint as they were, Mr. Breton, in the old days when I used to get fat fees out of men like your father. Nice man, your father. But," and he leered meaningly at his visitor, "when we do get a chance for a dollar I tell you we jump at it." He tipped back his chair against his half-filled book shelves and peered familiarly into Philip's stern face. "Why look at those dirty fellows back by the door. Time was I wouldn't notice a client unless he wore white collar and cuffs. But now for business. I suppose you were a little astonished to get my letter?"

"I should prefer not to have listeners," remarked Philip, coldly.

"Oh, well, I will finish with these fellows first, then. I thought you might be impatient."

"Not at all, sir."

The lawyer's clothes were threadbare and soiled, and the black felt hat that he wore, indoors and out, well slouched over his eyes, was torn in the crown. Philip compared him with his shabby-looking callers, and could not see but the clients looked as well as their patron. But at every sign of poverty and degradation his heart sank lower and lower, for the man must be reckless and hungry as a man-eating shark. If it lay in his power to rack the life out of a victim —the man could have no restraint of character or decency to hold back his hand. Could there be anything he knew about Bertha's past, that terrible gap Philip had not tried to look into? He dared not think. Impatient! he dreaded the moment when the lawyer should send away his soiled clients. Philip started each time he half turned, as if to come back. But when Giddings closed the door after the poor wretches, which was not until a little roll of bills had passed from their hands to his, and came back to his seat, the young mill-owner did not seem to observe him till the lawyer said,

" I have filled out a complaint but have not signed it yet."

Philip looked at him blankly. " What is a complaint?"

" Well, my dear sir, a man of your position might pass a lifetime and never know, ahem. It is a form of procedure that is generally understood to be applicable only to the poor. When a wretch has committed a burglary, for instance, some friend of justice, as I for example, goes before a magistrate and makes certain charges. Then the poor devil is arrested, dragged before the court and tried."

" Well, sir, what are your complaints to me?"

The lawyer smiled. " Strictly, nothing, unless you identify yourself with a woman calling herself Bertha Breton." He paused to notice the effect of his words.

" My wife," gasped Philip, " oh, for God's sake, speak quick."

" You have been lately married?"

" A week ago."

" The woman you have married has a husband already. By remarrying as she has done she has committed a felony by our laws. Some rather inaccurately call her crime bigamy. A states prison offence I suppose you know—I mean for her. The law of our state does not touch you."

"But she told me she was free to marry." How far off his voice sounded. Was it he, indeed, in a low attorney's office, discussing his wife whether she were a felon or no. It was like a horrible dream, too horrible to be anything but a dream, but he could not awake from it.

"No doubt she thought so," said the lawyer charitably, "but let me show you." He opened a drawer in front of him, and took out a long paper. "Isn't it odd, women have no notion of folding a legal document correctly. Did you ever notice it?"

"No, I never noticed it," answered Philip mechanically. He felt as if he were standing still, and the world was flying from under his feet.

"This is the marriage certificate. It is proper in form, you will see."

Yes, it seemed correct. Bertha's name was there, and Curran's; they seemed to leap out of the parchment as he read. And there were two witnesses. He rubbed his eyes, "Thomas Bailes"—that was the name of the servant he had turned away. Yes, it was not an hour ago he turned him away.

"Who is this Thomas Bailes?"

"He was a waiter at the 'Lockout House,' where the happy couple were made one."

The paper fluttered to the floor, the walls of the room seemed rushing in upon him, while the grinning face of the lawyer danced in hideous measure before his eyes. Was God, in his mercy, sending him death? When his brain cleared again the man was talking still.

"You will wonder how I happen to possess this paper, but you will recollect my advertisement at the top of my letter head? Well it seemed Mrs. Curran, excuse me, grew tired of her uncongenial husband, quite outside her sphere of course. A fine fellow that Curran was too. But the young lady naturally sighed for her old more refined associations. Her husband does nothing but shock her. She becomes wretched, her craze is over, the reality is not to her delicate taste at all. What next? She leaves him, fortune throws my advertisement in her way and I receive a letter from her address, then at Vineboro. Here was a short way out of it all, a divorce without trouble or publicity, for any cause desired. She would be free as air again, free to end her life, as she no doubt intended, in conventual retirement."

Giddings threw his feet upon the table, and smiled very slyly. "I undertook her suit. What better cause could there be than incompatibility. Oh, no, she need not come to Lockout, so there was no trouble, and as to publicity, why, will you believe it—" and the lawyer winked horribly at his visitor, "Curran himself was within twenty miles of Lockout during the pendency of the suit, and he never guessed his wife was being divorced from him, and I don't believe he knows it to this day, ha, ha." And he laid his head back on his chair and laughed till the tears ran down his face.

"But you procured her a divorce." It is almost worth pain to have the exquisite delight that comes with relief.

Philip felt ashamed that he had distrusted God so much. How much more joyfully he could cherish his wife than before. There was no blot of shame on her sweet name ; there was no page in her life the whole world might not look at then. And this man wanted a reward for what he had done, aye, and he should have it. There was no gift too great for him, who had turned this young husband's bitterest memories sweet, who had made his life and his love like that of other men. He reached forward, and grasped the lawyer's oily hand in hearty good will.

Gidding's stared at him in silence a moment. Then he moved uneasily in his chair and released his hand,

"I guess you don't understand," he had enough of his manhood left to hesitate, it was actually a more disagreeable business than he had counted on. "Such secret convenient divorces as I get, don't

stand in our courts. The whole thing is bogus, my
dear sir." Philip's face had become like a dead man's.
"Issued by the Supreme Juridical court of Utah—
it says on them, but there is no such court, and as for
the seal I keep in this little drawer. Besides, if there
were such a court, and its genuine seal were stamped
on a decree of divorce, it would amount to nothing
when both parties live in this state. Our state
makes its own decrees. Utah decrees, or the decrees
of any foreign state or territory are void here. Your
wife is Curran's wife yet ; she is as much married to
him to-day, as she has been at all."

"How am I to know but what you are lying to
me ?"

The attorney handed him over a file of letters
with a shrug of his shoulders. "You need not wade
through them all, the last is conclusive, I think you
will agree with me."

"MR. GIDDINGS :—*Dear Sir :*—I received this
morning, the divorce from the Supreme Juridical
Court of Utah, and you will find enclosed a draft for
the second half of the three hundred dollars agreed
upon. Of course I have to rely wholly on your assurance that my divorce is complete, and that I have
a right to resume my maiden name. I thank you
for the quiet way in which you have managed it. I
did not suppose it could be done so easily. I only
wonder Mr. Curran has taken it so calmly, he

seemed almost wild when I first left him. Yours
gratefully,   BERTHA ELLINGSWORTH."

Yes, there was no doubt about it.   It was Bertha's handwriting ; no forgery could have deceived
her lover's eyes.   How little she fancied he would
ever be reading it over, and cursing the first hour he
had ever looked on her dear face.   He watched the
attorney put it back on file again.   It seemed a des-
ecration to lay one of her notes in the stained, tin
box, with the ignoble company of lying and suppli-
ant letters.

" She seems to have relied completely on some
assurance of yours, that her divorce would be good."
Philip tried to speak calmly to this man, who held
his darling's fate in the hollow of his hand, but his
voice trembled, and almost broke.

"You are not well," exclaimed the lawyer, and
he opened another drawer in his desk, and drew out
a square shaped, yellow covered bottle. " Take a
swallow of this."

Philip clutched at it eagerly. He thought now he
could understand how a man might want to drown
all pride and sense in drunkenness. He poured the
crude stuff down his parched throat, as if it were
water. One swallow was not enough, nor two, but
when he set the bottle upon the table at last, the
lawyer resumed,

" And so it would have been good. nine times out of ten, good enough to make all parties concerned comfortable. A document is a document to most people, a seal is a seal. As a man thinketh, so is he. Parties divorced by my fiat alone, re-marry and raise children, and are as happy and clear of conscience as if they were not committing a sin every hour of their lives, unless it happens to come out."

" This has come out, I suppose, and Lockout is all agog with it." Philip's heart stopped beating while he waited for his answer.

" No, my dear sir, another mistake ; no one under heaven knows of it but me, and you now." Breton must have taken him for a fool.

Philip started from his chair like lightning. "Thank God, then Bertha is safe yet."

But Giddings attempted to look very stern. " Did you suppose I made out that complaint for nothing ? She is rich and beautiful and proud, no doubt, but the same law hangs over her as the rest of us. No one knows of her crime yet, but before the sun sets," the attorney rose, and cautiously put the table between himself and his guest, whose eyes seemed to him to gleam dangerously, " but before the sun sets," he continued, watching the other closely, " an officer with a warrant will call at your front door."

Philip lifted his chair high in the air, and brought it down like a trip-hammer, where Giddings had stood.   But the dextrous attorney had dodged aside, and left the chair to break into splinters over the table.

"Scoundrel, will you come with handcuffs and billets to take away my darling wife from my arms, for following your lying counsels? Is that your law?   Does it choose such ministers as you to break up peaceful homes, and shut behind bars a woman as innocent as an angel?"

Philip was advancing toward him when Giddings suddenly threw up the window and leaning out shouted to a policeman. Then he looked back to Philip.

"Another step—and your wife goes to jail."

"I won't touch you," and Philip folded his arms across his breast, while the red blood forsook his face at the threat. He was in this contemptible creature's power; he might grind his teeth at him; he must obey him.

"You seem very obtuse, Mr. Breton," explained the lawyer, from a respectful distance. "I have no ill-will toward Mrs. Breton, a very modest, and I may add—"

"As sure as there is a God, if you speak of her so, I will throw you from the window. Your secret will die with you then."

The lawyer smiled unhealthily. "I want money, that is all there is to it. You are rich—Mrs. Breton—well, well, don't be angry. In a word, I want to be paid to keep my secret."

Philip cast a glance of ineffable contempt at him. Then he put his hands behind him and walked slowly across the room. The price of life, of honor, of liberty, no money could measure it, but what trust could he rest in the fidelity of so base a creature as this? He would suck his blood forever, and forever cry for more; he would learn that his victim would make himself a beggar to save this woman, and he would beggar him without shame. He might not stop with money favors; he might require to be made his companion; to be invited to his table, and presented to his friends; to be godfather to his children; and at last in anger at his victim's incurable hate, or in some drunken debauch, the spy, who had embittered his life with daily humiliation, might bring or call down on him the ruin he had feared so long. His life-long slavery would have been in vain. Better a dungeon—no, Bertha must not be sacrificed. He turned on his heel and stopped before his tormentor,

"How much do you want?"

His glassy eye brightened. "Oh, I would not be too hard just because I have got the whip-hand of you. Say two hundred, and your secret is safe."

" For how long ? " sneered Philip.

" Forever," answered Giddings, with virtuous decision. " I swear before God I will never ask another penny of you ; and your secret shall die with me."

Philip had taken out his pocket-book. He found a fifty dollar bill; then he drew a check for one hundred and fifty dollars. The poor lawyer eyed the money with a great tenderness; his heart softened at sight of it, and the love of approbation, that never dies out of even the most degraded souls, stirred in his.

" I aint so bad a fellow, after all," he said, as he took up the money ; " I know lots of men who in my place wouldn't have let you off for less than a cool thousand."

" Your circle of friends must be very select." Philip was moving towards the door.

" To be sure, to be sure," but somehow the lawyer kept close to him, " I couldn't help feeling sorry for you ; and then your wife is such a nice woman ; it never seemed to me jails were made for such as she—"

" Stop your driveling," cried Philip, turning on him so suddenly the man fancied at first he had been struck, "keep your blood money ; but don't dare to breathe her name, even in your prayers."

The lawyer chuckled to himself when the door

closed behind his wealthy client. "I suppose I have considerable grit."

Then he pocketed the bill and scrutinized the check. "But I was almost too easy with him. Some fellows, now, would have just bled him."

CHAPTER XXIX.

The White Chamber.

THE five o'clock train drew up at the Bretonville station and the young husband alighted a
changed man. The brick walls of his mills looked
strangely unfamiliar to him. Was he indeed the
owner of them? Was that his house set like a
castle on the hill off to the left? It seemed impossible that any of his old acquaintances should recognize him, but here somebody was shaking hands
with him.

"What, so soon away from your young wife?"

"Business," muttered Philip, breaking away from
him impatiently. How the man's simple blue eyes
would start out of their sockets if he guessed what
the business had been. How he would regale his
eager family with the infamous story, and sleep more
complacently that night for the sudden calamity that
had fallen on the rich man's home, while he was safe
and his home spotless.

Another acquaintance drew Philip's hand through
his arm before he could reach his carriage. "Something very confidential," he whispered mysteriously.

Then Philip had bribed the greedy lawyer to keep a secret he had already feasted the whole country on. He glanced around him with a new hunted look in his face. He fancied he saw a peculiar expression in the eyes of the bystanders. Some of them appeared to avoid looking at him.

" It is this." Philip held his breath and the man laughed at his humor. "One would think you were scared to death. I was only going to say my wife and I want to call to-morrow on your charming bride."

" By all means," Philip answered huskily, and threw himself into his carriage. He had nothing to fear from this man at least, he clearly enough had not heard the news. People don't call on—it was too terrible! He let down the carriage window for fresh air. The village policeman stood by the roadside talking to a stranger. As the carriage passed they spoke of Breton apparently, and laughed. The man must be a detective, armed with the authority to break into his home and carry away his wife. They would shut her in the dock crowded close by murderers and foul-mouthed thieves. The court-house galleries would be packed with ruffians to stare at her sweet, frightened face, and her high bred friends would sit below and look insolent disdain at her and wonder how they ever escaped contamination from her.

"Drive faster," he shouted to the coachman. Perhaps they had not seized her yet and clasped their hideous iron bracelets about her dimpled arms.

"Faster, faster," he cried. If he were there they would not dare to touch her. Would they dare burst in his gate and break down his massive oaken doors, stride with their soiled boots through his parlors and tear her from his very arms. His father created their very town, and the men whom Philip Breton had befriended would rush to his help. Who ever heard of a house so grand as his being invaded by loud-voiced officers—of justice, they called it, to drag a wife from her home. Let them dare to do it.

"Faster, drive faster."

The carriage rolled into his grounds and he leaped out and looked about him. He saw no signs of a disturbance yet. The crowd of curious campfollowers that love to invest scenes of violence long after the echo of the screams of sufferers are still, had not come—not yet. His gardener was cutting a bouquet of roses. Bless his grey head, he would not be making bouquets for an outraged, plundered home.

"Whom are you cutting the roses for?" How heavy his master's hand rested on his shoulder.

"For the mistress, if you please, sir."

"Is she within then?"

"Can't you hear her playin', sir?"

Thank God for that gentle breeze that brought the music to his ears. It was that same familiar air from " Traviata," that she had played the night he had left her for the labor meeting before the first shadow had crossed her life. But she was safe yet.

He mounted the brown-stone steps, and unlocked the door. He closed it very softly after him and with noiseless step made his way to the drawing-room. The door stood half open ; he looked in at Bertha, his one week wife. She wore no cloak or hat to show she had soon to go, and her foot that rested on the pedal was slippered ; why not ? She had come to stay, night, morning, noon, always. She had come to stay.

But a sudden change passed over his face. That proud-faced woman—was a—they called it a criminal, a felon, on whose soft white shoulder any policeman in the state might freely lay his rude hand. She would look to him, but he could not help her ; he had undertaken to protect her, but he must stand back with breaking heart while they dragged her away. Could they not let him imprison her at home ? She should never go outside ; a cell, for such as she ! she would die—was there no pity in their iron laws ? To-morrow her name would be heralded abroad ; perhaps her sweet face, almost too fair for kisses, would be blazoned on the outside sheet of the lowest picture papers, and the dregs of the great cities would revel in its insulted beauty. Poor girl, she was thinking she had a right with him—that her home was in his arms, perhaps dreaming of a household whose queen she should be, of pretty, proud-faced boys and blue-eyed daughters who should sometimes cluster about her knees. She was living in a false world. Her children—God grant she might never have them—ah, the law had a bitter name for what their children would be. He was the wealthiest man in a hundred miles, and he could not give his children a name. Her children; how he could love them; but each young face, in turn, must mantle with shame. His love for them would have the same terrible mingling of pain that makes love more torture than happiness. And was there nothing he could do for this woman? She had given herself to him, all his vows were upon him.

"Bertha." She looked up and smiled on his stricken face and played on.

He came up behind her. She was his yet. He bent down and kissed her warm white neck beneath her red gold hair. The law had not claimed her yet, and all the rites of religion had once made her his wife. One moment he stood by her side; the next he fell upon his knees, and imprisoned the quick flying hands. He felt he could not bear the music now, it was a wild waltz she was playing; he bowed his head in her lap.

"Why Philip, are you so tired?"

"I am weary unto death," and his bent form shook with agony and baffled love.

Bertha's eyes rested calmly on his head for a moment, then glanced at the music sheet on its rack; not a spark of emotion showed in their clear depths. The perfect shape of her mouth was not hurt by one disturbing quiver of the rare red lips; they did not curve downward in gentle tenderness, nor part in sweet pity. There was not one shade more of color in her fair cheeks for this trembling heart-broken man whose whole soul seemed dissolving in love and sacrifice; who would have suffered a life-time to save her from the unguessed fate which hovered fearfully above her gold-crowned head.

It was two hours later that Philip saddled and bridled Joe the white horse, and set out for Mrs. Ellingsworth's. Strangely enough, as he sat at tea he had remembered the first malevolent expression in Jane Ellingsworth's face as his bride and he drove past that very noon. It had changed so quickly to smiles that he had doubted his eyes, but he trembled at his memory of it now, and the piece of paper that had fluttered to her feet, what could it be? Could it be she knew all; that while he was buying over the lawyer so that he should not use his terrible power, there might be near at hand an enemy to the death, who only toyed a moment with her poisoned arrow to shoot it when it would strike with deadliest effect?

Philip had parted with Bertha as painfully as if he were leaving her to die, and as he rode off he looked up and down the street as if danger lurked in every shadow.

Ought he not to have told her? But what good? She might enjoy a few more days of calm ; the worst could not be worse than such torture of fear and hourly dread as he suffered. She trusted him perfectly, and he believed he could fight best alone. He would ward off every danger human brain could foresee, and wealth and strength and ingenuity oppose, and then ; oh God, and then! But it could do no good to warn her ; she might flutter in her terror straight into the very jaws of destruction ; as for him, he could be cool and firm, though his heart was consuming within him. And who knows ; the hair that held the sword above her head might never snap, and at last after many years—what years of agony they would be to him—she might lie down at last in an honored grave. No, he would not tell her. If God in his mercy would permit him, he would thank him night and morning, and carry the burden of hourly terror, for her sake, alone.

The horse was not happy. His master had no kind word for him after his absence, not one stroke for his glossy neck. He sidled sulkily to and fro across the road and made but very slow progress, till a sharp blow of the hand that was used to pat him, sent him

bounding in great leaps on his way forgetful of everything except his own resentment. But when he
reached Mr. Ellingsworth's gate, Philip was sorry he
had come so fast, for he had not thought yet how to
conceal his motive in coming. But Jane received him
so cordially that he quite forgot he had anything to
conceal. Opportunities were not thrown away on
her. She had the art of appearing a lady so well,
none but the best trained eye, as her elegant husband's, for instance, could detect the factory girl
beneath. She had long since corrected all her inac-
curacies of speech; she could receive and dismiss a
caller to perfection. She had the proper gradations
in manner for the difference in wealth and position
of her acquaintance. Of books and art she knew
almost nothing, and cared as little, but she had picked
up the catch-words in vogue and it must be a very
discerning guest of her cultivated husband who discovered that learned talk and elegant criticism were
not alone unintelligible, but absolutely stupid to her.
She had learned among other things, that her parlor
furniture was bad, and everything had been changed
again. She had improved in her taste for ornaments,
too, and her heavy chains and bracelets were shut
away in a drawer up stairs. She had found it so
much easier to be a fine lady than she had supposed;
fine ladies are so much alike in the sort of things
they do and say, that all that is necessary is to do

and say things after a certain easy fashion, and it is accomplished.

This evening Jane Ellingsworth appeared at her very best. She made Philip tell her where he had been with his bride, on their short trip, and all they had seen, and was so charmingly interested that he imagined he was succeeding in quite winning her over in Bertha's favor. Then she hoped they would be so "very happy," and drooped her black lashes at last in a beautiful stroke of daring.

"Will you be sure and quite forget, I ever thought I disliked Bertha? I mean to be so very devoted now, if you, and she will let me."

"Do you?" he exclaimed drawing a deep breath of relief. "God bless you for it; make our house your other home." How he had misjudged this amiable girl. He would persuade Bertha to be very kind to her. How very fortunate women do not hold their hates as men do. While he had been speaking she had turned her head away, but as he said goodnight, she looked him in the face again.

"Why, what is the matter?" he said quickly, "your lip is bleeding."

"Oh, it is nothing, good-night."

The horse was put into the stall with his master's own hand that night, and rewarded for his services, at last, with the kind words that made him lay back his ears in content. Then Philip went into the house and bolted the doors with a new sense of possession. Bertha was within, with him ; the whole world besides was shut without, for to-night, at least. He hung up his hat and looked into the drawing-room. The gas was in full blaze, the piano open, and music sheets in place ; a book lay on a chair, as if just dropped there, but Bertha was not in the room. He turned out the gas, and stepped along to the library—he had been sure she would like that place, it was, somehow, exquisitely in keeping with her tastes, and her own classic repose. But it was dark, and no one was there. In sudden vague fear, he bounded up the stairs. She was not in her boudoir, and he pushed open the door into the white chamber. The gas was turned down low, but he put aside the curtains of the canopy, and there lay Bertha. Her lips were just parted in a sweet dream, and the delicious suggestion of a smile was in her closed eye-lids too. All the thunders of hell might be echoing around her, the dear head rested in perfect peace. A terrible fate trembled over her, but she was as unconscious of it as the babe of an hour. He bent over her with a yearning tenderness in his eyes. One white arm lay on the coverlet, he kissed it as softly as if it were a holy thing. He bowed his head low over her face, that seemed in her sleep to have a new gentleness and warmth in it. He drank her sweet child-like breath. What was she dreaming of, he wondered. He just touched her lips, when she moved uneasily in her sleep, and murmured his name.

"Bertha, you came to me pure, with no sin on your white soul. It is I who have put it there, I, who loved you better than myself, have put the sin upon you. And you never knew, my love, my darling, yes, my holy one, you never knew what you did." His slight form shook with a great tearless sob. Then he closed the curtains about her bed with lingering tenderness, turned out the light and left the room

It was at the same moment that Jane Ellingsworth drew a letter from her pocket, as she sat in the parlor where Philip had left her. She had read the letter a dozen times; it was the same that had fluttered to the floor when she had thrown kisses to the bridal pair, and this was the part that interested her so much:

"You ask me why I did not marry Bertha. Who has been insulting her then? She is my wife, so far as laws can make a wife. She left me because she no longer loved me. I suppose I was too illbred and common a man for her. If she had only known it before. I watched her in terror, as she began to awake from her dream of love. I tried to woo her again. I thought it might be I was not fond enough, and I became so tender, I wearied her.

I thought perhaps I was not gentle enough, and then I never spoke to her but in approval. But her beautiful face grew colder and colder every day. I saw the light of love that had made it an angel's fade hour by hour. Then I fell on my knees and prayed her to love me, but she only drew back her skirts; then I told her I must die if she were cruel to me, and asked—begged her to love me for pity, but when the tide of love begins to ebb, all the prayers and lamentations of a world cannot stay it. She was not like other women, she did not cry for her old associates, or for the fashionable society that once cherished her. She did not reproach me because I talked of nothing so much as the wrongs of my class, because I disliked the gay, false life she was bred in, and sighed to return to. But her face grew cold and hard, and the love died out of her voice. She never confessed she had mistaken herself in marrying me till the very hour she left me. Yes, she is my wife, and my heart aches always for her. Write and tell me where she is—perhaps sometime she may come back to me, for she once seemed to love me, and they say love cannot die.

CURRAN."

CHAPTER XXX.

Evil Eyes.

PHILIP BRETON began to notice in the next few days that a new spirit of discontent had come over the factory hands. Before the walls of the new mill had risen ten feet from its foundations, the smiles that used to salute him, and warm his heart, as he walked among his people and through the village that he had made smile too—had faded from averted, sullen faces. Once, the men and their women could find no words strong enough to express their love and gratitude to him. Now he heard constant complaints against the long hours that he still thought necessary; and against the smallness of their share in the profits of the mill. Did they not every one of them work a hundred times harder than he, who only seemed to have to look over a few papers; or lean back in his office chair and talk for a few hours, when he chose? Philip recalled with heart-sickness a great many times during these days, that paragraph from the Lockout Journal that seemed to have clung to his memory word for word.

"Mr. Breton's scheme encourages the spirit of restlessness among the working classes. He may think he gives them enough ; their wants and complaints will always keep just ahead of the favors granted them. They will grow bolder at signs of weakness, and he will soon find that they have passed beyond his power of restraint." Philip was fast losing his only hope and consolation. The dissatisfaction seemed to increase every day, and it was borne in upon him that his life in all its relations was to prove a complete failure. The people seemed to have forgotten how much better off they were than others ; to have forgotten the concessions he had given them, such as no other mill-owner thought of for a moment. There was so much more they wanted, that he had not granted. He had opened their eyes to their condition more than he had satisfied their ambition. They accepted the principle he had explained and illustrated to them, and carried it out in relentless logic. Philip thought they were more restless now, than in the worst days under his father's inflexible management ; there were more frequent meetings and bolder threats.

It was at this time, when the light of hope was almost faded from his soul, and when he was fearful of dangers on every side, that Bertha said she would like to see her husband's mill. He could not tell her that he did not dare to have her seen ; that he suspected her secret had spread among the villagers; and that he feared the people whose master he was.

"Isn't it too cold this morning," he answered, avoiding her eyes, while he cast about wildly for a pretence to keep her at home.

"I am not an invalid, Philip," she said smilingly, "and you have kept me shut up as if I were a prisoner. What crime have I committed?"

He tried to laugh, but a sorry thing he made of it.

"Well, shall we have the coupè?"

"Why no; you aren't jealous of me, are you?"

Surely it was no harm for him to kiss her even if—

In a few moments his beach wagon was at the door. He helped her in and taking his seat in front with a strange binding sensation in his throat, looked neither to the right hand or the left, but drove as if he were on a race course.

"Why, Philip, you take my breath away. Why don't you enjoy the morning with me?" How the people gathered in the windows to see them go by.

"I am in a hurry," he said.

"There is Jane signaling us; aren't you going to stop? Oh, yes, that is right. Here is a good chance to be friendly as you wished."

"May I ride too?" said Mrs. Ellingsworth, with childlike eagerness. One might have thought sometimes she had grown ten years younger with her new

accomplishments. The carriage drew up to the curb-
stone, and the usual greetings were exchanged.
" Isn't it delightful?" said she, as she took her seat
with them. Jane was all smiles and bright glances
this morning.

" How does it seem to be married, Bertha?"
she asked, with charming innocence. Philip caught
up his whip with a look so black Jane thought he
would strike her.

She saw he knew all; he had found it out some
way; but certainly not from Bertha, whose face
changed not in the smallest expression as she made
a graceful answer.

Jane was in a whirl of suppressed excitement at
the new position affairs had suddenly taken. What
a situation ! She must be more careful now in what
she said and did. Philip knew all and she knew the
rare making of the man; he would guard his unworthy wife as a lioness her young. He would
reckon of no account any sacrifice. The whole expression of his thin pale face had changed since the
day she had seen him gazing so rapturously at his
bride, when they drove past her window. His happiness was dead, his hope was gone ; he saw nothing
but shame and ignominy ; or a terrible daily burden
of fear and horror before him. But Jane knew the
man ; she had tried him ; he would not flinch. He
had set himself not only the task of defending her

from the punishment of her crime ; but even from the guilty consciousness of it.

While Jane Ellingsworth affected to be admiring the horses, she studied the stern set look of the face of this devoted husband, the deathly weariness about his mouth, the suspense in his eyes. Then she glanced at Bertha, the woman who now the second time had struck him ; this time mortally ; who had given him for the reward of his matchless love and tenderness first humiliation and loneliness, and now the hourly fear of infamy, certain to come in due time. Bertha was smiling idly at some children at play by the roadside ; the old indifference was on her face ; the old pride in the untroubled depths of her blue eyes. Well, let her wear it awhile, doubtless there was a shame that could touch her ; doubtless her cold heart could be racked at last, unshaken as it was yet by the ruin it had worked in three lives.

Philip pulled up his horses at the counting-room door.

"There are the mills," and he pointed his whip at the great brick buildings, that seemed murmuring hoarsely to themselves in their own strange language.

"But I want to go into them," insisted Bertha after she had alighted.

"It would not interest you," answered Philip steadily. "Would it, Mrs. Ellingsworth?"

Jane understood the looks and words, he feared for her, and glanced curiously at the woman who struggled so blindly against his protective love. The lower part of her face had become set and slightly unpleasant.

"It is very dusty and the smell of the oil would make you ill," suggested Mrs. Ellingsworth. They were standing at the edge of the piazza in full view of the windows of the workroom above, and the help were collecting curiously and looking down.

"Please come into the office." Philip laid his hand lightly on Bertha's arm, but she stepped a little away from him.

"No, I thank you!" she answered in measured tones. "I will wait here for you."

A gentleman whom no one noticed had come up the street, from the depot, and was just crossing over toward them.

"Please not wait here, my love," urged Philip, very gently. "Only see—the help from the windows above are all staring at you."

"It will not harm me. May I trouble you to help me into the carriage? I think I will sit there. Thank you."

Jane stood back a little, watching the unraveling of the plot, whose thread she held in her hands.

It was very thrilling. She saw the stranger come
up and lay his hand on Philip Breton's shoulder.
Who could he be with his mysterious air, his black
felt hat torn in the crown, and his shiny broadcloth
coat without cuffs? Philip had glanced again up at
the windows on the floor above, where a number of
the operatives had gathered. Behind them stood a
man who fancied himself in the shadow, but Philip
could see him point his finger at Bertha, and his
lips move. Then the rest looked back at him and
laughed and looked at Bertha, and laughed again.
The fellow peered forward incautiously and the
light fell upon the same malicious, distorted features Philip had seen reflected in the sideboard mirror the day he brought his bride home. It was
Thomas Bailes, one of the witnesses to Bertha's marriage with Curran. But Bertha sat superbly indifferent, the centre of their evil eyes, the mark of
their scurrilous words. Philip turned as the stranger's
hand fell on his shoulder.

"May I have your ear for a moment?" said the
ill dressed man in a low tone. Philip seemed to
stagger under a new blow. Jane's keen eyes were
very curious over this odd meeting, but Bertha
noticed nothing.

So three enemies to Bertha and his own honor
met by chance at the gate of his great mill yard,
ignorant each of the very existence and of the mo-

tives of the others, but each working for the ruin of
a life. Three mines were planted under one weak
woman's feet, but neither enemy knew there was another; they were plotters, but not conspirators, and
more deadly far. If she escaped one she must fall
by another, if one were melted by prayers, still two
remained ; if one were bribed with uncounted wealth,
still there was one unappeased. The woman sat the
focus of three pairs of hostile eyes, calm, beautiful,
unconscious ; the air might be thick with horrid hate,
she never guessed that even one shadow had fallen
across the sun's bright beams. But one man had
planted himself before her; he did not know how
many foes he must fight, he did not know their plan
of battle, but if sleepless guardianship and devotion
unto death can save her he will do it. He looks up
pitifully at her face averted from him in displeasure.
Ah, if she knew she would give him strength for the
conflict by a kind smile at least. But she preferred
to watch the impatient horses pawing the earth
beneath their feet, and Philip turned to the man who
had touched his shoulder. The man was staring
with insolent familiarity at Bertha, as if he had a
certain right of property in her.

"I am ready," said Philip fiercely, "come
inside." The paymaster called his name, but he did
not listen to him. He waited till the attorney, Giddings, passed over the threshold of his office, then he

25

locked the door and turned on him like an infuri-
ated animal.

" Do you dare look so at my wife ? Do you
think she is like the low creatures you associate
with ?"

The man's face grew a ghastly yellow, while his
eyes tried to seek out some safe corner in the room.

" My God," and Philip advanced upon the lawyer's retreating form till he shrank down in a chair,
and winced as if he already felt the threatening
blow. " I would kill you as I would a dog—" He
stopped, and the mad gleam died out of his eyes.
He threw himself into a chair, and covered his face
with his trembling fingers. " But one crime in a
household is enough." There was a dead silence for
a moment, then the lawyer, seeing he was out of
danger, plucked up courage.

"That was the very thing I called about."
Philip took his hands from his face, and his eyes
seemed to Giddings to be burning their way deep
down into his contemptible soul. Then he looked
at the man's frayed coat, frayed at the edges, and at
his torn hat that he kept upon his knee, and the
lawyer twitched uneasily under his scrutiny.

" I thought I was done with you forever," he said
with a bitter smile at last, " why, it was only a little
time ago—let me see—"

" I know it, I know it, but somehow my money

went pretty fast." And a new cunning leer came
into his face. He was beginning to feel at home,
though somehow, he could not look his victim in the
eye to-day. "But there is a new point I have
thought of since I saw you." He tried to look at
him, but could not get his eyes to stay any higher
than Philip's shoulder. The baptism of fire he had
suffered, had given a certain new dignity to the
young man's face, that cowed his visitor. " I mean
the risk I run ; do you know what the law calls
what I am doing?" Giddings lowered his voice to
affect a frightened whisper. "It is compounding of
felony. I was only thinking I ought to be paid for
my risk."

"Let me see," said Philip in stern irony, "two
hundred dollars for keeping your secret—now how
much for the risk?"

"Well," and the man grinned painfully, "you
might make it up to an even five hundred, all together you know, to include everything," Giddings
managed to raise his eyes, for an instant, to Philip's
face.

"And do you think there won't be any more
points? You know I can't submit to be bled at this
rate."

"Oh, no, I assure you, not another cent. I had
to pay debts with the first, you know, and buy
clothes." Philip was astonished at himself, but he

really had heart to smile as he looked the man over.

"Yes, you must have laid out the greater part of it on clothes." Giddings pulled his chair up to the table.

"I will sign anything you say." Philip had risen, and was crossing to the paymaster's office. "Wait," insisted the lawyer, "I will write an agreement in a minute."

"Your engagement, eh? No, I won't trouble you." He stepped into the paymaster's room, "Have you three hundred dollars in the safe, Mr. Smith? Coupon bonds will do. Thank you."

"Will you step in here as soon as possible?" said the paymaster, as he handed him the bonds. "There is a very important mat—"

"Yes, certainly. Please send up stairs for Bailes, I want to see him."

At the foot of the stairs Bailes and Giddings passed each other.

"Good morning, Bailes," began Philip, without turning his face to his discharged servant. "I suppose I was a little harsh sending you away as I did." He spoke hurriedly, as if it were a painful task he were performing. "Let this make it up to you," and the mill-owner threw a roll of bills on the table much as a man would throw a bone to a dog, though he would have been hearty if he could have forced

his tongue to do the false service. The man took
up the money with the air of the trained waiter taking up his fee. He asked no questions, he uttered no thanks. He understood. .Philip was filled
with shame, and the fellow's silence made it very
hard for him.

"If you are faithful to me," Philip looked fixedly
at the wall over the rascal's head, "I may be able
to do something handsome for you."

As Philip went out he glanced on neither side
but unhitched his horses and drove off as if a pack
of wolves were behind him. He never dreamed of
cause of fear from the pretty, black-eyed woman
who sat on the seat with him, who was amiable
enough to keep up the conversation all the way
home in spite of the ungraciousness of the others.
After Mrs. Ellingsworth had alighted at her house
Bertha said, in a displeased tone,

"I so wanted to go through the mill." But her
husband did not hear. He was thinking how mighty
his gold was. It had purchased them four weeks of
immunity, four weeks of honor; it was their honeymoon. It surely would control this dangerous
servant since it had worked so marvelously with the
lawyer.

"I am so anxious to see how cloth is made," per-
sisted Bertha, never losing sight of her object.

To be sure the servant had had personal offence

with his master, he might not unnaturally cherish
malice.   But gold is a sovereign balm for wounded
pride, only wouldn't it have been wiser to have given
him more since he gave him something?   He must
attend to the matter to-morrow.   Perhaps, after all
there might be some hope for his wife and for him.
How glorious it was to be rich and have power to
save her.   He would scatter his wealth like leaves
in autumn, for her sake.   His mill, yes, he would
even sell his dear old mill, and pay out its price as
the price of one year after another of respite, till
he and she grew so poor at last even their enemies
and tormentors would weep for them, and let his
beautiful bride lie down to die in peace.

" You really must take me through the mills to-
morrow."

Philip had alighted and held up his hands to help
Bertha to the ground.   She held back a moment
with a new pretty coquettishness.

" Will you?" she said.

He had not even heard her before.   He smiled
with his fine rare tenderness as he answered very
gently, " Anything you like, Bertha."   Then he
caught her into his arms.

CHAPTER XXXI.

Incautious Driving.

GOOD morning, my darling." But there was another letter at Philip Breton's breakfast plate,
and the old look of dread came back to his face—the
dark hollows under his eyes showed again. He had
forgotten for a moment, but he ought never to forget. How could he tell what moment he would be
called upon to strain every nerve to save his darling.
He tore open the letter in uncontrollable terror; oh,
it was only from Philbrick. Had Bertha noticed his
excitement, and would she question him in wifely
concern? He had so much to guard against. But
no, her graceful arm was raised to pour his coffee,
inclining her head prettily on one side, as women
always do at tea and coffee-pouring. She did not
watch his face as he did hers. She had not even
noticed the change that had come over him of late,
that shocked every casual acquaintance on the street.
But that made it so much the easier for him to keep
the secret from her; he told himself he ought to be
thankful for it, instead of ever permitting his foolish

heart to ache.   He ran his eyes rapidly over the letter his white-haired friend had sent him.

  "I suppose it is paper thrown away, but I want
to remind you once more of my offer, to take your
mill off your hands.   I have made up my mind to
try my scheme somewhere.   I am old and feel as if
I would like to do something for my race with my
money, which I have now well in hand.   Will you
let me have your mills for what I have got?   If not
I shall try elsewhere.   The reason I want your mills
is because I propose to give you a chance to take
part in my beautiful industrial plan.   I will pay you
one-third its valuation, one-third you shall keep at
four per cent interest till we can buy that in also, the
other third I am going to let you give in trust for the
benefit of the help as my discretion shall dictate.
This is a glorious opportunity, but I suppose I am
wild to expect you to take it, only that I have read
in the newspapers of growing discontent among your
help.   Various reasons are given for it ; my explanation is that a little leaven leaveneth the whole lump.
If you were working to stop complaints, you should
not have begun your reforms.   You may happen to
see things as I do, and be willing to let me try where
you have failed.   If so telegraph me at once and I
will come.

  Philip folded the letter thoughtfully and put it
back in its envelop.   No, he was not ready for that

yet. But he did not smile. If it should ever happen that he be called upon to sacrifice everything to save his wife—but Philbrick required that he accept at once. No he was not ready yet.

"Oh!" said his wife as if a sudden thought had struck her, "do you remember your promise, you are to take me through the mills to-day?"

"Did I promise that?" He put back his coffee cup untasted.

"Certainly, Philip, and I cannot let you off."

"But you must." His face grew dark at the thought that she should put at naught all his careful plans to secure her present safety. Bertha pushed back her chair and rising angrily to her feet, swept from the room without another word. Philip tried in vain to swallow the mouthfuls of food he so much needed, then he started on foot for the mill.

That Bertha should be angry with him seemed the last intolerable blow; was he not bearing enough before? He had made her unhappy, perhaps she was weeping hot tears of impatience now; she had thought he loved her enough to grant her every wish that might cross her heart. Philip was tempted to go back and explain everything, then she would not doubt his love, but she would have to share his agony with him; it were better to bear his burdens alone even to this last burden of her unmerited reproach. His sympathy for her grew stronger than his consciousness of his own unhappiness. Of course she would be hurt that he had denied her anything; if it had been a ribbon, it would have been the same. He was to blame for letting her leave him in vexation, he should have forgot his own grievances, and soothed her with gentle words till she smiled on him. It was not because she wanted the thing so much, but it was the first time he had ever crossed her wishes.

Philip was so absorbed in his thoughts that he did not observe that he was close upon an excited crowd of village people, till such words as these fell upon his ear :

" A noice friend of the poor man he be, with his four fancy hosses, his silver dishes to eat his victuals off of, and his house like a king's palace, while we lives and dies in dirt and poverty. Who made him better nor us? do he work harder? do he sleep less? No, but he have his venison and his game dinners, while us starves on tea and crackers ; he sprawls on his fine cushions, and sleeps in his soft beds, while we rots in close attics, and loafs in dirty saloons, the poor man's only home. What title have he got to have better than we, and give himself airs over us?"

Philip was astonished. The man who stood on the steps of one of the tenement houses, instructing an audience extending quite across the highway, was no other than the incendiary who had so nearly caused the ruin of the Breton Mills the night of the great fire. The fellow's hair was cropped as close to his bullet head as it was then.

The audience was mostly made up of old men, women, and children, with here and there an able-bodied man, who preferred talking about his rights to deserving anything. One or two had observed the young mill-owner, but they took no pains to spread the intelligence, and in a moment more the agitator had caught his breath and went on.

" He feeds his hosses more'n would keep two poor families. The wines he drinks every day cost enough to keep another two."

Perhaps the man was right in his tirade. Perhaps Philip Breton had only begun to grasp the first out-lines of the great question he had fancied mastered.

" But ye kiss his hand."

" No we won't," shouted the crowd. There stood Thomas Bailes, Philip's discharged servant, in the middle of the street, shouting with the rest. He could afford to be idle since his liberal present.

" Ye will thank him for his bein' so kind to ye."

" No, no," screamed the women. What a fool Philip Breton had been to count on gratitude. Human nature is too progressive to be grateful. Perhaps he deserved no thanks. He had done more than others for his help—the more fool he was, all sides would agree, unless he went further. He ought to have been either a thorough radical, or a thorough conservative. All parties abuse the half-way reformer, a vessel of pottery between two jars of iron, he is certain to be crushed.

A carriage was struggling down the street. How slow the crowd were to give way ; they were so much interested in their orator, they did not no-tice they were obstructing the highway.

"What good is such men as him? our women is stronger than them sort."

That horse seemed spirited, or else not properly guided. Ah, the driver ought not to use a whip in such a situation as this. Good heavens! the horse had become unmanageable. A man, it was Bailes himself, and a woman had been struck by the shafts and rolled under the feet of the horse, who was now rearing and plunging, while the crowd scattered in all directions with screams and curses.

Under the very wheels of the carriage lay a woman stunned and helpless from the blow she had received. Instant death threatened her, when a man's form rose suddenly out of the dust under the horse's iron shoes and caught the excited animal by his bit. The crowd gathered in more closely than ever, while a dozen hands dragged out the old woman from her terrible situation, and wiped the dust from her white ghastly face. The orator had ceased his eloquence, and all danger of accident seemed now averted, so Philip Breton was passing on his way.

But Bertha, for the occupant of the carriage was no other than she, found her way blocked in all directions by an angry mob.

" Pull her out, scarlet face," screamed the women. " Tear her pretty rags off from her." The barefooted children threw earth at her ; lean, dirty fingers plucked at her delicate skirts. How dared they touch her ! she shrank from the pollution of contact with such creatures as these, with a terror that would be inconceivable to a man. She saw them gather around the restive horse, who seemed as impatient of their touch as she ; they were beginning to undo his harness. In another moment she would be lost. But the horse was strong, could he not break through them? She did not care how many he should trample to death ; she would rather, a thousand times rather, die herself, than endure their insulting touch. But a rough hand caught the whip from her grasp ; the creature's unpared nails hurt her; another hand was on her shoulders ; and vile words, whose meaning she only felt, were on every tongue. Her heart grew sick ; oh, God would not let her faint ; oh, not now ; oh, not now ;—but her vision seemed failing, she could not see to the horse's head, and the terrible insults the people hurled at her grew indistinct, like a roaring of many waters in her ears. But she saw a hideous-faced hag reach her bare brawny arm into the carriage and clutch at her feet; they were lifting her out. But a hand like iron flung the virago back.

"Stand off. It is my wife!" The mill-owner's wife The crowd fell back for a moment, as if it was news to them; but Philip knew by instinct, the lull would only last for a moment. He must make the most of it. He had only time to refasten a little of the harness, when a sharp stone struck him on the cheek and drew blood.

"How many husbands can a woman have?" screamed a woman on the sidewalk.

"Jail's the place for her," growled a man at his shoulder. Then the crowd closed in again.

"Let go the bit," demanded Philip, never quailing. But Bailes only grinned at him, as Philip had seen him before, and tightened his hold on the horse.

"You're too small to give orders; I aint in your pay now." But before the fellow had time to put up a guard, his young master had struck him a blow in the face that fairly staggered him, large man as he was.

"Oh, that's your game, is it? Make way, boys, all I want is room. I'll finish him up quick."

The man wanted to make use of his weight and strength in the directest way possible, so he rushed forward to close with his antagonist, throwing up his hands to protect himself. But he miscalculated and his cheek bone fairly cracked with the force of the second blow. Bailes drew back for another attack; the smile of contempt was gone from his bruised and bleeding face, but a very dangerous look was in his eyes. His young master had lost his first paleness, a bright red spot burned in each cheek and his black eyes flashed forth defiance. The discharged servant ducked his head and came at Philip like a maddened ox. The crowd held their breath; the slight form of the master would go down, and the victor would pound his young life out of him. Was the lad crazy to invite a battle with a man of almost twice his weight? The young man did not flinch a hair's breadth. He raised his arm again. What good of battering against the fellow's thick skull? He was upon him—no, Philip had leaped aside at the last moment, and, as Bailes went past, had dealt him a blow in the temple that sent his great form reeling to the ground.

Before the crowd had time to move Philip had leaped into the carriage and caught the reins from his fainting wife. He turned his horse into an open space and the half fastened harness let the carriage run against the animal's legs. It was better than a thousand whips, and he broke into a wild gallop. Bailes had only time to get his feet and shout after the young mill-owner,

"This is only the first round."

Philip heard his words and muttered to himself, "I ought to have killed him, since I had to beat him; there isn't gold enough in California to buy him over now."

"What did they mean, Philip?" Bertha was lying on the sofa in her own little blue room. Philip had put a pillow beneath her tired head and was kneeling by her side watching for the color to come back to her frightened cheeks.

"Thank God she did not know, not yet."

He looked down at the veins in her pretty hands; how many there were to-day.

"It was only their senseless jargon. They are angry with me you know. Do not think about it again."

She opened her great blue eyes on him. She was going to thank him no doubt for her rescue out of the terrible peril.

"You look so small and weak. I wouldn't have thought you had any strength." That was all she had for him.

CHAPTER XXXII.

Ink.

PHILIP left his wife to fall asleep if she could, and made his way to his study where he and his father before him had fought out so many battles. His secret was out. The police might be at his door that very night to claim his bride back from him. He had beaten one man for her, but he could not defend her against the force they would bring against him. The air of his little village had grown close and suffocating. How long would it be before the storm would burst. He tried to calm himself and calculate how much time his crowding destiny would give him. He was rich and powerful and had many friends, and nothing that could happen to his wife could make him less formidable, though it might break his heart. There was not a soul in Bretonville but had something to hope of his favor, or to fear from his displeasure. He could shut up his mills and the village would become a desert; he could lower wages and send starvation knocking at every door. And there was not one creature in the village but knew his power. He had not used it to

25

harm them yet, but would a man not forget mercy
in defending his own home? And then what did
they know, after all, even the mob that had insulted
his wife? They might suspect, but suspicion was
not enough to give them courage to assail all the
bulwarks of wealth and respectability about such a
home as Philip Breton's. Even the discharged
servant, Thomas Bailes, did not hold the trump
card in this terrible game of life and death. No one
held it but Giddings the lawyer and he was provided
for as yet.

Philip paused before the window. There could
be no vital danger yet. It would take time. His
enemies were on the right track but there were
blind windings in it that would hinder the scent.
Hinder it, but at last what? His mills seemed to
hold him in bondage. His life work was here where
the danger was. He was to show the world what
an employer ought concede to his workmen. He
was to set a bright example to soften the rigor of
his class. Could he forsake his glorious work? To
be sure his workmen were proving themselves ungrateful, and murmured louder against him to-day
than ever against his father. They had taken their
children away from the schools to spite him, though
he would not suffer their little bodies to be tortured
in the mills any more. His cost stores were well
nigh deserted and the provisions spoiling on the

shelves, to punish him, it seemed, for ever trying to be kind to them. They begrudged him his luxuries, as if it were their money that bought them. There were no more smiles and hearty words for him from the poor he had done the best he knew for, and all the manufacturers around were laughing at his failure, they called it.

But a look of determination came over the young man's pale face. He believed he could plant his feet like the rock and wear out their impatience. The violence of his people should not make him tremble. He was their friend and they would come to believe it. He had not done all they wished, but he could not see any farther, and he would take no step blindly because of reproaches. If he was not right he was nearer right than thousands of his class. By-and-by their turbulence would subside, when it could not stir him, and his measures would have time to bring forth their certain fruit of smiles and prosperity. New blocks of mills would stretch away in all directions, and the homes of his working people would dot with happy cottages all the hills and valleys near.

But Bertha. Did he love his mills or her the more? She must not even guess her own terrible story or her life would be clouded like his. But the air of the village would soon be trembling with the news and the hand of pitiless justice would be laid upon her. And should he wait for it? God had granted him one week of peace, and now this month for warning. Was not the world large? Were there not high mountains and unpeopled deserts where they could be safe, where he could hide his darling from insulting looks and words, where no prison cells gaped open for her?

A sudden great light broke over Philip's face as he walked his little study with rapid turns. He could save her. The plan unfolded itself in his mind. He could save her. There was yet time if he were quick. He must give up his great plan for his workmen; he must sell his mill, but he could yet save his wife if she were willing. But she might refuse to go. Philip hurried to the room where he had left her and opened the door so suddenly that she started up in terror. Her nerves were so shaken that day, poor girl.

" Bertha, my love," he said breathlessly, " How would you like a trip to Europe?"

"You are joking, Philip." Was it eagerness or aversion in her eyes? he felt afraid to look and see. What resource was left if she would not go? " How can you leave your business?"

There was an inflection in her voice, that made him glance quickly at her face. The coldest women have their enthusiasms; he had touched on hers; he hardly knew her, her face had such a new vitality in it.

"And would you really like it so much?" he said, with his deep tenderness, that had a touch of reproach in it she was too dull ever to take. He came up to her, and explained what charming routes they should take, and what lovely lands they should see. Not France and Italy and the banks of the Rhine alone, but even Egypt and the far East, not a spot of beauty in the whole far-off world, but they would enjoy it.

A flush was on Bertha's cheeks, at last, and her eyes shone like a young girl's while a lover whispers the first romance into her ears. And Philip sat by her side only too happy to see her smile, and to touch her golden braids of hair.

It was after the table in Mrs. Ginness' factory boarding house had been set for next morning's breakfast, which was soon after tea this same day, that one of the boarders came into the dining-room and cleared away the dishes in front of him to write a letter. It was not a very highly ornamented room, but everything was painfully clean, that is reminding one painfully of the aching arms of some poor woman, everything but the table-cloth, and certainly no one ever saw a clean table-cloth in a factory boarding house. Clean linen is one of the most exclusive luxuries of the rich, the industrious poor may achieve shining floors, and glistening faces, but spotless linen is quite beyond them. But it made very little difference to this man to-night, for his eyes were swollen so that discriminating vision was out of the question.   He spread his paper before him, and after uncorking his ink bottle, made two or three abortive attempts to dip his pen.   Then Bailes, for it was he, looked around to see if anybody was laughing at him.   But the room was empty, all but a French girl and her lover in one corner, who were quite too much taken up with each other to take notice of anybody else.   Then he tried again, and this time inked not alone the pen and half the length of the holder, but the palm of his hand in addition, and as a natural but apparently not foreseen consequence, that portion of the table-cloth within his reach.   If it had been much that Bailes had cared to say, he probably would have given it up in despair, but it was only two lines, and even a blind man could write two lines, if he had a whole sheet of paper for leeway.   The two lines Bailes wrote were these.

" Curran.   You are wanted here at once!   A friend."

CHAPTER XXXIII.

Too Late.

IT was the afternoon of the Wednesday that the steamer "Salvator" was to sail. But Philip Breton and the woman he had hoped to save, were yet in their house in Bretonville, hundreds of miles from the pier. The clock in Bertha's drawing-room had struck three. It was the very hour; the last bell must be ringing now, and friends were saying their farewell words, handkerchiefs were waving graceful adieux, with here and there a teardrop. Home seemed very sweet at this moment of separation, and dreams of joys in strange lands seemed too vague to comfort many a heart that had been light and merry till now.

Philip had not slept these two nights for anxiety. The very air had seemed so full of danger, he had feared the storm would burst upon them before to-day. New haggard lines had come into his face. He had watched all the countenances of the villagers for signs and warnings; would his enemies give him time? Well, they had given him time, and yet he waited.

He had driven to every train for his old friend Philbrick, but he had failed him. He had strained his blood-shot eyes so eagerly last night to make him out of the solitary arrival on the evening train. If the old man had known how much depended on him, he would surely have hastened. Philip dared not trust his mills in any hands but his. The old man would be gentle with his charge ; he was patient, he had broader ideas than Philip Breton, he was less of an aristocrat. And his mills were very dear to Philip—only less dear than his wife. Perhaps the old man might come yet, before the next steamer sailed, but there were three long days for his terrible secret to work its way to the light— three long dark nights for a blow to fall.

Philip found Bertha in the drawing-room, waiting for him. She had not understood the delay, but never suspected that the steamer had sailed. The excitement that flushed her face, seemed to have smoothed out the lines of care, her eyes were brighter than love for him had ever made them. She seemed grown young as the first day in the garden she had fallen asleep on his shoulder. How the poor girl longed to go. He stood a moment before her, and love and sorrow swept over his soul in alternate waves. She was his beautiful wife, who looked to him for her only protection. And out of pity for the mob that had insulted her, he had let slip, perhaps, his last hope of saving her. What did the wretches deserve? and he had sacrificed his wife to them. He had made those sweet eager eyes weep forever; that queenly gold-crowned head must bow in humiliation. How the world would wonder that he had not saved her from a felon's cell, with such wealth and power as his to command. He had risked her salvation to soften the fate of the thousand ungrateful creatures in his mill who cared nothing for him.

"Oh, Bertha, forgive me!" he cried as if his heart broke that moment. All his hope seemed dead then; the waters of desolation were sweeping in ceaseless swelling waves over his soul.

For a moment the woman looked at him in silence, trying to interpret for herself the meaning on his wan, passion-marked face. It was for him the supreme moment of an agony such a soul as hers could not even conceive of. The man suffered more in that moment, than the foulest dungeon in the world, or the scoffs of a city rabble, or the contempt of every woman that ever spoke her name could hurt her. Then she drew herself back from him; she thought, poor creature, she understood the expression on his face.

"Then you have missed the steamer, and you knew, too, how much I wanted to go." He did not speak, but a pitiful look of confusion was struggling into his face.

"When can we go, then?" she asked coldly.

"The next steamer sails Saturday." Saturday! Poor girl, poor Bertha! the furies are folding their black wings this instant to settle about her soul. She only thought it was her pleasure trip was deferred, it was his plan to save her from impending ruin—failed. One of the ministers of evil was at the gate this moment—now at the door—in the hall. Then the servant announced a name, and Mrs. Ellingsworth stepped into the room.

She had been smiling her best, but every smile vanished at sight of the shawls and traveling bags. She looked sharply at Bertha, who was dressed in her blue traveling suit; her hat was on the sofa beside her. She glanced about the room; the chintz covers were over the damask upholstery; the piano was closed and packed. Bertha looked listlessly at her.

"Oh, won't you sit down." But this strange visitor stood as if rooted to her place.

"You are going away?" Philip turned a surprised glance at her, the tone she assumed was crisp and imperious. He saw the dangerous look come into the dark brilliant eyes, which forgot their dissembling for the moment. The woman knew everything. In some way she had learned the

secret. Would she dare denounce his wife before
him? Was he so poor a man a woman like this
dared to beard him? He did not speak. Her message of scorn and infamy would come in a moment,
she would tear down the veil he had spread before
his wife's crime; he saw her red lips fairly trembling
with the bitter words. Then Philip looked at her no
more, but his eyes rested pityingly on Bertha. How
would she meet it? would she flush into rare passion? would she turn pale and faint in overpowering
shame?

"Yes, we were going to Europe," answered Bertha, utterly unconscious of the hate that glowered at
her out of the flashing eyes. "Philip did not want
me to speak of it or I should have told you before;
but I suppose it don't make any difference now,
since we've lost the steamer. It left the pier an
hour ago. So we are not going now till Saturday.
Isn't that it, Philip dear? Why, you don't mind my
telling Jane?" It was Bertha's own words, then,
that had decided her fate. There had been some
hope before, Philip now remembered; but at last her
deadliest enemy knew everything. The mine would
be sprung before to-morrow's sun had set. He could
see it in the sudden triumphant gleam in the woman's
eyes before she thought to smile. But Bertha was
the only one who could talk, just yet.

"Won't you lend me a few things, to get me

over a few days, everything is packed up, and our baggage on the way, you know?" and Bertha went on to explain in detail her ludicrous necessities. "To-morrow will do."

"Certainly, I only wish you had let me help you get ready." But her light laugh could not deceive Philip again; only it was too late now to guard against her. "I will run right home and get the things you spoke of ready for to-morrow."

Yes, and there were some other things she had not spoken of, Jane Ellingsworth would have ready for to-morrow, too.

CHAPTER XXXIV.

The Last Straw.

"YOU are too late, my friend." Philip had been sitting in his study in the darkness which was not more black than his life. But he arose to give his cold hand to Mr. Philbrick, who had come at last.

"Why too late? This is only Wednesday. Have you changed your mind? I did not suppose there was so much hurry, and I wanted to have everything ready."

"It is too late," answered Philip gloomily. What use to tell the old gentleman that Philip Breton's wife was a criminal before the law, that the transfer of the mill property was only a part of his scheme to save her from an infamous penalty, that their deadliest enemy knew all their plans now, and no doubt her sleepless eyes watched their every movement, lest they should escape her hate.

The servant came to the door, "I suppose you will have lights, sir. Some men from the mill folks want to see you."

"Oh yes, show them in," he said carelessly.

There were not chairs enough for the four workmen who came stumbling in like pall bearers at a country funeral, but Philip did not even seem to look at them. One took his place by the window, and soiled the curtain with his hands; another, apparently the spokesman, disdained to lean against anything, but stood stock still in the centre of the room, bent forward a little in an attitude borrowed from the prize ring. His feet were planted well apart, and his arms bowed out at the elbows.

"I suppose you have some complaints to make," said the young mill-owner, with a gentleness of tone that was quite misunderstood by the delegation, who immediately tried to look very fierce.

"Ye're right sir," answered the man in the centre of the room. "Ye know yerself, ye aint doin' the right thing by us."

Philip did not speak for a moment, and Mr. Philbrick would have thought he had not heard the fellow, only for a little twitching at the corners of his mouth. Apparently the young man was deeply hurt by his failure to satisfy his men.

"I have done the best I knew."

"Wal, we kin tell yer, if ye don't know no better," resumed the workman insolently. Philip's eyes flashed at him, then dropped to the carpet again. "Pay us more wages for one thing, shorten up our hours for another."

"You fare better than others. I divide the profits

with you. You thought I was very good to you
once." The young man's tone was not argumentative, it was too hopeless for that.

"Yer don't divy even ; our share don't 'mount to
nothin'," put in the man who was soiling the window
curtain.

"I am sorry for you, but you can't expect me to
make you all rich." There was such a sadness of reproach in Philip's voice, that a mist gathered before
Philbrick's kind eyes. But the workmen got the idea
they were frightening the young master.

Then Philip rose wearily to his feet and turned
his grave troubled eyes almost wistfully to one after
another of the visitors.

"I have gone as far as I can see my way. Don't
you think you had better be patient with me?"

"Be you goin' to raise our pay?" Philip shook
his head thoughtfully.

"I cannot understand it is my duty or my right."

"Are you goin' to shorten up our hours?" asked
the man at the window.

"I cannot—"

The chief spokesman turned to his companions.
"Ther aint no use. Wal squire, to-morrow you may
wish you had. Come along, boys."

Philip had dropped back heavily into his chair.
He seemed to have forgotten the presence of Mr.
Philbrick, till that gentleman began to explain his

more perfect system. Then he looked at him vaguely, as if he were trying to understand the man's
object in distressing him. Had he not told the old
gentleman he was too late?

" How can you expect your help to be satisfied,"
Philbrick was saying; " even if they were well paid it
would be small object for them to be shut up all their
lives, as if they were convicts. But you don't pay them
either. It isn't because the business don't pay, for
your father's profits and yours were enormous. It is all
the result of a false valuation of the worth of services.
Now I shall seek to remove the burdens that crush
the people and restrict their natural development,"
went on Mr. Philbrick as he rose to his feet and bent
eagerly over the table toward his young friend.

" Their own energies will accomplish more than
any plans of mine can effect, in ways we cannot foresee, but it will only be through the elevation of the
common people, as we call them, that this world will
become a fit place to live in. The progressive energy
of untrammeled nature will bring about all beautiful
results."

Mr. Philbrick did not appear to have understood
his meaning, but Philip said nothing at first. How
well his old friend had kept his enthusiasm through
all the years of his life! Well, it would do no harm
to let him talk on.

" You will ask me for details." Mr. Philbrick

took his seat again and drew up to him a sheet of paper and a pencil. " You will ask what burdens they are that are on the million, only the common necessary burdens of human nature. I will tell you the principal burden, it is the intolerable tribute to accumulated capital laid upon the working classes, which makes a tyrant of the man who has saved a surplus out his wages, and causes the hopeless *vis inertiæ* of poverty. Like all forms of slavery its effects are great apparent luxury, which never penetrates below the very surface of society, and tireless industry which earns nothing for the workers but food barely enough to support his day's work. It is benefit enough for the man who has saved money that he can work to better advantage ; it is a lever in his hands. If we permit capital to take such enormous profits as it does, every day and year it increases, as wealth increases, the crushing tax on labor. Instead of the wealth that is vaunted so much helping the poor, every pound additional, with our high rates of interest, makes the day laborer's life more hopeless. The rich man who has a surplus may spend it and thus live on it. His wealth stands for so much labor, and he may live in idleness on the strength of his former labor if he spends it, otherwise somebody must work the harder on his account. If he keeps his money and charges interest on it, the burden he ought to bear is handed

27

down from class to class till it can go no lower, and the poorest men in the great city toil in rags and squalor to support the jeweled aristocrat who would not throw them a crust to satisfy their hunger. I shall pay you but two per cent on the money I shall owe you on account of the mill property. The rest of the income of the business above two per cent, belongs to the laborer."

The reformer glanced expectantly at Philip. But the dull hopeless look that was on his face an hour ago had not changed.

" I am not sure but that is too much," pursued Mr. Philbrick, "but it will only be a little while before I shall pay up the debt."

" How will you divide your profits?" asked Philip, gravely. "Wouldn't you leave anything of my pretty system?" He smiled very sadly.

"Certainly," argued Philbrick, "I shall declare dividends just as you did, only semi-annually. The wages will remain at market rates, and each man will receive a dividend in proportion to his half year's work. But another thing. I don't want any tenements for the help. I mean to have each family own its home. We can't expect family virtues and graces or a hundred other fine qualities from tenements. I shall mean to apply a certain part of each dividend on a house lot which I shall hold by mortgage at two per cent till paid for."

There was no use in stopping the enthusiastic
old gentleman, whose great heart was a fountain of
human kindness. It would be time enough for
Philip to tell him that he had changed his plans,
later.

"As for your cheap stores, I shall keep them,"
continued Mr. Philbrick, in high spirits, "but I shall
go farther and furnish the help with amusements,
lectures, newspapers, even pictures, on the same
method. One important cause of high prices of
such things is the uncertainty in market and in pay-
ment; those that buy and pay have to pay enough
to make up for losses. This element of cost I shall
be able to save the village. But I shall also shorten
the hours of work. Six hours of confinement in the
mills is enough, and without leisure all the advan-
tages I can give my work people will be of little
avail. I can let different sets of hands relieve each
other if it seems necessary, or build new mills and
take in a thousand more hands to share the blessings
of justice."

Mr. Philbrick leaned back in his chair and a great
light of benevolence shone in his face. It was a pity
to disappoint him.

"This is an opportunity I have hoped for a whole
lifetime. I can show the world that labor ought not
and need not be wretched and famished. It is more
blindness than wilful cruelty that delays great re-

forms.   If I can once show the world what justice is
and how it works it will not be long before "—

"But my dear friend," said Philip, dropping his
eyes to the floor, " did I not tell you it was too late.
I am not going to sell.   You will have to select some
other spot for your Utopia."   The young man spoke
bitterly.   Unconscious of his selfishness he begrudged
the rest of the world the happiness he had missed.

Then came a moment of intense silence which
was broken at last, not by a voice but by the loud
ringing of a door-bell.   It rang so violently the
great silent house echoed again.   Had the end
come then?   Philip leaped to his feet.   Wild
thoughts of desperate expedients rushed through
his feverish brain, but he yet stood like a statue
when the study door opened behind him.   He tore
open a telegram and read aloud,

"Steamer Salvator delayed till to-morrow morning at three."

For a moment he did not take in its meaning.
Then he caught Philbrick's arm so tightly the old
gentleman almost cried out.

"Do you want the mills as you said?   You were
not joking, oh, you were not joking?"   Philbrick
gazed at him in astonishment.   Philip seemed in
such a terrible state of excitement.   His pallor
was replaced by a burning flush, his eyes that had
been so dull shone with unnatural brightness.

"Your plans will succeed better than mine and you can't find such a good place as this. You will take my mills."

"Of course I will, but I thought you said"—

"Never mind," cried the young man, "never mind what I said. Draw the papers at once. But no, I cannot wait." Philip turned on his heel as if no earthly power could detain him a moment longer.

"But the papers are all ready." And Mr. Philbrick took a bundle of documents from his breast pocket, and laid them on the table.

"Where shall I sign them—quick?"

"No, no, not there, that is my note to you; sign here, and here, and here."

"I can hardly see; everything dances before my eyes. Is it all done now?"

He hardly waited to take the papers Mr. Philbrick had signed for him. Then without another word he rushed from the room and bounded up the stairs. Freedom! safety! oh, thank God, thank God! He could save her yet. A castle on the Rhine, a palace in Venice; he would find the rarest homes for her. How sweet it would be to hide with her. The awful sense of hourly peril would lift from his soul; how long it had been since he breathed a full breath.

He pushed open the door of the white chamber. Bertha had been sleeping. The tear marks were on

her cheeks that had lost their beautiful flush. She
was so disappointed, poor girl, and yet she never
guessed—

"Wake up, wake up, my darling." She started
from the bed, and fell to weeping on his shoulder.

"I dreamed they were taking me away from you,
Philip." But he dried her tears with merry kisses.

"We are in time yet. The steamer don't go till
three to-night."

CHAPTER XXXV.

Unwelcome Visitors.

THE watchman at the mills was not a little surprised, as he went his first round that night, to see a man's figure leaning against a pillar in one of the weave-rooms. The fellow did not appear to mean any harm; he was not breaking any thing or stealing any cloth, but how could he have found his way inside? The watchman felt a little uneasy in spite of himself; it was such a thing as had never happened before.

" Hello! what business you got there?"

But the interloper did not appear to hear him. How oddly he looked at the looms, as if they were living things that he loved. He had not spoken, and his hat shaded his eyes, but the expression of the attitude was so plain, that even so rude a man as the watchman could read the tender reminiscence in his heart. Perhaps the fellow might be crazy, but this was no place for him. " Oh! I didn't know you, Mr. Breton. It is a nice evenin', sir."

But the mill-owner did not even answer him, and moved away toward the window as if impatient at being interrupted. The moon was full, and the sky was clear, only for a few silver-edged clouds. One, he fancied a ship sailing over the sea, but how slowly it glided; could it go no faster? Ah! suddenly it parted into bright fragments, and the wind scattered them pitilessly. He looked across at the other mills; the moonlight kissed their grim walls fondly, and sparkled in their windows like a hundred brilliant lamps. Why, here were his fire escapes, close to the window coping—his first business venture. Philip raised the window and stepped outside.

It was a wonderful night. Why couldn't people sleep by day and awake for such glorious nights as these? He looked down at the rising walls of his new mill, whose foundations might have been on his heart, so crushed it was to-night. It had risen three stories high, and every brick ought to have been gilded, to be as bright as his dreams for his new mill. But it looked terribly like a tomb to him to-night, within its wide walls were his buried hopes. But the work would not stop, he was but one, and that mill was for thousands. Others would admire its proportions, others, more blessed than he, watch over its uses and rejoice in its happy throngs of workmen. They would have but a scoff or a jest for him, only too glad henceforth to hide from renown. How many times he had walked the worn path in front of the mills, when grateful faces had only smiles for him. But he would be forgotten as if he were dead, that is what he must hope for. It seemed hard to believe that his mills could run on without him, that the great wheel would turn as willingly for another as for him.

How old and crooked the mills looked. Was it a trick of the fantastic moonlight, that made the roofs look broken and the bell towers leaning, or was it his own morbid fancy? But how terribly bright it was, what a misfortune if a man were fleeing from a relentless enemy such a night as this. Why from his post he could see the winding roadways glistening like running streams as they left the village and crossed the plains on every side.

It must be nearly time for Bertha to come with the carriage, as he had arranged. No, there was half an hour yet. But Philip closed the window behind him and went down the silent stairs. To-morrow morning they would be crowded with weavers again. How the girls would chatter. "The master has run away." Would to God they would have it to say, and not "they have caught them." If it were not so light now—But it was so still; surely there could be no danger to-night.

He went into his office, he would wait there for the carriage, it would not be very long, and then there was one last duty he must attend to. He struck a match and the gas shot up so brightly it dazzled his eyes. He turned away for an instant.

A massive form stood in the doorway. Philip must have left the counting-room unlocked when he had come in. Some one had followed him, apparently. But the young mill-owner took only one step toward the intruder. It was no stranger that crossed his threshold, but a man whose name was burned into his heart. It was the rightful husband of Philip Breton's wife—Curran. His hair had grown long and almost straight about his neck. His cheeks were thin and haggard, and the form that had been like a proud oak, was bowed as if it had been weighed down by a burden too heavy even for a giant to bear. Philip stopped short and looked at the man with speechless terror. He had supposed him hundreds of miles away. Perhaps the outraged husband had never left the village since their last meeting. Perhaps his flashing eyes had watched Philip wooing his wife a second time, and begrudged him his few cold kisses. Perhaps he had peered in through the windows of Philip's home; had he not a right to look at his wife, and followed them forth on every walk and drive, waiting to strike till the blow should fall most deadly. He had chosen his time well. Poor Bertha, with her dreams of Como and Chamouni. But what would he do? Leap upon his enemy and kill him? The man in the doorway looked

too pale and ill for such violence ; would he then
heap curses upon him, the bitterest human lips ever
uttered ? But Curran advanced into the room with
outstretched hand.

"Don't you know me, then, friend ? "

Philip hesitated again. There might be a grain
of hope yet ; he would surely never have given the
young man his hand if he had known—or called him
friend.

"Some one wrote me to come. I don't know
what he wanted," Curran explained wearily. "They
expect so much of a man ; they want him to be a
God ; and if he were they would crucify him."

Philip was recovering his composure. At first he
had felt a wild impulse to confess everything to the
wronged husband. He seemed so grand, so magnanimous ; he would not be cruel. But then his reason
came back to him. In such a case as this there could be
no amends. Innocently, Bertha and Philip had done
him a terrible wrong—and themselves ; forgiveness
could not blot it out. God in his mercy might
spare them the penalty of infamy ; but the injured
husband had no choice but vindicate his honor,
when he came to know.

"You look ill," said Philip at last, drawing him
out a chair. Should he detain him ? Bertha might
come before her time and break in upon them, the
two men she had injured so terribly. Oh ! that

must not happen.   Was not that a step in the passage now?   Should he let Curran go, then?   The
first man he met would pour the story of his
shame into his ears, and then the catastrophe.   He
must not go—but he must not stay.   Philip looked
out into the passage.   No one was there.   Curran
had dropped into the chair Philip had offered him.

" Do I look ill?" he asked, pushing his long hair
back from his forehead.   " Did you ever love a
woman who hated you? did you ever want to pour
out your life for her, and she despise you?   You
know whom I mean.   Why I once fancied you
and she were lovers, till she told me not.   I mean
Bertha."   He spoke the name so tenderly, a thrill
of shame passed over Philip.   Bertha was this man's
wife.   Had he not a right then to speak her name
tenderly?   And so Curran had fancied Bertha and he
were lovers till she told him not—ah, Bertha.

" She has left me," Curran went on in the same
soft, tender tone.   " I don't suppose it interests you.
But if I could only see her now, I have such a
strange feeling that I might win her back.   She
made such a tender sweetheart."   Then he lifted
his eyes more firmly to Philip's face, set like a wall
of rock.   " Is there any trouble among your help?"

"Yes, they have flung all my offers in my
teeth."

"It must have been that made them send for

me. I had hoped, or feared, I hardly know which, it might be something of Bertha. It is queer, isn't it, a woman like her should turn my head so completely? What is there about her, did you ever think of it? Of course you haven't." Curran seemed to make an effort to dismiss all thoughts of her that unmanned him. " You needn't be afraid of me ; I thought you seemed a little strange when I came in."

Philip started involuntarily, but Curran continued, " I sha'n't encourage any strikes against you. God will bless your life for your work for the poor. If He hasn't yet, he will give you a happier love than he has given me." Then he rose with new energy to his feet. " I must go and stop the mischief. I can do more with your laborers for good or evil than any man in the world. I suppose they may be in the hall to-night?"

"Yes." But Philip hurried up to him, and laid his hand on his arm. " But don't go, not yet."

" I must, shall you be here long? Well, I will see you again to-night."

" God grant not," murmured Philip Breton, as the door closed after him. Then Philip unlocked the great safe and swung back its green door of iron. He took out a packet and then locked the safe again and carried his packet back to his office. He turned the gas still higher and held the packet

in the flame, till all that was left of it was a little
heap of charred paper on the floor—all that was left
of Philip Breton's Will. With that act he closed up,
as he believed, all that part of his life worthy to be
remembered. He was young and strong, but he had
failed. Henceforth he must look on while others
worked ; they had taken his work away from him.
He must sit back on the seats with the women and
children, and look on and applaud when great deeds
were doing. He would have liked to work too, but
perhaps others would do his work better.

"Hallo, hallo, Phil, don't you work pretty late?"
It was Giddings the lawyer in a condition of decided
intoxication. "I'll bet yer dollar you don't know
what I came for! ha ha ha ; you think money; don't
you? more money? But I aint that sort of a feller."

Philip had been simply disgusted at first, but
there seemed a terrible leer in the drunken eyes.
Could it be the man had come to expose him? What
was the use of struggling against his destiny any
longer? If he could have gone yesterday, he would
have saved all risks. But he had waited just too
long. Curran had returned to claim his wife ; Jane
Ellingsworth had discovered everything, and now
this Giddings in his drunkard's foolishness was threatening what ruin he could bring.

"You are not going to do anything rash are you,"
said Philip dropping his eyes in humiliation.

But Giddings came close to him and laid his hand
on his shoulder. Then he put his face close to
Philip's, with a drunken man's false measure of distance. The young man writhed at his touch, and
held his breath to avoid taking the hot fumes of bad
liquor the fellow exhaled. But he did not dare to
anger the low creature.

"Did you think," continued Giddings with gush-
ing reproachfulness, "that I aint got any conscience?
You're doin' wrong, Mr. Breton. I aint got no right
—no right to let it go on. Did you think I aint got
no conscience?"

Philip shook him off and his face grew so terrible
that the fellow winced, as he had done before at
that look.

"Don't strike—don't kill me Phil—Mr. Breton,
I was only jokin'—can't you tell when a man's jokin'.
Got any money 'bout clothes, say fiffy dollars,'m awful
hard up. I wouldn't hurt you, your altogether too
nice feller." He leered affectionately at the young
man, then suddenly he winked frightfully. "And
'sides where would my pocket money come from? he,
he, he. Your the goose you might say or the gander,
no that won' do, I mean your the goose that lays my
golden eggs, see, my boy. I wouldn't harm yer mite,
only juss squeeze yer little sometimes, he, he, he."

Philip threw him a roll of bills. It was the last
blood money the scoundrel would ever draw. By

to-morrow morning Philip Breton and his wife would
be beyond the reach of harm, or beyond the reach of
help, one or the other.   " There is a hundred dollars, take it and go, I have business."

The drunken man looked suspiciously at his victim, his professional instinct was warned in spite of
his intoxication. The young man was too eager. But
Giddings' brain was too befogged for a long train of
reasoning.   He was suspicious, but his suspicions at
present got no farther than the roll of money.   He
concluded Philip Breton was trying to cheat him,
and began to count over the bills with set staring
eyes, that had a strange look of blindness in them,
and with forehead hideously wrinkled in the effort to
be sober.

" Ten, twenty, and twenty makes thirty, ten, and
twenty and twenty, here aint but eighty dollars.
Thought I's too drunk to coun' did yer."

" There is a hundred dollars there."

" 'S lie. Yer takin' vantage me cause I'm drunk."

Giddings burst into maudlin drunkard's tears and
missing the chair he tried for sat down on the floor.
Philip pulled him to his feet.   Bertha might be here
any moment.   This creature must be away if it cost
a thousand dollars.   He crowded another twenty
dollar bill into the fellow's clammy hand.

" Now go, or you'll stay longer than you want
to "

Giddings dried his tears and gathered his limp joints together to go. But he insisted on Philip's shaking hands. "No ba feelins you know. You aint such ba feller, Misser Breton, but I should thought you'd got a pootier woman for all your trouble, there I didn't mean 'n-harm. Goo-bye Misser Breton."

But even after Giddings had got into the hall Philip heard the fellow muttering to himself. He stepped hurriedly to the door of his office to catch the words, but could not. If Philip had been a little quicker he would have heard this.

"Somethin' up, I aint so drung but I ca' see that. Guess 'sil g'up to the boy's house. His wife 'll knew me, he, he."

Would Bertha never come? If they escaped it would be but by a hair's breadth. Ruin would be close upon them. For the adjustment of a ribbon she would sacrifice everything. It seemed a great while since Curran had left the office for the labor meeting, and he had not so far to go. Something might have delayed the terrible disclosure for a few moments, but by this time he must surely have heard the whole story of his shame and dishonor. It would stir him to madness. His noble eyes would flash lightnings, and thunderbolts of hate and scorn would drop from his lips. No human being could stand against the divine dignity of such a man's

28

righteous wrath. Philip fancied the mob sweeping up the road after this outraged husband, seeking out his wife for the doom that would satisfy his mad thirst for vengeance. Now, perhaps, they were bursting in the gates, now breaking down the oaken door. Ah, Philip would not be there this time to protect the beautiful woman who had only sinned through love for him. How the color would flee her cheeks as she looked out on the pitiless faces of the frenzied mob. There was no arm now to shield her, none but Curran's, whose love was now embittered into hate. There was no pity in his white, wasted face, only insulted love, only scorn that could grind her fair life, without one throb of tenderness, beneath his feet.

Why did she not come! Philip was almost wild with mingled terror and hope. He walked the room like a caged lion. Now he rushed to the door and glanced desperately up and down the street.

His horses were champing their bits at her door, but the light yet burned in her chamber. There was hardly time to catch the train at the Lockout station. The wild mob with the maddened lover, the most terrible of enemies, at their head, would be at her door in a moment. Still other dangers Philip did not guess threw a gathering shadow across her path. But she lingered yet.

CHAPTER XXXVI.

A Popular Leader.

MARKET HALL was full of excited workmen when Curran pushed the door open and
stepped in. Some would-be orator was trying to
voice the wrongs of the people, but when the whisper ran along the seats that Curran was at the door,
every head was turned. Then as if by a common
impulse the whole audience rose to their feet, and
the building seemed to tremble with the cheer that
burst from the brawny throats. Here was an orator
indeed, a man who could set before them their sufferings, and wring their hearts with self-pity; who
could make each soul of them wonder at his own
patience.

All they needed was a leader, there were enough
of them to bear down all opposition; they lacked
neither in courage nor endurance, but only in unity.
There was no leader to bind them to a resistless
purpose.

The poor from unnumbered betrayals have learned
suspicion; they commonly distrust every man who
would rise above their hopeless dead level. The great

man who would crush them, they yield to; but the man of themselves who longs to work with them and for them, the man who alone could direct concerted action, such as is employed against them, they meet with hate and suspicion. Their labor movement which might sweep everything before it, drifts helplessly with every gust of changing passions like a Great Eastern with unshipped rudder.

But some way Curran could conquer their distrust for a little while at least. They called him their pride and their delight, his marvelous magnetism could disarm their envy at least while they listened to him. To-night they would have followed where he said, if it had left a track of ruin behind them.

He made his way slowly up the aisle with simple greetings for his friends, as they stretched out their grimy hands to him; but his smile was so sad and hopeless that every glad face sobered as he passed. He mounted the platform and turned his face toward them. He seemed but the ghost of his former magnificent manhood, but the people cheered him again and those in the rear leaped upon their seats in their eagerness to see their hero. Then all held their breath to listen; even the girls in the gallery stopped their excited whispering while they waited for his grand ringing tones that had thrilled the faintest hearts so many times before. Would he never begin?

" What is this meeting for? "

The orator his coming had interrupted, was only too glad to explain.

" We don't get our rights. We get a little, but that's all, and we mean to fetch the young boss to his milk to-morrow; don't we, lads ? "

A shout of eager assent went up from the crowd. Then all was still again. Now would come the torrent of words of flame. Yes, Curran had stepped forward to the very edge of the platform, in his old habit. But who was the fellow with bandaged head, pushing his way so rudely up the main aisle, as if he bore tidings ? It must be ill tidings to make him in such haste. But Curran had begun to speak.

" You are making a mistake, my friends—a great mistake. The young master has done well by you, and he will do better, if you will give him time to think. Such mighty ideas as have got into his mind, can't be stopped ; they will not let him halt long, he must be swept forward. But you must wait for him ; you have waited for your cruel and heartless masters thousands of years. Will you only show yourselves impatient and insolent to the first one who shows himself kind toward you ? Do you want to make his name an example and a warning for his class ? I have heard their scoffs and taunts already—the air is full of them. Look, they say, the way the people treat the man who tries to help them. Friends, you are making a terrible mistake."

The light of the man's noble genius had flushed his pale cheeks, and flashed beautifully in his steel blue eyes. His voice that had seemed weak and unsteady as he began, rang out its bell-like tones again, as he saw the sullen faces soften under his matchless power.

"He has made your village blossom by his love; he has brought smiles to your weary children's faces; he has planted hope in a thousand desperate hearts. Do you ask me how I know? I see it in your eyes. I see it in the way your heads rest on your broad shoulders. And will you use your new manhood to do him injury?"

But the man with the bandaged head had reached the platform, and at this very moment when the orator paused to let his meaning sink into the hearts of the people, he touched Curran on the shoulder, and whispered a few hurried words in his ear.

The people saw their hero's face blanch. He turned to the fellow with a look that would break a man's heart, and seemed to be asking him a question. As he listened to the reply, his knees trembled under him, and he sank into a chair, and still the messenger of evil bent over him, and kept whispering with poisonous breath into his ear. At last Bailes stood back from his victim, who bowed his head upon his hands. Curran's whole body shook with the violence of his passion.

The inert people waited. They knew nothing else to do. Their hero might have died before them, they would never have thought to stir from their seats. But he rose at last, and Bailes grinned diabolically behind him. They would have another story now.

"Friends, you have heard what I said." He spoke as if a great weight was upon him and his voice came slowly. "I repeat it, be patient with your young master; he means well by you."

But Bailes rushed forward and, tearing the bandages from his head, threw them upon the platform at his feet. Disease had settled in his bruises and his face was frightfully swollen and disfigured. He might have been a ghoul or a gnome instead of a human being.

"Revenge him, men," he screamed, throwing up his arms, "if you have any spirit in you. I have just told him—some of you knew it—how that boy has stole his wife and spit on the laws, as if they were not for the rich like him."

It was more like a groan than a shout that went up from the crowd before him, that only waited a word from the bowed, broken man they loved, to become a blood-thirsty mob. Would he give them their word? He had leaped to his feet and thrown out his long right arm in his grandest gesture, and the murmur of the people died down. His face was as white as a dead man's, an ashy white, but his eyes flashed lightnings.

" Whose wrong is it then, this hideous creature's or mine ? I will settle my own grievances, I need no mob to right me." Then Curran paused a moment. When he began again it was in a lower tone. " Besides, the man is wrong," his voice trembled like a child's, " I have no—no," he almost broke down, " I have no wife—I am—I am not well, I must go to my bed, but before I go I want to be sure you will make no mistake to-night or to-morrow." He folded his arms across his broad chest in a sublime effort of self-control. His blood boiled in mad fever, every moment was worth a world to him, agonizing pictures floated before his dimmed vision, but he would not stir from his post till he had conquered this mob. " Philip Breton has shown himself fair to you, be fair with him. If he never did another thing for you he —he has yet deserved your—your patience. You will excuse me now, I will see you to-morrow, but I need rest. Can I depend on you ? " He did not even look at them ; his attitude, as he waited with downcast eyes, was of a man walking in his sleep.

" Yes—yes," shouted the people, and then he turned and stepped off from the platform. He came down the aisle very strangely, at first he would hurry and notice no one, then, as if by a mighty effort, walk very slowly, then faster again, then he

would stop short and put out his hand to some perfect stranger.

Many eyes watched him curiously when he sep-
arated from his eager friends at the door of the hall
and walked rapidly away. If Curran had turned off
to the road that led to Philip Breton's house on
the hill, he would not have gone alone, but he did
not even look that way so long as the half-tamed
mob could see him. So the people scattered in disappointment to their homes.

But Curran is no longer walking in his first direction; he has turned on his heel and made a route for
himself across the fields; his face is pointed towards
the lights that yet shine down at him from the stone
house on the hill. And the roads are not straight
enough for the errand he is on, nor is walking fast
enough, he breaks into a run. Now he falls over a low
fence so violently a limb might have been broken,
but he only loses his hat and runs on, his long hair
shaking down over his pale set face as he runs. His
breath comes like the puffing of a locomotive, he can
hear his heart throb louder than his footfalls.

What does he seek, what will he do when he
looks again on his faithless and dishonored wife and
on the man who has put this deadliest shame upon
him? Punishment can wipe out nothing, vengeance
never assuaged one pang of human anguish yet.
But mercy or pity or reason are fled from his maddened soul to-night while the furies whip him on.

CHAPTER XXXVII.

Too Fond a Husband.

THE drunken lawyer very nearly fell as he tried to step off the counting-room piazza, and almost made up his mind it would be more desirable to lie down in some soft spot and go to sleep, than take the long walk he had set himself. But the cool breeze seemed to refresh him marvelously, and in another moment he despised the green hollow under the elm that had looked so inviting, and hurried up toward Philip Breton's house. He shook his head wisely as he walked. It took a pretty smart man to get ahead of John Giddings, drunk or sober. The young mill-owner wasn't nearly as frightened as usual. Something was in the wind. He ought to have watched him closer lately, but Giddings concluded he was in good time yet with Breton at one end of the village his wife at the other and himself, the acute lawyer, between them.

The lawyer had walked as far as Silas Ellingsworth's house, when he caught sight of a pair of horses on a fast trot, drawing a close coupè. Elegant pairs and chariots of that description were not so common in Bretonville as to make it doubtful who might own this one, and besides it must have been an occasion of peculiar necessity that called for such unaristocratic haste. Giddings was perfectly delighted with his own sagacity.

He knew human nature pretty well. When a man gets another in an unpleasant situation, he must count on the unfortunate struggling to escape, if it happens to be a woman, he need not be so watchful, —women are all fatalists. But it takes a pretty smart man to get ahead of John Giddings.

"Whoa, whoa, I say." The lawyer had thrown himself in front of the excited horses, and the driver had to pull up to keep from running over him. "Whoa, I say."

Then he stepped to the door of the carriage and turning the knob threw it wide open. The moonlight revealed a woman surrounded with carpet bags and shawls. A thick brown veil concealed her features, but Mr. Giddings took off his hat to her.

"Mrs. Breton, I believe."

"Why yes," she did not recognize him, "but I am in a hurry," she said nervously drawing back. "Drive on Henry."

"No, you don't," insisted Giddings, mounting the steps. "I guess you don' know me." His liquor began to overcome him again, "name's Giddings, aint goin' far are you?".

" To Europe," she answered quickly, recognizing him at last. " I have no further occasion for your services, I have paid you, haven't I ? "

" Not s'much as your second husband's paid me since," he gurgled. " If you're goin' so far, guess I'll go too, I like your family, Miss Breton."

" Drive on, I command you," she screamed, and the horses started. Giddings lurched forward, and Bertha put out her white hands, and tried to push him back. He clutched, with an oath, at something to hold to, but she loosened her India shawl, and the man carried it with him into the ditch. But he leaped to his feet.

" Hold ! stop ! police, police !" but Giddings had no sooner spoken than the village policeman laid his hand on his arm.

" Here I am, sir, what'll you have ?"

" Stop that carriage ; arrest that woman, she is a criminal." Giddings had shaken off the policeman's grasp, and started to run after the carriage.

" You must be very drunk," said the other, over-taking him, " that is Mr. Breton's wife."

" I know that," screamed the lawyer, " and I tell you, stop her, let me go."

" More likely you're the criminal. Hallo, what you doing with that Indy shawl. Guess I'll have to lock you up. Come along quiet, now."

But Giddings was perfectly frantic. He fought

with his feet and hands, and with his teeth, kicking, tearing and biting like a wild beast.

"Don't let her escape, I say, never mind me, I'll give you a thousand dollars. I'll tear your heart out, you villain. Stop her, stop her!" The officer grew angry at last, and drew his billet, but still the fellow struggled and screamed like a wild creature, till blow after blow paralyzed his arms, and finally stretched him unconscious and bleeding on the ground.

"Tremens," growled the policeman, as he lifted him to his feet soon after, and led him along, subdued at last.

But a woman had stood in her window as the carriage had rolled by, and she had recognized the equipage, too. A sudden change came over her face.

"Where are you going, Jennie?" Her husband looked up calmly from his paper.

"Out a minute," she hardly looked at him, "that is all."

"But it is almost nine o'clock, my dear, what can you want out?"

Her breath came fast, and two bright red spots burned in her cheeks. Mr. Ellingsworth had never seen her so pretty. He must keep her so a few moments. He stepped to the door and turned the key, then he put it in his pocket and threw himself back in his chair again.

She faced him with flashing eyes.

"How dare you—am I your slave? I want to go out."

Her husband settled down cozily in his seat, and smiled his old brilliant smile. She had never seen him laugh any more than the rest of his acquaintances. He might perhaps, have laughed before an intimate, but men like Silas Ellingsworth have no intimates.

"How lovely you are when you are angry. I see I have made a mistake in being so amiable with you. What treats I have lost. Why, you are better than an actress, my dear. Such coloring as yours does not hurt the complexion."

Precious time was flying; the carriage had rolled away out of sight; her victim had outwitted her—her hate would be balked forever, and all for her husband's foolish caprice. She stamped her foot at him. "I must go." There was yet time to rouse the villagers, and fetch back the fugitives from justice. Oh, what devil of stupidity had possessed her wise husband to-night? "Give me the key." She had come close to him, but she did not scream when she was angry, her voice grew low and almost hoarse, "or I will leave you forever."

He had laid aside his paper now, with quite a serious air; and Jane felt vaguely frightened; she had never seen him sober with her. Could he do any more than others when they are angry? She did not reason about it; she only began to be afraid of her own words. His was the only nature in the world could have tamed her so completely.

"That is just the trouble." Then he smiled as brightly as ever his keen cold smile. "You want to leave me now, but I love you too well to let you; come kiss me and I will."

Every moment Philip Breton's carriage was bearing the woman Jane hated, to safety and peace that her false heart had never deserved. But there were fleeter horses in Bretonville than his; they could be pursued; they could be overtaken and dragged back in greater ignominy than ever. It would be more terrible for Bertha than if the blow had come while she sat serene in her own home. To be overtaken in flight would cap her shame. Jane threw herself into her husband's arms. She kissed his eyes, his mouth, his white neck; she covered his smooth hands with kisses; twining her arms about his neck, she lavished the tenderest of caressing epithets on him. Then she drew herself away. Her black hair had been partly loosened, and as she stood hung well down her flushed cheeks. She had raised her hands, and clasped them over her bosom; her lips parted; surely no human being can resist such wistful beauty as hers.

"Please let me go."

But before he could answer, she heard a noise like thunder and rushed to the window. She sees nothing, but the sound comes on nearer and nearer; it comes from the hill. Something white gleams in the moonlight.

"What do you see?" asked Mr. Ellingsworth, carelessly, returning to his newspaper.

She holds her breath, nearer it comes, Philip's white horse Joe on a mad gallop. But Philip is not upon him. Who is that wild rider, with long uncovered hair, and pale haggard face? He strikes the maddened animal every moment for better speed, though now they seem flying faster than the wind. The man is Curran. Let him be his own avenger, then.

CHAPTER XXXVIII.

The Price of Happiness.

THE Breton carriage had passed the last house in the village, when Philip leaned out for one last look at the home of his childhood and the scene of the only work he should ever do. He was almost a boy yet, it seemed only a few days since he had looked at the great world only as a play-ground. It was a short work he had done in the few days of his manhood, and even that had been condemned. Dear old mills, with their bold towers and massive walls, but his no longer. His heritage was sold, his birth-right lost. He turned his eyes away, it was more than he could bear. On the hill back above the village he saw for the last time, as the road wound off toward Lockout, his house, that was. "Deserted" seemed written on its stone walls. It had never looked so noble to him, a sort of halo seemed to float above it. He could see the window of the room where he was born, but for what a worthless life.

"Good-bye," he murmured. The road as it followed the winding river made another turn, and the

29

lights of the village were shut away from his misty
eyes.

The horses were trotting at their best. There
was none too much time.

It was far better than he had hoped. The
dangers had gathered so thickly, there had seemed
at one time hardly more than a chance for escape.
Peril seemed on every hand, enemies to spring from
every covert, and stretch out their hands to stop the
fugitives. But the village was far behind now. A few
moments more, and the steaming horses would draw
up at the Lockout station, and they would be whirled
away faster than any pursuer, to peace and safety
and honor.

" How odd it all is, setting out in this way as if
we were eloping."

Philip was reaching forward to take her hand, but
he drew back, as if he were stung. How terribly
thoughtless she was.

" I explained about the steamer's early start."

" Do you know," resumed Bertha softly, " how
pleased I am to have this trip to Europe? It is a
sort of wedding journey isn't it ? "

How good God had been, to let him keep the
awful truth from her. It would have crushed her,
the very thought of her shame. It was crushing
him.

" I shall enjoy it very much," she said putting

out her hand to him, in unusual fondness. "I
am afraid I haven't returned your goodness very
well." No more she had, but it was not her fault,
poor girl.

"Where shall we go first?"

"To the south of France, God willing," he added
solemnly.

Bertha looked at his face with a new anxiety.
The moonlight seemed to bring out all the marks of
his terrible care and suffering. But he gazed at her
in astonishment, he had never seen an expression so
near love in her eyes for him. Was her heart softening, would she yet make up to him in her new love,
all that he lost for her sake? But her lips were
moving.

"I shall be better with you than I used to be.
I—I"—she dropped her eyes before his passionate
joy, the sadness had gone in an instant from his
face, his future seemed beautifully radiant again. "I
feel different toward you, dear."

He bent forward to draw her to his heart. He
was paid for everything. He had taught his wife to
love him as he dreamed she could love. She had
lifted her rapt face toward his. It had come, the
moment he had given his life for. But suddenly his
heart stopped beating, there was a sound of a gal-
loping horse. Philip kissed his wife, but as solemnly
as if she were dead, and put her away from him.

He leaned forward and looked back over the road they had come.

He saw nothing at first but he heard the sound of a horse's hoofs. He put his head far out. It might have been a white speck in the road, but as he looked the speck became larger and clearer. It was a white horse, at a dead run, on their course. Philip Breton's heart, that had just been almost bursting with its new happiness, was a great cold stone in his breast. And he had fancied he could escape, with enemies like his and a whole village against him. He could see only one pursuer. Ah, he knew who it must be, and he grew nearer every moment.

"Drive faster," he shouted to the coachman, "run the horses."

How like the wind his pursuer came. Philip had thought there was but one horse could leap so mightily. Why this was that one, his own horse Joe. Why it might be a servant from his home with something that had been forgotten. It need not be the worst peril his fancy could picture? But he dared not hope.

"Isn't this delightful," exclaimed Bertha. "There can't be any danger of our missing the train at this rate."

The carriage rocked from side to side; a dozen times it seemed turning over, but still Philip leaned

far out of the window, and as he saw the great white
horse gaining at every mad leap, he shouted to the
driver between his set teeth,

"Whip your horses; don't spare them—faster."

If anything should break, their troubles would all
end that night. And the strain on the harnesses
and the groaning axles was beyond all calculation of
the makers. The horses, too, had got past the control of their driver. He had no more occasion to
urge the wild creatures; instead he was pulling at
the reins with all his strength but to no purpose, only,
so far, he had kept them in the road.

The rider of the white horse was hatless and his
long, loose hair and his swinging hand as he struck
the panting white flanks of the horse gave him an
uncanny look as if there were no deed of horror too
blood curdling for him to do. The horse dropped
big flakes of foam from his mouth, foam mingled with
blood; his eyes and nostrils were dilated with agony;
his breathing was like fierce gusts of wind in a tem-
pest. Philip Breton knew the rider as well as the
horse. His pursuer was Curran; and the implacable
laws made him yet the husband of the woman whom
Philip Breton had made his wife.

They were almost at Lockout. The carriage gave
a terrible lurch at a turn in the road. The horses were
almost taken off their feet but still there was no accident; the windows of the carriage grazed the solid

wall of rock without being broken, and in a moment the horses, now subdued, were trotting down the hill toward the city.

But the fugitives had hardly escaped the cut through the rocks, when the pursuer entered it. He had almost overtaken them. He struck the horse's white flanks a pitiless blow. It was at the very spot where Curran had saved Bertha's life from the mad dog, that the old horse, forced beyond his strength, stopped as if lightning had struck him. The blood welled in torrents from his mouth and nostrils; he quivered like a leaf, and then fell dead in his tracks. The rider shot over the creature's head with the gathered momentum of that mad race, and struck the jagged rock with a sickening crash.

CONCLUSION.

AS the dawn broke in the east that Thursday morning, Philip Breton stood on the deck of the steamer "Salvator." The look of feverish watchfulness, that had never left his face for so long, was gone at last. The great fear that had chased smiles from his lips, had given place to a great hope. A divine calm and peace had come at last upon his soul. Fate had seemed invincible. He had pitted his beautiful mills and his home and his hopes of glory against it, all for the love of a woman who had no heart for him. He had conquered; and he did not begrudge the price, this royal lover; for he had won the love of his bride at last.

Below in her stateroom, weary with her unwonted excitement, Bertha was sleeping; sleeping like a child unconscious of the terrible peril and infamy she had escaped by only so much as a hair's breadth. The hurrying ship rocked her gently in the great cradle of the deep and bore her to lands of undreamed beauty; where the light of a new eternal love would be on everything.

THE END.

PUTNAM'S ART HAND-BOOKS,

Edited by SUSAN M. CARTER, Superintendent of the Woman's
Art School, Cooper Union

I. Sketching from Nature. By THOMAS ROWBOTHAM. Reprinted
from the Thirty-eighth English Edition. 27 Illustrations. 16mo,
boards, ... 50 cents.

'It is a model of clearness and conciseness, and even the unartistic need have no
difficulty in understanding its contents."—*Library Table.*
" This is an excellent little book, which we heartily commend to amateurs."—*Yale
Courant.*
" Cannot fail to make a good landscape sketcher of anyone who is skilful in the
use of the pencil."—*Albany Argus.*
" It is full of useful hints, simply stated."—*Boston Commonwealth.*

II. Landscape Painting in Oil Colors. By W. WILLIAMS. Reprinted from the Thirty-fourth English Edition. 16mo, boards, 50 cents.

" Every young artist should possess the volume, which will be found readily to be
worth ten times the amount for which it is sold."—*Boston Traveller.*
" Will be found a valuable adjunct to an art education."—*N. Y. Evening Express.*

III. Flower Painting. By Mrs. WM. DUFFIELD. Reprinted from
the Twelfth English Edition. 12 Illustrations. 16mo, boards, 50 cents.

"It is a thoroughly scientific and practical treatise."—*Boston Watchman.*
" Its instructions are clear, condensed, and sufficiently minute."—*Detroit Post and
Tribune.*
" The instructions include everything that needs to be known regarding the art of
painting flowers in water colors."—*Buffalo Express.*
Of the Series the *N. Y. Tribune* says: "* * * cannot fail to command the at-
tention of art students."
The *Christian Union* says: "* * * We can, from personal knowledge,
recommend them as excellent hand-books for amateurs."

IV. Figure Drawing. By C. H. WEIGALL Reprinted from the
Twenty-first English Edition. 17 Illustrations. 16mo, boards, 50 cents.

V. An Artistic Treatise on the Human Figure. By HENRY
WARREN, Prest. of London Institute of Painters in Water Colors.
(In preparation.)

PUBLICATIONS OF G. P. PUTNAM'S SONS.

I. Tent Life in Siberia. ADVENTURES AMONG THE KORAKS AND OTHER TRIBES IN KAMSCHATKA AND NORTHERN ASIA. Fifth Edition. 12mo, cloth extra, ... $1 75

"We strongly recommend this book as one of the most entertaining volumes of travel that has appeared for some years."—*London Athenæum.*

II. Travels in Portugal. By JOHN LATOUCHE. With Photographic Illustrations. Octavo, cloth extra, . . . $3 50

"A delightfully written book, as fair as it is pleasant. * * * Entertaining, fresh, and as full of wit as of valuable information."—*London Spectator.*

III. The Abode of Snow. A TOUR THROUGH CHINESE TIBET, THE INDIAN CAUCASUS, AND THE UPPER VALLEYS OF THE HIMALAYA. By ANDREW WILSON. Square octavo, cloth extra, with Map, $2 00

"There is not a page in this volume which will not repay perusal. * * * The author describes all he meets with on his way with inimitable spirit."—*London Athenæum.*

IV. The Life and Journals of John J. Audubon, the Naturalist. Comprising Narratives of his Expeditions in the American Forests, etc. 12mo, cloth extra, with Portrait, . $2 00

"It is a grand story of a grand life; more instructive than a sermon; more romantic than a romance."—*Harper's Magazine.*

V. Notes on England and Italy. By Mrs. NATHANIEL HAWTHORNE (wife of the Novelist). Third edition. 12mo, cloth, $2 00 Illustrated edition, with 12 Steel Plates. Octavo, cloth extra, gilt edges, ... $5 00

"One of the most delightful books of travel that has come under our notice."—*Worcester Spy.*

"The grace and tenderness of the author of the 'Scarlet Letter' is discernible in its pages."—*London Saturday Review.*

VI. Recollections of a Tour Made in Scotland in 1803. By DOROTHY WORDSWORTH (sister of the Poet). Edited by PRINCIPAL SHAIRP, LL.D. 12mo, cloth extra, . . . $2 50

"The volume glistens with charming passages, showing how rich in 'Wordsworthian' fancy was this modest sister."—*London Athenæum.*

VII. Bayard Taylor's Travels. Complete in 11 vols. Containing works upon Africa; Egypt; Iceland; California and Mexico; Greece and Russia; India, China and Japan; Palestine, Asia Minor, Sicily and Spain; Sweden, Denmark and Lapland; Europe, etc., etc. Per volume, ... $1 50 Or, 11 volumes, neatly put up in box, ... 16 50

"There is no romance to us quite equal to one of Bayard Taylor's books of travel."—*Hartford Republican.*

PUTNAM'S HANDY-BOOK SERIES.

A Manual of Etiquette. With Hints on Politeness, Good Breeding, etc. By "DAISY EYEBRIGHT," One vol., 12mo, boards,   50 cts.

The Mother's Register. Current Notes on the Health of Children. Part I.—Boys; Part II—Girls. "The Mother records for the Physician to interpret." From the French of Prof. J. B. FOSSA-GRIVES, M.D. 12mo, cloth, ... 75 cts.

Hints on Dress. By an AMERICAN WOMAN.

Outline History of Dress. Economy and Taste.
Things Indispensable. What we Mean by Dressing well.
Estimates of Cost. Color, Form, Suitability.
How and What to Buy.

12mo, 124 pp., cloth, ... 75 cts.
"This little volume contains as much sense as could well be crowded into its pages."—*N. Y. Evening Mail.*

The Home: Where it Should Be, and What to Put in It. Containing Hints for the Selection of a Home, its Furniture and internal arrangements, with carefully prepared price-lists of nearly everything needed by a housekeeper, and numerous valuable suggestions for saving money and gaining comfort. By FRANK R. STOCKTON, (of *Scribner's Monthly*). 12mo, 182 pp., cloth,   75 cts.
"Young housekeepers will be especially benefited, and all housekeepers may earn much from this book."—*Albany Journal.*

The Mother's Work with Sick Children. By Prof. J. B FONSSAGRIVES, M.D. Translated and edited by F. P. FOSTER, M.D A volume full of the most practical advice and suggestions for Mothers and Nurses. 12mo, 224 pp., cloth, . . . $1 00
"A volume which should be in the hands of every mother in the land."—*Binghamton Herald.*

Manual of Thermometry. For Mothers, Nurses, Hospitals, etc., and all who have charge of the sick and of the young. By EDWARD SEGUIN, M.D. 12mo, cloth. . . . . . . 75 cts.

Infant Diet. By A. JACOBI, M.D., Clinical Professor of Diseases of Children, College of Physicians and Surgeons, New York. Revised, enlarged, and adapted to popular use by MARY PUTNAM JACOBI, M.D. 12mo, boards, ... 50 cts.
"Dr. Jacobi's rules are admirable in their simplicity and comprehensiveness."—*N. Y. Tribune.*

How to Make a Living. By GEO. CARY EGGLESTON, author of "How to Educate Yourself." 16mo, boards . . 50 cts.
"Shrewd, sound and entertaining."—*N. Y. Tribune.*
"An admirable little treatise, full of sound practical advice."—*Christian Union.*

Manual of Nursing. Prepared under the instructions of the New York Training School for Nurses. By VICTORIA WHITE, M. D., and revised by MARY PUTNAM JACOBI, M. D. . . 75 cts.
*** Better adapted to render the nurses a faithful and efficient co-operator with the physician than any previous manual of the kind we have seen.—*Home Journal.*